UNLOCKING THE MYSTERIES OF

GENESIS

HENRY M. MORRIS III

HARVEST HOUSE PUBLISHERS
EUGENE, OREGON

Cover by Left Coast Design

Cover image © AstroStar / Shutterstock

UNLOCKING THE MYSTERIES OF GENESIS
Copyright © 2016 Henry M. Morris III
Published by Harvest House Publishers
Eugene, Oregon 97402
www.harvesthousepublishers.com

ISBN 978-0-7369-6798-3 (pbk.)
ISBN 978-0-7369-6799-0 (eBook)

Library of Congress Cataloging-in-Publication Data
Names: Morris, Henry M., author.
Title: Unlocking the mysteries of Genesis / Henry M. Morris III.
Description: Eugene, Oregon : Harvest House Publishers, 2016.
Identifiers: LCCN 2015049208 (print) | LCCN 2016014522 (ebook) | ISBN
    9780736967983 (pbk.) | ISBN 9780736967990 (ebook)
Subjects: LCSH: Creationism. | Bible. Genesis--Criticism, interpretation,
    etc. | Evolution. | Bible and science.
Classification: LCC BS651 .M697 2016 (print) | LCC BS651 (ebook) | DDC
    231.7/652--dc23
LC record available at http://lccn.loc.gov/2015049208

Printed in the United States of America

16 17 18 19 20 21 22 23 24 / LB-JC / 10 9 8 7 6 5 4 3 2 1

CONTENTS

Creation or Chaos

Nothing captures the minds of human beings more than the question of where we came from. The oldest writings ever uncovered have dealt with that issue, and it is no exaggeration to say the question still causes heated debate today. In our era of scientific inquiry, the majority view insists everything is the result of eons of chance interplay between physical forces and random collisions between various atoms and molecules—all with no design or purpose, just the happenchance of blind natural processes.

The secular theories of origins are many, complex, and technical, but the common theme among them all is that there is nothing—absolutely nothing—supernatural in the equations. Everything must be explained in natural terms. All that can be understood about the past must be delved from the examination of present processes and scientific reasoning. Anything even hinting of a miracle, anything that cannot ultimately be explained by natural laws, must be rejected. The one absolute is that there is no supernatural involvement by a deity of any kind.

Oh, it is generally accepted that one can be agnostic about the possibility of a being or a mind of some sort within the vast reach of outer space. But if such a person or being exists, it would be both impersonal and detached from any involvement in the interactions of the forces within our universe. Some would conjecture that such a Force (capital F) might have caused the initial singularity of that super-dense pinpoint of mass-energy that exploded in the Big Bang some 13-plus billions of years ago. But if so, whatever that may have been, it has long since dissociated itself from our reality.

Our universe is all there is. That is where the mainstream of academic thought is positioned today.

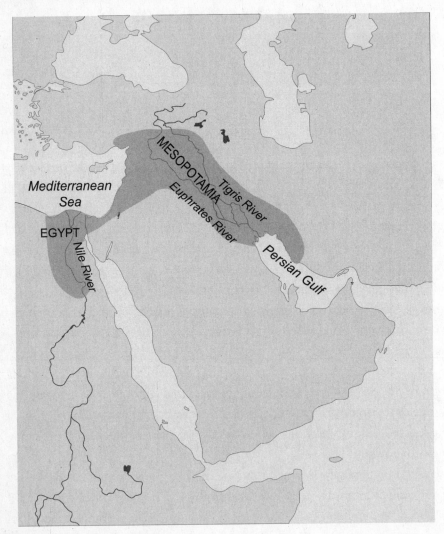

Figure 1.1—The Fertile Crescent

The Past

It was very different in the recent past. Up until the surge of scientific thought in Europe in the sixteenth and seventeenth centuries, most of the various centers of civilization held to some form of polytheistic or pantheistic explanation for the universe. Beginning with the organized people groups around the cities of Babel and Nineveh in the Fertile Crescent, various forces of nature were personified as deities or demigods, or the universe was seen as an Over-mind or Force that controlled everything. As these explanations gained prominence, they became religions with a plethora of gods and goddesses who held court on certain high places and dabbled with the forces of nature and the lives of humans.

The Egyptians developed a sophisticated system of temple worship that mingled the ruling dynasties with various deities—usually Ra, the sun god. The Nile, so important to their economic stability, was given deification in a series of gods and goddesses associated with the river, the fish in the river, and the annual inundation that fertilized their fields. Literally every facet of their daily lives was intertwined with gods or goddesses who at their whim could make life prosperous or miserable. There was no question in the minds of the Egyptians that supernatural forces were necessary to bring about the universe they lived in.

The Assyrian and Babylonian empires that followed were very similar. The names changed with the language and cultural emphasis, but gods and goddesses were still at the core of their world, making sure that all was developing according to their plan. Humanity could beg for insight from various oracles and pray to the gods, but it was the personified forces that ruled the universe. And the human rulers sought to identify with the most powerful god, often taking either a high-priestly role or, in some cases, claiming deity for themselves.

The Greeks and the Romans were great mimics of previous religious systems, often combining and assimilating the deities of earlier cultures or conquered territories into their pantheon, giving names to the deities of their more famous rulers or military generals. The Caesars of Rome typically deified themselves and demanded total allegiance, as well as claiming miraculous powers to keep rebellions in check.

Ultimately, each of these empires crumbled under the weight of misman-agement—and in some rather startling events, by the intervention of the very God of the universe whom they were all denying.

Ordinary Observation

The common denominator among all the various religious systems and the sequence of empires and tributary nations was this: The reality of our world is so complex, so intertwined with order and purpose, so obviously full of observable cause-and-effect relationships that supernatural power was required to create it in the first place and to keep it from falling apart over time.

Today, we would recognize such observation as a key part of the scientific method.

The more humanity learned about the sciences (mathematics, astronomy, medicine, engineering, etc.), the more people came to the conclusion that the makeup of our universe was so intricate and so endued with unknown and inexplicable energies that something or someone outside and beyond our universe had to be involved. Thus, the gods and goddesses took on a greater reality as people's understanding of the enormity of the universe expanded.

Every culture even had some kind of "super-god" or "all-knowing god" that was a catchall deity who took care of the mysteries. As the apostle Paul once declared to the scholars in Athens:

> Men of Athens, I perceive that in all things you are very religious;
> for as I was passing through and considering the objects of your
> worship, I even found an altar with this inscription: TO THE
> UNKNOWN GOD (Acts 17:22-23).

Engineering Design

Even the most uneducated person knows that things don't "just happen." All our experiences in life verify that somebody made the things we use and play with. Red wagons and rag dolls do not pop out of raw dirt. Somewhere, someone makes them. There is a manufacturing process. Even if it is little more than our mother or father, somebody makes the things we come in contact with every day.

Once we enter formal schooling, and ultimately when we enter the workforce, we become more and more aware that the houses we live in, the food we eat, the tools we use, the cars we drive, and the clothes we wear all come from a source, a place, a store, a company, and even a specific person or persons who are responsible for making them.

Everyone knows that!

What is it about the unknowable—like where the stars came from or how life got started—that makes us leap out of reality to suppose that those things happened by chance over long periods of time? Why is it that we absolutely *know* that the red wagon was made by somebody but are willing to believe that the far more complicated aspects of even the simplest life forms "just happened"?

Think with me a little bit.

In order for something to come into existence—such as a red wagon or a computer—a series of events have to happen in a specific order, controlled by a process that itself must be controlled. All of the technologies we use are designed by rather sophisticated and highly educated people using equipment and processes that have been previously designed by other people.

We are pretty good at understanding things today. Our microscopes and telescopes and measuring instruments are quite advanced, and we have been able to get at the core working parts of almost everything we can touch—and much of the universe that we can't. The human race has come a long way from the Dark Ages, when very few people could read or write and social structures were barely functional.

We're good at making things. But just what does it take to make something?

- There has to be a purpose for what we want to make. Usually there are multiple parts working together to accomplish a goal.

- Each piece must have a specific design that suits the purpose of the overall design.

- Each of the parts must have a precise size and shape—or they won't fit together.

- The fit must suit the purpose—or the pieces will come loose and fall apart (stop working).

- Finally, there must be a definite sequence for correct assembly. Each part must be specifically arranged and attached in the proper relationship with its mates or the purpose will not be accomplished. The thing won't work.

All of this seems rather obvious. That's because everything that exists follows this procedure all the time, whether we are talking about a peanut butter sandwich or a Boeing 787 Dreamliner jet.

Evidence for Design

The fundamental principle of science is *observation*. In fact, one of the main objections of scientists and philosophers who hold to naturalistic evolution—the view that everything in our world came about by chance over eons of unimaginable and unmeasurable time—is that creation is based on faith and is *not* observable. While it is true that the processes of the original creation are no longer observable, it does not follow that we cannot observe the *design* that is inherent in everything we can access in our universe.

It seems to defy the very logic we proudly depend on to say that even when design is obvious, the designed object has not been actually designed. Richard Dawkins is one of the more famous modern scientists. Here is the way that he expresses his blatant refusal to accept what is designed: "Biology is the study of complicated things that have the appearance of having been designed for a purpose."[1]

Perhaps it has become "scientific" to deny observations and insist on beliefs!

What Is Obvious?

As has been discussed, science is about observation. It is important, however, to distinguish between *empirical* (operational) observations and *forensic* (historical) observations. Empirical science is based on observable facts that can be seen, measured, and recorded. Forensic science is based on *un*observable and *un*repeatable events of the past. Empirical science observes current events and attempts to determine how or why such events can be repeated or applied. Forensic science observes the results of a past event and attempts to figure out what made the past come about.

Empirical (operational) science begins with a measurement of currently observable events that is followed by analysis, hypothesis building, and testing. Repeatability of observations and measurements is what establishes scientific fact. Forensic (historical) science begins with the results of an event that is neither observable nor repeatable. Scientists must therefore make multiple assumptions, inferences, extrapolations, and conjectures about past events before a plausible explanation for the event can be developed.

Although both disciplines search for knowledge, only empirical science has the capacity to develop laws of science through the observation, repeated testing, and verification of results. Forensic science is often used to speculate about past possibilities and has gained a large measure of popular acceptance through the use of dramatic visualization through video animation. As a common example, various programs such as *NOVA* are well-known for showing how stars formed or how a planet became part of a solar system. But all of that which is presented is pure speculation and hypotheses. None of it has actually been observed by any human being living today.

The New Horizon probe's 2015 flyby of the dwarf planet Pluto was made possible by an enormous amount of engineering skill and mathematical planning. The data captured by the instruments on the spacecraft were stunning! We now have more empirical data about that part of the solar system than ever before—but speculation about how Pluto was formed or why the various moons were "trapped" around it (and other such questions) amounts to nothing but sophisticated guesswork. We know certain facts, but it is foolish to assert that we know how stellar bodies came into being in the first place. No human being was alive at the time of star formation, whether on Day Four of the creation week or billions of years ago of supposed evolutionary time. Certain scientists may assert knowledge they don't have, but no one *knows*.

Figure 1.2—Pluto

Overwhelming Evidence for Design

We have a mountain of observable and verified data about a stupendous number of magnificently designed objects and living animals on Earth. The scope of this book will not permit any kind of comprehensive listing, but a few of the more obvious and beautiful are worth reviewing. The following examples are taken from articles that present the science in such a way that most of us can recognize the wonderful mysteries that have been "unlocked" for us to see. Each example could be multiplied many times over, and more detailed information can be accessed through ICR's website, www.icr.org.

Amazing Animal Eyes

Animals benefit from a variety of unique eye designs, but where did eyes come from? Most vertebrates have the classic "camera eye," which uses a transparent cornea and convex lens to bend images onto a light-sensitive layer of tissue called the *retina* that lines the back of the eye. That's the way our eye is designed.

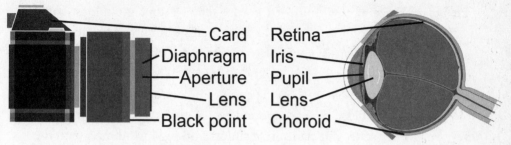

Card   Retina
Diaphragm   Iris
Aperture   Pupil
Lens   Lens
Black point Choroid

Figure 1.3—Camera and Eye

This camera eye is a whole lot more complicated than that, but the basic design is common among many land-based creatures. For example, spineless squids and octopi possess the same basic camera-eye anatomy as vertebrates—albeit with a few optimizations for life underwater. Even some jellyfish have small camera eyes. But if you would like to look at an exciting example of how the human eye works, check out ICR's DVD series *Made in His Image: Exploring the Complexities of the Human Body*. Random evolutionary accident? Unlikely!

Other life forms with an internal backbone use completely different eyes. For instance, the deep-sea spookfish uses reflective mirror lenses, not refractive lenses. The chameleon has a pinhole eye design that uses concave lenses instead of convex lenses. These lenses spread out a narrow section of incoming light onto a broader retina. Similar eye designs, but unique features that "just happen" to fit the lifestyle and needs of the specific creature. Similar designs, but very different animals. Interesting.

The classic and unique compound eye works very well, as anyone who has tried to catch a fly knows. The many refractive lenses fit into round or hexagonal light-sensitive, tiny, tube-like units called *ommatidia*. The fly is part of a group of living things called *arthropods*. But some arthropods have completely different eyes. Odd. If natural selection is "selecting" for certain kinds of life, why would a single animal grouping possess a variety of radically different eyes?

In fact, compound eyes seem to pop up here and there without any particular preference to environmental needs—or to animal groupings. Some worms have compound eyes. Sabellids are marine tube worms, and each of their ommatidia consists only of two cells. Similarly, "most known starfish species possess a compound eye at the tip of each arm, which, except for the lack of true optics," resembles the compound eye of the fly![2] And clams from the family Arcidae have compound eyes. Other than their compound eyes, worms, sea stars, and clams have almost nothing in common with the arthropod body plan. Yet giant clams have pinhole eyes. The chambered nautilus, a cephalopod along with squids, hunts its prey with pinhole eyes without lenses.

Animals within one group use very different—and always fully formed— eyes, and certain animals from very different groups share the same basic eye structure.

What is going on here?

The observations (the facts) do not fit the evolutionary expectation. So, those who do not believe in an omnipotent and omniscient Designer must speculate that the same eye designs evolved multiple times in separate organisms. And, since there is absolutely no evidence for any kind of multiple evolutionary episodes, the academic literature is full of magic words like "emerge," "evolve," and "appear" instead of a realistic explanation for each supposed gradual step in eye evolution. No wonder Charles Darwin wrote to American botanist Asa Gray in 1860, "The thought of the eye made me cold all over."[3]

Beetles, Birds, and Butterflies

A very interesting spectacle leaps out at those who love the brilliant colors among living things. The surprise is that common color schemes are found across widely different types of animals. A strikingly iridescent blue is seen in some butterflies, beetles, and bird feathers. Although the color is very obvious, no blue pigment can be found! These very different creatures, and even some plants, reflect or absorb certain frequencies of light with the external chemical composition of their body.

Figure 1.4—Butterfly

The South American butterfly *Morpho rhetenor* has a regular grid of precisely constructed wedge-shaped ridges on its upper wings spaced at intervals of about 0.00022 millimeters. This pattern is repeated so accurately that the maximum deviation is only 0.00002 millimeters. No earthly workshop would be able to make one single wing scale with this required precision. Male peacock plume colors are due to variations in the tiny barbules of the magnificent feathers. Beetles of the genus *Hoplia* found in France have tiny scales within the exterior cuticle—scales so small that it takes a microscope to see them. All of these marvelous devices are tuned to specific light frequencies and absorb all of the light spectrum—except that which is reflected back in brilliant color.

There is no "survival" need here—just a flash and dash of beauty. One wonders how blind nature came up with these spectacular displays of color!

Spiral Spider Wonder

There is incredible detail and beauty in a typical spider web. How did these critters learn to make their webs? What trial-and-error process was necessary for nature to "select" the perfect design that would allow these marvelous creatures to trap their food? What was happening to the countless generations of evolving spiders that did not have the right tensile strength (too much or too little) in their web strands? Fossil spiders look just like today's spiders. Where did the first spider come from? Nobody seems to know.

Figure 1.5—Spider and Web

Scientists have found that web strands are comparable in strength to fused quartz fibers. Zoologists discovered that spiders have one to four pairs of spinnerets located in their abdomen (the usual number is three pairs). In addition, there are seven silk glands, each making a strand for a unique purpose. Many dozens of tiny tubes lead to these specially designed abdominal glands. In a process not completely understood, a special scleroprotein-based substance is released as a liquid that then seems to harden as it is pulled from the spinneret.

One silk gland produces thread for cocoons, and another for wrapping up the prey. The two seem to be the same, but they require especially designed silk. Other glands make the walking thread so the spider doesn't get snagged herself, while still another makes the sticky material that captures the juicy dinner. Some of the finer threads are almost invisible to us unless the light is reflected just right. Yet spider silk is strong! Typically it has a tensile strength five times that of steel and elasticity—strong enough to stop a lumbering bumblebee at full speed.

Each spider engineers a style of web characteristic of its species and builds it perfectly on the first try. These complex glands and intricate design patterns have every evidence of design. It is obvious that the spider does not have the intelligence in its brain to learn how to do this. It is equally obvious that the ability to create webs is already designed into the genetic instructions that were placed in the original spiders by their Creator.

Unlocking the Mysteries of Design

What we see around us gives overwhelming evidence of having been designed by "super" intelligence in the past. It is obvious the Designer is not creating things now, but our universe is filled with engineered systems of magnificent design.

Jesus Christ stated, "You shall know the truth, and the truth shall make you free" (John 8:32). If truth is knowable, then it should follow that there would be ample evidence of truth in and around our universe. While we each have unique, subjective experiences, there is an absolute, objective truth that is manifest to everyone.

Inescapable laws in nature exist for our benefit, our advantage, and our protection. We can observe these laws in action all around us. Scientific knowledge requires an absolute standard of truth that can be discovered. Such knowledge is not a collection of subjective opinions. Rather, it is a collection of explanations about objective reality that is based on observed or predicted phenomena. In addition, these explanations must be verified repeatedly to confirm they correctly model reality.

As our technical ability to observe reality improves, we are able to increase the quality and quantity of our observations. Better-observed data can challenge our explanations, some of which will no longer fit the observed facts. New theories are then formed and either verified or discredited. While our scientific knowledge changes rapidly, the absolute reality being modeled has never changed. The scientific method assumes an absolute reality against which theories can be checked.

The scientific method compares our limited understanding with reality. This method requires that a scientist test a theory based on observation or a predicated hypothesis. The scientist must formulate a theory or hypothesis based on what has been observed, then design a test by which the theory may be verified as valid or not. If that theory produces observed events that correspond with what was predicted beforehand, then the scientist has a serious beginning point from which to claim further science (knowledge) about the specific test.

Over the last several hundred years, a number of theories have been tested and verified so often that they are now considered scientific laws. Scientists are confident that these laws correctly model reality. Should someone claim they have had a subjective experience that contradicts one of these laws, the burden of proof is on that person to prove that they can repeatedly demonstrate that the previously observable law is wrong in some very important way. The standard of measurement remains true about reality, verified through repeated observation.

How to Evaluate the Past

Past events are different from events that are repeatable and observable. The scientific method is limited to what can be tested, reproduced, and falsified. What lies outside these parameters is not empirical science but passes into the realm of historical science or speculation.

Untestable assumptions about the past must be based either on the presumption of uniform natural processes that are believed to be consistent over all time, or the presumption that there is an eyewitness revelation of an intelligent being who was present when the past events were unfolding. Obviously, the first presumption is that there is no such eyewitness—and all that we can depend on are the current processes of nature. The remaining presumption is that there is an omnipotent, omniscient, and transcendent Creator.

Neither position is "science." Both positions are belief systems. Both positions are mutually exclusive of the other. One must believe that the observable design that surrounds us in everything that we see demands a Designer—or one must reject that presumption and embrace the idea that everything we see has come about purely by natural processes with no intervention on the part of anyone or anything other than nature.

The assumptions the scientist brings to his or her study can obscure their interpretations of the evidence. Untestable events do not benefit from the repeatable observations that have served as the cauldron that verifies scientific knowledge, but science can test an assumption by evaluating the accuracy of the predictions of different ideas. The model (theory, belief, revelation) that best predicts what is observable is the more credible model of reality. However, because new observations cannot be made about past events, verification is limited.

Observable Cause

The best explanation for the cause of the reality we experience is an all-powerful, all-present, all-knowing, and loving God. While absolute proof of the existence of God cannot be realized by any human being—it is not possible to "test" omnipotence, omniscience, or transcendence—the great weight of evidence, when rationally evaluated, clearly balances the scales heavily in favor of God. We can demonstrate beyond a reasonable doubt that "He is, and that He is a rewarder of those who diligently seek Him" (Hebrews 11:6).

God has promised numerous times that He will help us understand what He has done for us. Indeed, there are promises that ensure our discovery of God's existence—if we really want to know the truth.

> For I know the thoughts that I think toward you, says the LORD, thoughts of peace and not of evil, to give you a future and a hope. Then you will call upon Me and go and pray to Me, and I will listen to you. And you will seek Me and find Me, when you search for Me with all your heart (Jeremiah 29:11-13).

If that promise is true, we ought to be able to "see" God in the physical world in such a way that knowledge of God would be obvious or intuitive through our everyday experience. In fact, that is exactly what God promises:

> Since the creation of the world His invisible attributes are clearly seen, being understood by the things that are made, even His eternal power and Godhead (Romans 1:20).

Even the "invisible things" are clearly seen by what is available to all of us. Are you aware that all science rests on an invisible law of science?

Cause and Effect

The most certain and universal of all scientific principles is that of causality, or the law of cause and effect. The implications of this principle have been fought over vigorously in theological and philosophical disciplines, but there is no question of its universal acceptance in the world of experimental science, as well as in ordinary experience.

During the first century AD, a high-ranking Jewish leader named Saul of Tarsus—also known as Paul—became so convinced that Jesus is the Son of God that he spent the rest of his life as a Christian activist. In fact, he became so famous that on his trip to Athens, the intellectual elite of that sophisticated city invited him to speak to the philosophical leaders at Mars Hill, next to the Acropolis. During his discourse, Paul told these men that they were looking for spiritual satisfaction in all the wrong places. The evidence for God was all around them—even in their own humanity:

> Therefore, since we are the offspring of God, we ought not to think that the Divine Nature is like gold or silver or stone, something shaped by art and man's devising (Acts 17:29).

Scientific interpretation: Since we are here, the cause for humanity must be greater than, but similar to, us.

Everything Has a Cause

In ordinary experience, one knows intuitively that nothing happens in isolation. Every event can be traced to one or more events that preceded it and, in fact, caused it. We ask, "How did this happen?" or "What caused this?" or "Where did this come from?" Sometimes we try to get at the beginning cause (or First Cause) by asking, "When did it start?" or more incisively, "Why did this happen?"

When we try to trace an event to its cause, or causes, we find that we never seem to reach a stopping point. The cause of the event was itself caused by a prior cause, which was effected by a previous cause, and so on. Eventually, we must face the question of the original cause—an uncaused First Cause.

A scientific experiment specifically tries to relate effects to causes in the form of quantitative equations, if possible. Thus, if a scientist repeats the same experiment with exactly the same elements, then exactly the same results should be produced. The very basis of the highly reputed scientific method is this very law of causality. Effects are in and like their causes, and like causes produce like effects. That is, everything that happens contains the "stuff" that made it happen—and the happening looks an awful lot like the stuff that made it happen.

Your kids look like you!

Science in the modern sense would be altogether impossible if cause and effect should cease. This law inevitably leads to a choice between two alternatives: (1) an infinite chain of nonprimary causes (nothing is ultimately responsible for all observable causes and effects), or (2) an uncaused primary Cause of all causes (the one absolute Cause that initiated everything).

The Effect Problem

Rationally, it must be concluded that all things began with a single uncaused First Cause, an all-powerful and all-knowing transcendent God who is above all and existed before all other causes. This universal law demonstrates the existence of an uncaused source or a First Cause by which all observable effects came about. In simple terms, every cause must be at least as great as the effect that it produces and will, in reality, produce an effect that is less than the cause. That is, all effects must have a cause that is greater than the effect that was produced.

But there are also two more related universal laws that are demonstrated in everything we examine in the world around us. There is no new mass-energy coming into existence anywhere in the universe, and every bit of the original mass-energy is still here. And every time something happens (i.e., an event takes place), some of that energy becomes unavailable.

These two laws are well known as the First and Second Laws of Thermodynamics.

The First Law of Thermodynamics tells us that matter (mass-energy) can be changed but can neither be created nor destroyed. The Second Law tells us that all phenomena (mass-energy organized into an "effect") continually proceed to lower levels of usefulness. When this universal law is traced backward, one is faced again with the possibility that there is an ongoing chain of ever-decreasing effects resulting from a chain of nonprimary, ever-increasing causes. However, what appears more probable is the existence of an uncaused and ultimate Source—an omnipotent, omniscient, eternal, and primary First Cause.

The Logical Implications

Everything we can observe—up and out to the seemingly infinite reaches of our universe or down and into the miniscule pieces of the world of the nature of matter— is exceedingly complex and fascinatingly related to everything else. All of our scientific intelligence is attempting to find the unifying principle of reality. Everyone knows that it exists; secular academia is sure that there is a foundational "god particle" of some sort, a cause from which everything else emanates. But while atheistic academia searches for the "unknown God," all of empirical science depends on this absolute fact: Nothing can come from nothing—everything has a cause.

Applying these principles of cause and effect, it is clear that scientific logic indicates that the cause for the universe in which we live must trace back to an infinite First Cause of all things. Random motion or primeval particles cannot produce intelligent thought, nor can inert molecules generate spiritual worship.

- The First Cause of limitless space must be infinite.
- The First Cause of endless time must be eternal.
- The First Cause of boundless energy must be omnipotent.
- The First Cause of universal interrelationships must be omnipresent.
- The First Cause of infinite complexity must be omniscient.
- The First Cause of spiritual values must be spiritual.
- The First Cause of human responsibility must be volitional.
- The First Cause of human integrity must be truthful.

- The First Cause of human love must be loving.
- The First Cause of life must be living.

We would conclude from the law of cause and effect that this First Cause of all things must be an infinite, eternal, omnipotent, omnipresent, omniscient, spiritual, volitional, truthful, loving, living Being! Perhaps the words of the Creator Himself are worth quoting as we wrap up this chapter on design:

> For the wrath of God is revealed from heaven against all ungodliness and unrighteousness of men, who suppress the truth in unrighteousness, because what may be known of God is manifest in them, for God has shown it to them. For since the creation of the world His invisible attributes are clearly seen, being understood by the things that are made, even His eternal power and Godhead, so that they are without excuse, because, although they knew God, they did not glorify Him as God, nor were thankful, but became futile in their thoughts, and their foolish hearts were darkened. Professing to be wise, they became fools, and changed the glory of the incorruptible God into an image made like corruptible man—and birds and four-footed animals and creeping things.

> Therefore God also gave them up to uncleanness, in the lusts of their hearts, to dishonor their bodies among themselves, who exchanged the truth of God for the lie, and worshiped and served the creature rather than the Creator, who is blessed forever. Amen (Romans 1:18-25).

CHAPTER 2

Origin of Life

Two fundamental questions regarding life remain unanswered from the perspective of secular scientists. First, and most often discussed, is "When did life begin?" The second, and more profound, question is "What *is* life?"

Most of those who do not give the biblical message any credence on this matter would suggest that life began with "curvaceous, worm-like strings of microfossils" that were discovered in ancient fossil beds said to be some 3.5 billions of years old.[1] Obviously, both the date and the fossils have generated a lot of discussion, with little agreement on the specifics except that life "happened" a long time ago.

Basic Story

I suspect you are familiar with the basic story that has been told and speculated about for nearly 200 years—especially since Darwin's theory of a common ancestor for all life was generally accepted by academia. Essentially, the majority opinion is that inorganic chemicals came together to form amino acids, which then somehow bonded together to form proteins, which then (again somehow) began to replicate and connect together in a certain manner to form a living cell.

After a couple billion years of random replication, there was an "explosion" of life about 540 million years ago during the Cambrian period. Very complicated marine invertebrates suddenly appeared in the fossil record—with no evidence of any change in the previous life ancestors. This is certainly a curious thing, but the story insists that such indeed did happen. Then, over the next 50 million years or so (a very short period of evolutionary time), most major phyla of the life forms now known appeared.

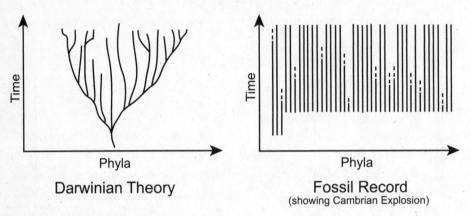

Figure 2.1—Fossil Tree and Lawn

After this explosion of living animals, the various "eras" or "epochs" of life began to diversify, finally coming to the apex of complexity with the development of mammals and man within the last two to four million years or so, depending on who is making the estimates. Each of these eras has its specialized types of life forms, with the more well-known period of the dinosaurs covering 230 to 66 million years ago during what is known as the Mesozoic Era.

That is a short version of the story that is most often taught and believed in the educated societies of the world. Similar stories have been around in more popular forms for millennia, however, with the ancient Egyptians, Babylonians, Greeks, and Romans having variations of a pantheon of gods who were responsible for the long development of the planet and its creatures. Evolution is not a new concept, simply a new word for an old story. It has just become more sophisticated in the past two centuries as scientists have sought a nonsupernatural explanation for the functioning life and processes around us.

ICR founder Dr. Henry Morris suggested in his commentaries and articles that the idea of an evolutionary development out of a watery chaos originated with none other than the great archangel Lucifer, who was the first created being to rebel against the Creator.

It is intriguing to note that God created the angels when there was only water all around them, probably on the first day of creation week...Among all these "angels of light" (note 2 Corinthians 11:14), none was more glorious than "Lucifer, son of the morning" (Isaiah 14:12), who was evidently the "anointed cherub," hovering over the "holy mountain of God" in the heavenly "garden of God" (see Ezekiel 28:13,14)...

Since his first consciousness had been of the pervasive waters surrounding him and the other angels, as well as the throne of God, he must have assumed they all had in some mysterious way been "created" by the waters themselves. It was perhaps by such reasoning that he could rationalize his otherwise completely irrational rebellion against his Creator, a rebellion which is still continuing today.

It is probably no coincidence that all the ancient pagan cosmogonies—most notably those of Samaria, Egypt, Babylonia, and Greece, as well as others—taught that the world, with all its systems and inhabitants, evolved out of an eternal primeval watery chaos. The "deceiver of the whole world" (Revelation 12:9) has deceived himself most of all.[2]

Thus Lucifer became the first evolutionist, and this great lie by which he deceived himself became the basis of his later deception of Eve and then of the founders of all the varied pantheistic religions of the world, as well as modern evolutionism and "New Age" philosophies.[3]

Yes, those ideas are speculative—but no more so than the idea that there was no Creator! One would anticipate that any speculation based on a scientific methodology would have some evidential basis. All that we know is that life comes from life! Many, many experiments have been performed in attempts to demonstrate how organic chemicals could arise from inorganic matter. At best, the answers are not satisfactory. Everything we know, everything we can observe, everything we can test in a laboratory—all demonstrate that we must have a living cell to get life.

Geneticist Dr. Jeffrey Tomkins said:

> The question of how life first arose on Earth is perhaps the greatest obstacle for the evolutionary paradigm. While the whole concept of biological evolution itself is full of serious problems, the origins of the first biomolecules and the first cell (not to mention the enormous amount of information contained within the cell) is a complete impossibility from a naturalistic perspective. In fact, without a plausible explanation as to the origin of the first cell, the whole evolutionary story collapses![4]

Basic Science

As mentioned in the last chapter, the First Law of Thermodynamics states that matter can neither be created nor destroyed (the law of conservation of energy). The Second Law of Thermodynamics says that all processes tend toward a state of increasing entropy (the law of deterioration of energy). The First Law insists that the universe could not create itself. The Second Law maintains that the universe could not be infinitely old. The First Law tells us that the amount of energy in the universe remains stable. The Second Law tells us that the energy in the universe is becoming less and less available for work as time goes on. The First Law has demonstrated that nothing can come into existence by itself. The Second Law demonstrates that everything is dying.

Scientific Law	Creation Implication
First Law of Thermodynamics: Energy cannot be created or destroyed.	The universe could not create itself.
Second Law of Thermodynamics: The energy of a closed system will constantly decrease.	The universe could not be infinitely old.

Figure 2.2—Scientific Law

This is particularly significant when considering the origin of life.

To begin with, all living things are exceedingly complex. We now know, of course, that the DNA and RNA of living creatures are informational systems of the first order. To suggest that these unimaginably complex systems of chemical messages just "happened" is challenging, to say the least. The First Law would appear to prevent any form of "new" information coming into existence (it should have been there at the beginning), and the Second Law would seem to destroy any information that happened to be available—certainly over millions of years of deterioration!

It is possible, of course, to invent a workaround to all the problems in an evolutionary story. The multiple thousands of pages in secular textbooks that contain such explanations are a testament to that possibility. However, all those explanations are exceptions to the observations. That is, we do not find any observable data that provide evolutionary evidence for the so-called "explosion" of life recorded in the Cambrian strata. Nor do we find any observable evidence for a general "upward" shift of new or additive information in the DNA of living organisms over the supposed eons of evolutionary time. As already noted, the First Law would limit the addition of any new mass-energy, and the Second Law would generate an inexorable force toward disorder.

The laws of science are against the story of evolution.

Evolutionists often note that order can arise in one area as long as the rest of the universe loses more orderliness than is gained. But this phenomenon fails to connect the gain in one area to the loss in another. A growing plant will organize energy into new tissue, but this comes about through the complex and wonderful process of photosynthesis. Intelligent and well-educated engineers can design machinery to convert certain energies into a more organized format, but these events come about by purposeful design, not random interplay across a mysterious universe.

The argument that the laws of science stand against "big picture" evolution remains fixed.

The Origin of Life

But this book is not about exposing the flaws of evolution, although there are many and they are obvious. The focus of the book is about unlocking the mysteries of Genesis. What, then, can we learn from the book of Genesis about the origin of life?

Creation

The Bible opens with an amazing declaration: "In the beginning God created the heavens and the earth" (Genesis 1:1). That statement is both unique and profound. It is unique in that no other religious book begins that way. It is profound in that it is both clear and precise, with an economy of words.

Many have tried to add to or subtract from it, but doing so requires long treatises or tomes to make it tell another story. The statement is purposely designed either to be accepted at face value and believed or rejected in its entirety. There is no room for a middle ground without going to great lengths to explain away the words used or to design a reason why the words do not mean what they obviously mean.

God created!

Many years after those words were recorded by Moses, the psalmist wrote a hymn of praise to the Creator, noting:

The heavens declare the glory of God; and the firmament shows His handiwork. Day unto day utters speech, and night unto night reveals knowledge. There is no speech nor language where their voice is not heard (Psalm 19:1-3).

Just what is it that the universe "says" to us? Please recall the First Law of science: Everything that exists is in a state of conservation. Nothing can be created or destroyed. The various forms of energy can be changed, augmented, or transferred from other sources, but the amount of that mass-energy remains the same. If anything can be called an absolute fact, this First Law is as sure as anything we can know.

This information is really important! That law tells ("speaks to") us *nothing* that exists today could cause itself to come into being. There must have been a beginning. And that beginning would have to involve processes, information, and energies that we have absolutely no knowledge of. Scientists argue all the time about how and when the beginning may have happened, but everyone knows that there must have been one.

The Second Law of all science has also been proven. Every time work is done in the universe—every time anything happens—some of the energy necessary to make the event happen becomes "used." Some portion of the constant quantity of energy in the universe (the First Law) becomes unavailable for further work. The energy turns inward—the *quality* deteriorates. That measurable deterioration is called *entropy*, and it always increases over time, causing everything in the universe to "die"—slowly, but surely. Again, if there is anything that can be called a law of the universe, this Second Law is demonstrated in everything all the time. Some things can be maintained for a time (using mass-energy from other sources), but eventually everything wears out. Everything goes toward a state of disorder and ultimately becomes unusable. Everything! No exceptions.

There is no *ex nihilo* ("something out of nothing") creation going on now. But here we are! We live, we think, we see—we gaze into the vast universe and see untold and uncountable galaxies of billions of stars, and we peer into the microscopic world of the molecule and are stunned with the complexity and vast interrelationships of the "world within." Here we are! Here it is! How? When? Why? These questions blaze in our minds, and we sense the omnipotence and omniscience of the Cause of our universe.

And here is another universal "language" of the universe—the law of cause and effect. Simply stated, it is this: Everything that happens is caused by something else. Every event has a cause that produces an effect. The source (the cause) of the event must have sufficient power and information to produce the specific effect. Even an apparently random event like an explosion (let's say the Big Bang) has to have the confined energy necessary to produce the explosion and the trigger necessary to start the explosion.

- The space our universe occupies is essentially limitless. The cause of that infinite space must of necessity be without measure.

- The reservoirs of energy in our universe are essentially immeasurable. The cause of that amount of energy must itself be essentially infinite.

- The interrelationships of all matter and energy require that the cause of such conditions must be everywhere present.

- The inability of our minds to conceive of an end to time requires that the cause must of itself be eternal.

- The very fact that humanity can think and reason requires that the cause of such phenomena must be rational.

- The inconceivable complexity of the universe—of life itself—must have a cause that is omniscient.

The existence of life, and especially human life, demands that the cause of living beings must be alive. In fact, that is precisely what we discover in the laboratory. Even though recent headlines touted that scientists had created life in their lab, the hyperbole was rampant. Geneticists had merely made exact copies of the DNA already present in the bacteria. These "creators" merely copied what was already created! In literature we would call that plagiarism, not creation.

Life itself is required before another life can be made to begin.

Life Is Created

As was discussed in the first chapter of this book, everything that we can see and measure has all of the elements of being designed by a Master Engineer and Planner. There is no evidence of haphazard or random relationships.

Yes, some things are difficult to understand, and there is a lot of evidence of bad things happening, but that does nothing to override the reality of order and purpose. If anything, those bad things only verify and hasten the impact of the law of entropy!

Creation is an act of omnipotence and omniscience. Creation requires the bringing into existence of something that did not exist before. Creation even requires a unique word to define it!

Most of us are aware that the older books of the Bible were written in the Hebrew language. Genesis certainly was, as were—with the exception of a few sections or verses—the remainder of the 39 books that have come to be known as the Old Testament. These books comprised the Bible of the Jewish nation, Israel. In that ancient language, that Hebrew word translated "create" is *bara*.

The term appears 54 times in the Hebrew text of the Old Testament. God is the only subject of the verb in all but four figurative uses of the word, and it is absolutely clear from the biblical text that God is the Creator who creates something from nothing using power and processes that we know nothing about.

> By faith we understand that the worlds were framed by the word of God, so that the things which are seen were not made of things which are visible (Hebrews 11:3).

> ...God, who gives life to the dead and calls those things which do not exist as though they did (Romans 4:17).

The New Testament stresses the creative power of God applied to the twice-born process that "creates" an eternal life where nothing existed before except something that was "dead in trespasses and sins" (Ephesians 2:1). All of self-conscious life will one day acknowledge that such action is unique to the Alpha and Omega of eternity. All will worship and confess that God alone is able to create—man is the created, not the Creator.

In simple language, only God can create. *amen*

You may recall that after God had created the universe on Day One, He "made" and "shaped" the stuff of the universe over the next three days. He made an expanse between the watery matrix that held the earth inside space on Day Two. Then he made the dry land and the seas along with the plants that were

③   ④

to be for food on Day Three. On Day Four, God made the lights (light holders) of the heavens that were to be for timekeeping. *Sun, Moon, Stars*

God had created (something from nothing) on Day One. God had then used the material of Day One to make everything else, including the stars, the sun, and the moon. *Amen*   ①

⑤ On Day Five, God created life. First were the water creatures and then the
② air creatures—"abundantly" throughout the planet. These living things were
created, not made. On Day Six, ⑥ He continued creating the "cattle," "beasts of the field," and "creeping things" that would live on the dry land. They were very different from the air and water creatures, but they shared the created life that set them apart from the food that had the ability to reproduce "after its kind."

Then God paused for a very specific purpose. He would create a being that would bear His image and be in His likeness. A male—and then a female—who would be delegated the authority to rule over the planet that had been "created and made." You may recall that God took some of the dirt that was created on Day One and formed the body of Adam. Here again, God used the "create" verb, but He also used a very personal term—God "sculpted" this body with His own personal involvement and breathed into this unique body (God made only one) the "breath of life."

There is an old joke that may help us grasp the significance of the concept of creating as opposed to merely making or shaping—or even sculpting.

The Bible lets us know that the angelic beings were brought into existence sometime before the third day of the creation week (Job 38:7). Lucifer, the chief angel (Isaiah 14:12-14), was a created being (Ezekiel 28:13-15). All these angelic creatures watched from someplace outside the universe as these events were transpiring, and apparently Lucifer, who seems to have been the most brilliant and powerful of all of these spirit beings, thought he could do everything that he saw God doing.

The joke goes something like this:

Lucifer: "I watched you make Adam from the dirt. That was no big deal. I can do that."

God: "Okay. Have at it. Let's see what you can do."

Lucifer reaches down to the ground and grabs a fistful of dirt.

God: "No, you don't. Get your own dirt!"

And therein lies the difference between creating and making. God created the heavens and the earth. Lucifer was merely mimicking what he saw God making. Yes, the great Adversary is a powerful being and is far superior to our own abilities and understanding. But:

> You believe that there is one God. You do well. Even the demons believe—and tremble! (James 2:19).

> I am the LORD, and there is no other; there is no God besides Me. I will gird you, though you have not known Me, that they may know from the rising of the sun to its setting that there is none besides Me. I am the LORD, and there is no other (Isaiah 45:5-6).

> There is one God and one Mediator between God and men, the Man Christ Jesus (1 Timothy 2:5).

Life Is Unique

Animal and human life is different from that of the plants and vegetation of Earth. But we have so comingled the terms that we often overlook the fact that the Bible text uses a unique word for "life" that is never applied to plants and vegetation.

The first use of such a term is in Genesis 1:20-30, where God describes His creative action on Day Five. The word choice of the Holy Spirit is the Hebrew term *chay* (and its derivatives) and occasionally the word *chayah*. Together, those words are used 763 times in the Old Testament—never applying that quality to plants or vegetation.

> Then God said, "Let the waters abound with an abundance of *living creatures*, and let birds fly above the earth across the face of the firmament of the heavens." So God created great sea creatures and every *living thing* that moves, with which the waters abounded,

according to their kind, and every winged bird according to its kind. And God saw that it was good...

Then God said, "Let the earth bring forth the *living creature* according to its kind: cattle and creeping thing and beast of the earth, each according to its kind"; and it was so. And God made the beast of the earth according to its kind, cattle according to its kind, and everything that creeps on the earth according to its kind. And God saw that it was good...

Then God blessed them, and God said to them, "Be fruitful and multiply; fill the earth and subdue it; have dominion over the fish of the sea, over the birds of the air, and over every living thing that moves on the earth...

Also, to every beast of the earth, to every bird of the air, and to everything that creeps on the earth, in which there is *life*, I have given every green herb for food"; and it was so (Genesis 1:20-30).

Please note that last phrase. The beasts, birds, living creatures, and various creeping things were to find food from the "green herb." In no place in the Scriptures are plants ascribed the life that living creatures possess. Plants are food. They do not possess the life of animals and man. They are, indeed, marvelous, beautiful, complex, and able to reproduce "after their kind," but they are designed by the Creator to be a source of energy to maintain life—they are not alive, as we will soon see.

Life Has Independent Movement

This may seem like either an obvious point or an irrelevant one. However, one of the descriptive terms that the Creator applied to living creatures was "moves" or "creeps."

God created great sea creatures and every living thing that *moves* with which the waters abounded, according to their kind, and every winged bird according to its kind (Genesis 1:21).

Then God said, "Let Us make man in Our image, according to Our likeness; let them have dominion over the fish of the sea, over the birds of the air, and over the cattle, over all the earth and over every creeping thing that *creeps* on the earth" (Genesis 1:26).

Then God blessed them, and God said to them, "Be fruitful and multiply; fill the earth and subdue it; have dominion over the fish of the sea, over the birds of the air, and over every living thing that *moves* on the earth" (Genesis 1:28).

"Also, to every beast of the earth, to every bird of the air, and to everything that *creeps* on the earth, in which there is life, I have given every green herb for food" (Genesis 1:30).

The Hebrew word here is *ramas*, used 17 times in the Old Testament—never of plants or vegetation of any kind. It is used to describe birds gliding through the atmosphere. It is used of insects "sneaking" around on the floor of the earth. It is used of large beasts "stalking" and moving freely through the wild lands of the earth. It is never used of trees, plants, grass, or vegetation of any kind.

Living things move. Not just swaying in the wind, not just spores drifting along or pollen hitching a ride on bees, but independent, conscious, willful movement. Almost all plants are rooted to the earth—they are "sprouts" of earth. Plants do not travel from one location to another—except on the backs of animals or carried by water or wind or in trucks driven by humans. They are rooted. They do not have the power of *ramas*.

Science has had an interesting time trying to sort out some of the smallest of moving things. Most of us have looked through a microscope at the "wigglies" in a drop of pond water. They are amazing critters! Some of them ooze, like the amoeba; others bounce around, like the *Paramecium*. If we are able to watch long enough, we can see them split into two—reproduce right in front of our very eyes. Fascinating!

But there are real questions about the myriads of organisms in the microscopic domain. Most scientists would appear to agree that bacteria are alive (that is, they move and reproduce rather normally). Viruses, on the other hand, don't seem to behave at all like bacteria. Some viruses are more dangerous, and we have a much more difficult time controlling or overcoming their harmful effects on living bodies. There is much we do not know about the microscopic world. The Creator has designed these miniscule elements for purposes not yet fully discovered. The damage appears to be the result of mutation, and that phenomenon seems to have arisen at God's judgment on Earth because of Adam's rebellion (Genesis 3:17).

But what we do know, what we have observed and tested repeatedly, is that living things have the ability to move independently—and plants do not.

Life Has Blood

"The life of the flesh is in the blood," announces Leviticus 17:11. There is so much in the Scriptures about the significance of blood as the evidence of life that it seems somewhat superfluous to speak of it. The bulk of the sacrificial system under Mosaic law was centered in blood sacrifice. Again and again, the dictates of that law required the shedding of blood to kill (execute) an innocent animal in a temporary substitutionary atonement (covering) of the sins that people had committed.

The whole Christian gospel is founded on the necessity of the shedding of the Messiah's blood during the crucifixion as evidence that His life was given on behalf of the "sins...[of] the whole world" (1 John 2:2). The death of Jesus Christ was made necessary, "for it is not possible that the blood of bulls and goats could take away sins" (Hebrews 10:4). These are broad and oft-repeated principles.

When God was instructing Noah about his responsibilities after the global Flood of cosmos-destroying judgment, God insisted that "you shall not eat flesh with its life, that is, its blood" (Genesis 9:4). The sacred life that was contained in the blood was so important that God even insisted that "surely for your lifeblood I will demand a reckoning; from the hand of every beast I will require it, and from the hand of man. From the hand of every man's brother I will require the life of man" (Genesis 9:5).

The dietary laws of the nation of Israel specifically restricted any consumption of blood in their meals. The blood was the life source of all living things, and was, therefore, to be held sacred.

> ...for it is the *life* of all flesh. Its *blood* sustains its life. Therefore I said to the children of Israel, "You shall not eat the blood of any flesh, for the *life of all flesh is its blood*. Whoever eats it shall be cut off" (Leviticus 17:14).

> Only be sure that you do not eat the blood, *for the blood is the life*; you may not eat the life with the meat (Deuteronomy 12:23).

Those restrictions were a far cry from the blood drinks and blood puddings of the pagan societies of their day—not to mention the practice of bloodletting that abounded from ancient pagan Egypt until the "enlightenment" of naturalism and medical practice in our own country. Had the Christian physicians of earlier centuries observed the clear principles of God's instructions to Israel, many would not have needlessly suffered and lives might well have been extended during the "Dark Ages" of history.

The concept was pretty simple. If a moving creature had blood, it was alive. If it had blood, it had life. This is not very difficult to understand, but it is often either ignored or disputed.

Life Has Nephesh

This Hebrew word is used 753 times in the Old Testament and is translated by the English word "soul" 475 times. Another 117 times the translators chose "life" as the best way to express the term, but there is no doubt that the basic idea is that *nephesh* speaks of the noncorporeal part of life—perhaps best equated with the self-conscious awareness that "I" exist. Frequently, *nephesh* seems to be used to express the emotive side of living things as opposed to the thinking side.

Figure 2.3—Romans 6:23 says, "The wages of sin is death." This means that there could be no death of nephesh *creatures that have blood (Leviticus 17:11) before Adam's sin.*

> My *soul* shall be joyful in the LORD; it shall rejoice in His salvation (Psalm 35:9).

> The *heart* knows its own bitterness, and a stranger does not share its joy (Proverbs 14:10).

> I will greatly rejoice in the LORD, my *soul* shall be joyful in my God; for He has clothed me with the garments of salvation, He has covered me with the robe of righteousness, as a bridegroom decks himself with ornaments, and as a bride adorns herself with her jewels (Isaiah 61:10).

Nephesh is often used in the same context as the "heart" of man—that mysterious inner part of us that responds and reacts to events as well as seems to be the place where we make (or at least treasure) long-term commitments.

> Only take heed to yourself, and diligently keep *yourself* [*nephesh*], lest you forget the things your eyes have seen, and lest they depart from your heart all the days of your life (Deuteronomy 4:9).

> You shall love the LORD your God with all your heart, with all your *soul*, and with all your strength (Deuteronomy 6:5).

Now set your heart and your *soul* to seek the LORD your God
(1 Chronicles 22:19).

As he thinks in his *heart* [*nephesh*], so is he. "Eat and drink!" he
says to you, but his *heart* is not with you (Proverbs 23:7).

They eat up the sin of My people; they set their *heart* [*nephesh*] on
their iniquity (Hosea 4:8).

Whether *nephesh* is translated as soul, life, person, mind, heart, creature,
yourselves, desire, or appetite, it is never used of plants. Ever.

Life Has Ruwach

The other noncorporeal term used by the Holy Spirit to describe and define
life is the Hebrew word *ruwach*. Of the 389 times the word or its derivatives
appear in the text of the Old Testament, it is translated "spirit" 232 times, "wind"
92 times, and "breath" 27 times. The clearest connection between *ruwach* and
life is the phrase "breath of life."

Behold, I Myself am bringing floodwaters on the earth, to destroy
from under heaven all flesh in which is the *breath* [*ruwach*] of life;
everything that is on the earth shall die (Genesis 6:17).

They went into the ark to Noah, two by two, of all flesh in which
is the *breath* [*ruwach*] of life (Genesis 7:15).

All in whose nostrils was the *breath* [*ruwach*] of the spirit of life,
all that was on the dry land, died (Genesis 7:22).

These sweeping statements, made by God Himself and by Noah, who wit-
nessed the events, are clearly inclusive of every kind of living creature that lived
on the dry land and breathed air. The only creatures not included would have
been plants, marine animals, and some insects that neither breathe air nor have
blood (as we know it).

Several passages suggest that the "spirit" of man and of animals is more than
merely the ability to breathe.

Blessed is the man to whom the LORD does not impute iniquity, and in whose *spirit* [*ruwach*] there is no deceit (Psalm 32:2).

All the ways of a man are pure in his own eyes, but the LORD weighs the *spirits* [*ruwach*] (Proverbs 16:2).

Who knows the *spirit* [*ruwach*] of the sons of men, which goes upward, and the *spirit* [*ruwach*] of the animal, which goes down to the earth? (Ecclesiastes 3:21).

The burden of the word of the LORD against Israel. Thus says the LORD, who stretches out the heavens, lays the foundation of the earth, and forms the *spirit* [*ruwach*] of man within him (Zechariah 12:1).

Several other passages seem to differentiate between the *nephesh* (the soulish part of life) and the *ruwach* (the mental/intellectual part of life).

They were a grief of *mind* [*ruwach*] to Isaac and Rebekah (Genesis 26:35).

The Spirit of the LORD fell upon me, and said to me, "Speak! 'Thus says the LORD: "Thus you have said, O house of Israel; for I know the things that come into your *mind* [*ruwach*]"'" (Ezekiel 11:5).

What you have in your *mind* [*ruwach*] shall never be, when you say, "We will be like the Gentiles, like the families in other countries, serving wood and stone" (Ezekiel 20:32).

Then his *mind* [*ruwach*] changes, and he transgresses; he commits offense, ascribing this power to his god (Habakkuk 1:11).

Life Summarized

There are several key elements to life that distinguish it from all the other molecular forms and compounds of Earth. To begin with, although Earth was created along with time and the heavens on Day One, the making and shaping of that which was created did not require another *bara* (creation) until Day Five. On that day, after the earth and the universe had been prepared in such a way that environment, time references, and food sources were available and fully functioning, God created:

- Life itself—*chay*
  Self-contained, independently functioning, reproducing "kinds" of living creatures

- Things that *move*
  Self-directed, independent movement

- Things that have *blood*
  Blood is the source for life

- Soul—*nephesh*
  Self-aware, feeling, emotively responding

- Spirit—*ruwach*
  Mental consciousness, intuition, instinct

Figure 2.4—Life Nouns in Hebrew

In none of the hundreds of biblical passages that deal with living creatures are plants ever declared or compared to that which God created to carry His life force. Plants were made from the raw dirt of Day One and were specifically designed to be food for the life that was created on Days Five and Six.

Here's the dilemma: In modern scientific terminology, we apply the term *life* to almost everything that reproduces. We study the ever-expanding knowledge of plants and call it botany. *Plant life* is such a common term that we never give it a second thought. And indeed, the absolutely wonderful, beautiful, and amazing complexity of plants is stunningly exciting!

It wasn't until the mid-1700s that the process of photosynthesis was discovered by Jan Ingenhousz. Until then, we just ate the plants. Now we know that we literally could not live without them. That food takes in carbon dioxide and gives back some of the oxygen we need to survive—both as a people and as a planet. That makes plants pretty important. They feed us. They shade us. They protect us. They hold our planet together—and they even please us!

Who doesn't love to get or give flowers? When Jesus was living, He suggested that we "consider the lilies of the field, how they grow: they neither toil nor spin; and yet I say to you that even Solomon in all his glory was not arrayed like one of these" (Matthew 6:28-29). All over this planet, the magnificent blooms and arrays of color and structure strut like peacocks in full majesty. Yet they exist for only a few days or weeks "and tomorrow [are] thrown into the oven" (Matthew 6:30).

We spend billions of dollars of research funds and multiple thousands of highly educated man-hours trying to make a better peanut or a juicer tomato. Many of the economies of the world are based around growing, harvesting, and distributing plants. Everything we *know*, everything we *observe*, is that plants are *food* for living things—just like the Bible says:

> God said, "See, I have given you every herb that yields seed which is on the face of all the earth, and every tree whose fruit yields seed; to you it shall be for food. Also, to every beast of the earth, to every bird of the air, and to everything that creeps on the earth, in which there is life, I have given every green herb for food"; and it was so (Genesis 1:29-30).

Although plants are absolutely wonderful, complex, beautiful, and necessary for the functioning of our planet and for all living things, they do *not* have life! When we eat salads or cook veggies, we do not *kill* the lettuce or the broccoli. They are reproducing "earth" that the Creator of Earth caused to have "seed [within] itself" and to be able to replicate "according to its kind" (Genesis 1:11-12).

Yes, I know that this distinction goes against the majority of modern classifications of biology. However, it is theologically very important. If Earth is billions of years old, then there has been billions of years of death and destruction—before man and, according to the Scripture, before sin (Genesis 3:17-19; Romans 5:12-19; 6:23; 1 Corinthians 15:21).

One of the "proofs" given for death being a normal part of creation is the logic that plants are alive. Except for the record in the Genesis account, in every scheme of development plants were around for a long time before any kind of animal life—even the so-called explosion of life during the Cambrian Era. Every scenario of naturalistic development (even the theistic evolution and day-age theories) insists that plants were living and dying for eons prior to animals of any kind. Thus, if plants die, then death is a normal part of creation—and such a Creator would have made death the mechanism of bringing into existence the better (the "fittest") things.

If indeed death is normal and necessary, then a whole array of Bible teaching is negated. Death is certainly not the wages of sin (Romans 6:23). Neither is death the last enemy that must be destroyed prior to the new heavens and new earth (1 Corinthians 15:26). The whole concept of immortality, eternal life, and the victory of the resurrection becomes meaningless (1 Corinthians 15:51-57). But far more important than that would be the unnecessary "mistake" of the death of the Lord Jesus on the cross (1 Corinthians 15:3-4). If death was part of God's creation, if God created death, then He (the Father in heaven) executed His only begotten Son for no justifiable reason at all!

Yet it pleased the LORD to bruise Him; He has put Him to grief.
When You make His soul an offering for sin, He shall see His

seed, He shall prolong His days, and the pleasure of the LORD shall prosper in His hand. He shall see the labor of His soul, and be satisfied. By His knowledge My righteous Servant shall justify many, for He shall bear their iniquities (Isaiah 53:10-11).

One of the most observable and provable of all scientific principles is that life is so unique that it is absolutely necessary to have life to produce life. No scientific experiment has ever produced it! None. Not one. Many have tried, and countless millions of dollars have been spent on efforts to get life out of non-life. All have failed. Even after the greatest brains and research labs of the world were able to clone life, they still had to start with a living cell.

The Bible simply puts it this way:

In the beginning was the Word, and the Word was with God, and the Word was God. He was in the beginning with God. All things were made through Him, and without Him nothing was made that was made. In Him was life, and the life was the light of men (John 1:1-4).

CHAPTER 3

Human Life

Secular scientists will openly admit that uncovering a reasonable theory for the origin of life is very difficult. As we discussed in the last chapter, the enormous differences between inorganic chemicals and a functioning and replicating cell are too vast a gap to contemplate bridging naturalistically. That's why many of our more reputable academic scholars are going back to some form of panspermia—the theory that life was brought here from some distant galaxy where more highly evolved intelligent beings were experimenting with "seeding" life throughout the universe.

In his interview with Ben Stein in the movie *Expelled: No Intelligence Allowed*, Darwinist Michael Ruse mentioned the theory that life began from nonlife through a bunch of chemicals getting together "on the backs of crystals."[1] Actually, that theory is not at all new. It was initially promoted by Scottish chemist A.G. Cairns-Smith in a paper in 1966. Several books about it followed, and the idea was favorably mentioned by Richard Dawkins in his book *The Selfish Gene*.[2] Essentially, the crystal theory was based on the idea that the core of all life is the ability to copy portions of its information, and since there are many forms of copying in crystalline formation, the idea was proposed that this innate characteristic might well be the beginning of nature trying to evolve life.

Interesting, to say the least!

Although there are many, many theories about how the first life came into being, most evolutionary theories make the assumption that human life evolved through various stages from apelike ancestors. The most recent of our "relatives" is favored to be chimpanzees. And, as one would suspect, because the evidence for such a relationship is predominantly circumstantial, there are detractors.

I suspect you have heard that humans are the current apex of evolutionary development and, though highly evolved, are really nothing more than advanced mammals. Creatures that became humans and apes are thought to have split about 20 to 25 million years ago from those early mammals that gave rise to the monkeys of Europe, Asia, and Africa. In this scenario, humans and great apes—orangutans, gorillas, and chimpanzees—share a common ancestor that existed around 13 million years ago. Human ancestors diverged from the ancestors of chimpanzees around seven million years ago, and *Homo sapiens* (you and I) most likely descended over the last two to three million years from those supposed ancestors.

At least, that's the party line.

Lots of debate, however, has gone on among the scientists who study fossils. The various branches of the human family tree have been sliced and diced every which way, with every new discovery bringing new ideas about how humans evolved from one branch or another. Some paleoanthropologists (scholars who study humanlike fossils) are talking more now about a bush than a tree since the fossil data are so diverse and partial that there is little agreement among them—other than that *Homo sapiens* did, in fact, come from an apelike ancestor.

What's the Evidence?

Just what is the hard evidence that you and I evolved from apelike ancestors? Well, there are a bunch of fossils, that's for sure. Many primates and other fossils are considered to be in the family tree of humans. Most of their remains are fragmentary and often consist of only partial bones or isolated teeth. More complete skulls and skeletons are very rare. A few, however, are quite interesting.

Figure 3.1—Lucy

Lucy is the most famous, discovered by Donald Johanson in 1974 and designated *Australopithecus afarensis. Pithecus* is Latin for "ape," and *austral* means
"southern." The bulk of the fossil find was in Hadar, the Afar Region of Ethiopia. Thus, the full name means "southern ape from Afar." She was 3 feet 6

inches tall, estimated to weigh 65 pounds and to be between 3.9 and 2.9 million years old. At the time of her discovery, many evolutionists considered *Australopithecus* to be a "long-armed, short-legged knuckle walker."[3] There is no question that Lucy was far more apelike than humanlike, but evolutionary scientists' need for transitional evidence is very pressing. Some have concluded that Lucy was some form of extinct gibbon, with the possibility that she *might* be one of our ancestors.

Other fossil discoveries over the next decades pushed Lucy further and further from our direct line of supposed ancestry. However, she is still included in our evolutionary family tree—by those who "know" that humans descended from some form of apelike creature.

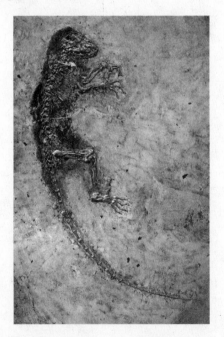

Figure 3.2—Ida

Then along came Ida. She was discovered near Darmstadt, Germany, in 1983 and named *Darwinius masillae*. Estimated to be some 47 million years old, Ida was a tiny little thing, only 19 to 21 inches long, and might have weighed 10 pounds. Ida hit the press as an international "earthshaking" discovery. She was analyzed by a top-level international team that boldly declared Ida was the

"'Rosetta Stone' for understanding...primate evolution."[4] Soon, however, the scientific community admitted that Ida was some kind of lemur and was "not even a close relative."[5] In fact, Dr. Erik Seiffert of Stony Brook University in New York said that Ida "is as far removed from the monkey-ape-human ancestry as a primate could be."[6]

Ida's discovery was followed by Ardi (*Ardipithecus ramidus*), a female dated about 4.4 million years old. She stood about 4 feet high and was thought to weigh around 110 pounds. Ardi represented another class of extinct ape; she was found among at least 35 different individuals during 1994 in Ethiopia. One of the more famous scientists who analyzed Ardi was Dr. C. Owen Lovejoy, Kent State University professor of anthropology. Lovejoy insisted that Ardi "changes what we know about human evolution."[7] A *Science News* article opined that Ardi was "one of the most controversial proposed members of the human evolutionary family, considered an ancient ape by some skeptical scientists...a mix of monkey, ape and hominid characteristics."[8]

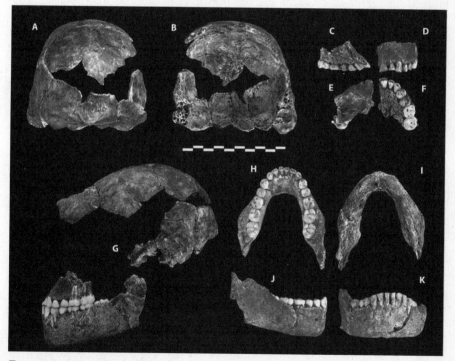

Figure 3.3—Homo naledi

Scientists so firmly believe that human evolution is a proven fact that all they have to do is develop a theory out of fossil parts and *voila*—a missing link! One wonders how far this will go. Well, maybe one doesn't have to go too far— just over to Washington, DC, and the Smithsonian Institution. There you can see these fossil "beings" in full diorama—cave man, cave mama, cave dog, cave cat, cave paintings, cave food—everything in living color!

Except it is not real.

Out in Glendale, California, the technique is known as Imagineering.[9] The best that can be said of these fossil discoveries is that the creatures are unusual and extinct. They are not human—not even close. Yet the story is told so often that everyone just seems to believe it to be true.

What Does the Bible Teach?

While the information in Genesis about the creation week is historical and narrative, it is designed to give us major insights, not details. God recorded the significant events and results. He did not describe the specific processes and procedures that were involved in "creating" or "making."

For instance, as was mentioned earlier, there were only three days during which God was *creating*, bringing something into existence where nothing existed before. The other three days God was making the structure and features of the universe from the material that was created previously.

On Day One, God created the space-matter-time universe. Prior to that first "evening and the morning" there was no universe as we know it. God existed, but our reality did not. There was a creation of the invisible, omnipresent background of all things—the heavens.

DAY 1	DAY 2	DAY 3	DAY 4	DAY 5	DAY 6
Create	**Make**	**Make**	**Make**	*Create*	*Create*
Universe	Division of water	Land plants	Sun, moon, stars	Life Air/sea	Land animals Man in the image of God

Figure 3.4

Days Two, Three, and Four were days of making and shaping—days of structuring and formatting the "heavens and earth" that was created on the first day. These were days of order and purpose, days of setting in place the structure that would be sufficient for the life that would inhabit Earth. The text of Genesis 1 does not provide specific details of how the waters were divided or just where the dry land was positioned on the planet, but the results were made clear. God made an expanse between the waters created on the first day, preparing the planet for suitable habitation. God separated the waters from the dry land and caused the earth to sprout several kinds of replicating food that would provide for the ongoing energy needs of living creatures. Then on Day Four, God made lights that would provide a means of timekeeping.

While these feats are far beyond our understanding and required the omnipotence and omniscience of the Creator in order to take place, they were not created in the sense of being brought into existence from nothing. The First Law of mass-energy had been established on Day One. No matter was being created or destroyed during Days Two, Three, and Four. These days simply saw the omniscient engineering feats of the Master Designer on display.

But on Day Five, God created life! We spent most of chapter 2 trying to understand something of this mystery. As was pointed out, the plants (the food) of Day Three were not alive in the sense that animals are. On this fifth day of the creation week, the Creator brought into existence air and water creatures that were *living*. This is when the five characteristics of life were brought into existence: independent movement, self-consciousness, blood, the soul, and the spirit.

These characteristics were also included in the land creatures on Day Six, but the final creation act was to bring into existence a creature that would bear the image and the likeness of the Creator Himself.

Man Was Created

The magnificent variety of the air, water, and land creatures was and is wonderful. But God brought each creature into existence by the hundreds, if not thousands. The waters were to "abound with an abundance of living creatures" (Genesis 1:20). Great sea creatures sprang into being as "every winged bird according to its kind" flew across the sky (Genesis 1:21). Then on Day Six, God brought the "cattle and creeping thing and beast of the earth" (Genesis 1:24) into being, all of them sharing the life that God had in Himself (John 5:26).

No doubt, had we been able to watch as the angels watched, we would have burst into song as they did as the absolutely unfathomable "science" of the Creator was displayed (Job 38:4-7).

Image and Likeness of the Creator

These special biblical terms—*image*, a representative form of another form, and *likeness*, a copy (stronger word)—are used only of humans. While that may not seem significant, consider that there are a lot of Bible passages that speak of animals. None of them ever speak of any animal as having the image or likeness of God. On the other hand, in those places where the role of man is discussed, there are often references that compare the work God intended for man to do with the responsibility to "take over" God's creation and function as the steward in God's place.

That is never even hinted at for animals.

Whatever this involves, it does not apply to animal life. When the Creator came to the time on Day Six when He determined to make man, He made only one male and one female. All of the living animals in the air, in the water, and on and under the earth were made at least in the hundreds of pairs, if not thousands. They were "abundant" and "filled" the air, sea, and land.

Not so with Adam and Eve.

> The LORD God formed man of the dust of the ground, and breathed into his nostrils the breath of life; and man became a living being (Genesis 2:7).

> The LORD God caused a deep sleep to fall on Adam, and he slept; and He took one of his ribs, and closed up the flesh in its place. Then the rib which the LORD God had taken from man He made into a woman, and He brought her to the man (Genesis 2:21-22).

Image

The shape and capabilities of man are unique. The word "image" is most often used in the Bible to describe idols. Idols were physical representations of a spiritual god or goddess the pagan culture used to give focus to their worship of natural phenomena. So, when we read that God formed the body of Adam from the dirt of the ground and later made the body of Eve, we are being told that these two living creatures were unique among all of the rest of creation.

The Holy Spirit specifically used the Hebrew word *yatsar* to describe what God did to bring about the body of Adam. *Yatsar* is a "hands-on" verb used to describe personal involvement, like an artist painting a picture or a sculptor developing a figure. This was the first man (1 Corinthians 15:47) and was unique from everything else that had been made up to that point in the creation week. Apparently the many air, sea, and land creatures were spoken into existence. Adam, however, was personally sculpted by the Creator.

> He who *planted* [*nata'*—fastened] the ear, shall He not hear? He who *formed* [*yatsar*] the eye, shall He not see? (Psalm 94:9).

Then the Creator took some "rib" from Adam and made a woman:

> The LORD God caused a deep sleep to fall on Adam, and he slept; and He took one of his *ribs*, and closed up the flesh in its place. Then the rib which the LORD God had taken from man He *made* into a woman, and He brought her to the man (Genesis 2:21-22).

The English translations don't quite do justice to the record. *Tesla* is the Hebrew word that is translated "rib." Every other time this word appears in the Bible, it is translated "side." Surely what God took from Adam would have included a rib, but there was muscle and other tissue as well, which is why Adam later said, "This is now bone of my bones and flesh of my flesh; she shall be called Woman, because she was taken out of Man" (Genesis 2:23).

When Scripture states that God made the body of the woman from the side of Adam, it uses the Hebrew word *banah*, which conveys the idea of constructing things like houses, cities, towers, and altars. The word insists on a complex process. It is often used with descriptive explanations—sometimes with great detail, like Solomon building the Temple. Occasionally the term is used to describe a long process, like building a nation. But it always demands personal, intelligent design!

In both cases, with the handful of dirt and the piece of Adam's side, God formed and made the independent and unique bodies of Adam and Eve.

Likeness

Both Adam and Eve were created in the image of God. That is, they both had a physical identity that would be recognizable by all of the creation as similar to the Creator. The words "image" and "likeness" are synonyms in that they both stress "looking like" something else. Of the two words, the Hebrew word *dᵉmuwth* ("likeness") is the stronger term. Where image could be inferred to represent an idea or concept in a general way, likeness demands a physical similarity.

That likeness may help underscore the importance and distinction of the human as much as anything else the Bible teaches about the significance of man.

The difference between man and animals is *not* merely quality or superior abilities. Man's body is similar but still unique. There is a wide gulf between apes and man even in their physical appearance. Man's soul (emotion) certainly sets him apart as unique from animals. All animals reflect emotional ups and downs, but the vast range of feelings and reactions in the human being is easily observed. Man's spirit (intellect, self-consciousness) exceeds that of animals by an unbridgeable chasm. The human ability to reason, construct abstract thought, plan, imagine, sing, play, and worship—to love and hate and help and hinder—all of these aspects of humanity are so easily observed that it takes a real and conscious effort to deny them!

Everlasting Relationship

One of the great mysteries of Scripture is that Christians (twice-born humans) will have an immortal body that is like the resurrected body of the Lord Jesus (1 John 3:2). That promise is built on the twin facts that the Lord Jesus is "all the fullness of the Godhead bodily" (Colossians 2:9) and that when

He returns to bring us to the new heavens and the new earth we will be "raised incorruptible, and we shall be changed" (1 Corinthians 15:52).

There is a lot of biblical support for those facts. The Lord appeared in human form to the patriarchs several times during the formation of the nation of Israel, and later to the prophets. Every time the Bible records such an incident, the image and likeness were human. And when the Messiah "became flesh" (John 1:14), He was fully human! We can't go into the theology of these facts here, but this image and likeness were in the triune nature of God in eternity past (Philippians 2:6-8; Hebrews 10:5).

Because of Adam's sin, our bodies are burdened with the death that will ultimately destroy them. But that death is an intrusion! Death is the enemy that God will finally destroy with the resurrection of all humanity. "Do not marvel at this; for the hour is coming in which all who are in the graves will hear His voice and come forth—those who have done good, to the resurrection of life, and those who have done evil, to the resurrection of condemnation" (John 5:28-29).

What is of consequence here as far as the image of God in man is concerned, however, is the clear acknowledgment in Scripture that our current earthly bodies do not fit the requirements for the new heaven and the new earth that are coming. What we possess now will be changed before we can be "as he is" during eternity. The face-to-face fellowship that Adam and Eve knew in the Garden prior to their rebellion (Genesis 1:29; 2:8, 16; 3:8-10) was taken away, and the relationship between the Creator and His crowning creation needed to be reconciled.

Everything that the Bible tells us about the age-long salvation effort on the part of God toward man is that after we have been drawn to the Father (John 6:44) and given the faith to believe in what has been done by the Lord Jesus on our behalf (Ephesians 2:8-9), we are a "new man which was created according to God, in true righteousness and holiness" (Ephesians 4:24). Something Adam and Eve possessed at creation, before their fall, is restored at the moment of the new birth. That something was at least part of the image of God. That something may well have been the eternal and spiritual part of humanity that we *do not* possess prior to salvation.

Three Important Points

All of these varied and scattered points throughout Scripture seem to indicate three very important points about the image of God that was created in both male and female on Day Six of the creation week.

- One: There was an eternal part to us that no longer exists until we are given eternal life at the point of salvation. Apparently, Adam and Eve possessed that quality when they were created.

- Two: The form of the human body is directly connected throughout Scripture with the incarnation of our Lord Jesus, both in His appearances prior to His entry into this world and after His resurrection.

- Three: After the terrible curse rendered in Genesis 3, the mortal body humanity is now born into must be changed into a suitable immortal body that will be compatible with the eternal body of the Lord Jesus.

Whatever God did for Adam and Eve that made them in His image, He did not do it for the entirety of the rest of creation. As marvelous as their many life forms, shapes, functions, and reflections of God's attributes are, none of the sea, air, or land creatures can fellowship with the Creator—except man. One day, every tongue in the universe will confess the lordship of Jesus Christ in an open assembly around the throne in heaven (Philippians 2:11). Now, however, mankind alone is afforded the opportunity to be redeemed and reconciled to the great Creator.

The image that was made "dead in trespasses and sins" (Ephesians 2:1) because of the horrible rebellion of Adam is now given the opportunity to receive the "guarantee of our inheritance until the redemption of the purchased possession" (Ephesians 1:14) "for salvation ready to be revealed in the last time" (1 Peter 1:5). We humans—and humanity alone—can be born again.

Dominion Mandate

Many of the books that deal with religion have little to say about creation. Those that don't give much attention to the uniqueness of man. The Bible, however, seems to go out of its way to present the creation of Adam and Eve as unique above that of all other creatures—and indeed endows them with dominion authority over all other life.

> God said, "Let Us make man in Our image, according to Our likeness; let them have dominion over the fish of the sea, over the birds of the air, and over the cattle, over all the earth and over every creeping thing that creeps on the earth." So God created man in His own image; in the image of God He created him; male and female He created them. Then God blessed them, and God said to them, "Be fruitful and multiply; fill the earth and subdue it; have dominion over the fish of the sea, over the birds of the air, and over every living thing that moves on the earth" (Genesis 1:26-28).

Something very special is delegated from the Creator to the created. Please notice the authority. Man was to "have dominion" over all other life, to "fill" Earth, and "subdue" the planet. Those terms are intense. Not only is the Creator's final creative act to bring into existence a being that would bear His image and likeness, but those unique beings would have broad authority over the entire planet.

> You have made him a little lower than the angels, and You have crowned him with glory and honor. You have made him to have dominion over the works of Your hands; You have put all things under his feet, all sheep and oxen—even the beasts of the field, the birds of the air, and the fish of the sea that pass through the paths of the seas (Psalm 8:5-8).

That first command to man is often called the dominion mandate. If we are to understand the uniqueness of human life, we must first grasp the significance of this authority. There are three biblical factors to keep in mind.

1. All authority is *delegated* authority—God the Creator is still the owner.
- His authority is the basis for action (Matthew 28:18-19; Daniel 7:14).
- His Word is still the source of ultimate truth (John 14:6; 17:17).
- His steward (man) is still responsible to the Creator (Isaiah 45:18-22).

2. All physical, biological, and spiritual processes are now dominated by sin and the judgment that was pronounced on man as a result of his rebellion against the Creator.
- Evil is ingrained in fallen man (1 John 5:19; Romans 3:10-11).
- Good is the result of redemption (James 1:13-20), not man.
- Death is the constant burden and ultimate end of this current life (Romans 8:22).

3. The operative force now in nature is *conservation*, not *creation* (Colossians 1:17).
- Conservative force is supernatural (2 Peter 3:7).
- Conservative force is covenantal (Genesis 8:22; 9:9-17).
- Conservative force is not the "key to the past," as uniformitarianism holds (2 Peter 3:3-5).

What About Empirical Science?

In spite of the academic shouting, posturing, and foot stomping, there is a good bit of hard scientific evidence that you are *not* an animal—especially not anything like a chimpanzee. Let's explore the basics.

Common Design

The observational evidence is overwhelming—everything that we can observe and test has clear evidence of design and purpose. Since that is so evident, we would expect that land animals (especially mammals) would share some common designs. For instance, the internal skeletons of land animals are strong and sturdy, designed to carry weight and allow for repetitive motion. It should be no surprise, then, that bipedal animals like primates and humans have similar skeletal features. Nor should it be a surprise that land animals would have internal and external characteristics that are pretty much the same, especially those that share similar lifestyles. Muscular structures and internal organs would be similar since all of these creatures have active lives, eat, sleep, and reproduce with basic functions that require common designs.

It should be no surprise to scientists, then, to find a commonality in the design programming—the DNA. Genetic similarities between chimpanzees and humans would be expected since both have many similar characteristics, but drawing the inference that humans have, therefore, descended from the same ancestors as chimps is a bit of a stretch.

In fact, several studies have shown that humans have genetic data that are very similar to mice and kangaroos. Not much appears in the popular press about our relationship to either of these animals, however, because that doesn't fit the majority opinions of the academics. More interesting yet is that some researchers have found we share half our genes (DNA) with the banana. Well, since both chimps and humans eat bananas, why not? As long as the comparison is based on selected "lettering" of the DNA strands, just about any conclusion is possible.

Empirical DNA Research

It is rather common today to compare DNA similarities among humans to determine relationships. The more similar the patterns are, the more closely related the people are to each other. More often than not we hear such stories from various court cases or paternity searches. That really works well—from human to human. But when one tries to apply the same logic from human to chimp—or from human to kangaroos, mice, or bananas—the testing logic breaks down.

To begin with, the testable data (lab work) must be interpreted. While we can be relatively sure that calculations of the genetic similarities between certain creatures can be accurate, the relationship between those creatures depends on the assumptions that are made about them. With human beings, we have a good bit of written records (archives, birth records, etc.) that helps us establish relationships among humans. Those historical accounts give more certainty to the conclusions of the test data.

Once we get beyond known records, however, we are inferring and assuming relationships based on the extrapolation of our known data. With humans, we can be fairly sure. With ancestry beyond written records, we must base the conclusions on interpretative inference. In science, the difference is called *operational science* versus *historical science*. Operational science refers to testing performed according to the scientific method (observing, testing, reproducing the same test and getting the same results). Historical science is a form of forensic study—that is, using either eyewitness accounts (if available) or clues that must be interpreted.

Figure 3.5—According to new scientific research, humans and chimps are no more than 86 percent similar.

Since no one observes an ape producing a human today, the scientific method is not possible to use. What can be, and is, done is to compare the DNA information of humans with chimpanzees and interpret the results based on the clues of similar anatomy and design. Much of the work that has been done over the past decade has concentrated on specific areas of the DNA chemicals that impact observable changes. Within the past few years, many studies have concentrated on blood chemistry and brain cells—assuming (correctly) that the blood and the brain have pretty important functions! Differences, therefore, might provide clues to the relationships between various creatures.

Dr. Jeffrey Tomkins ran one of the largest gene sequencing labs in the country at Clemson University. Dr. Tomkins now heads up ICR's research on human-chimp similarities. Many scientific research programs are funded by the government and are therefore made available to all scientists. Dr. Tomkins has taken the data uncovered thus far and has found some startling admissions by certain researchers. Instead of the fabled 98 percent similarity between humans and chimps touted in the popular literature for many years, those researchers are now admitting that the differences are much wider—as much as 14 or more percent wider! And those differences are among the key genes of the blood and the brain.

I won't attempt to list all of the technical data. You can find this on the ICR website if you are interested.[10] Suffice it to say, dramatic differences exist! The research has been tissue-specific (same types of cells and locations). For instance, white blood cells from living humans, chimps, and orangutans were compared because they are the most similar type of cell known between humans and apes. The scientists were surprised to find that in more than 1500 different regions, major differences were obvious between the human and ape cells.[11]

In 2012, a series of studies was performed on the genetic chemistry in brain cells that impact neurological disorders and cancers. Overall, 1055 genes demonstrated significantly different patterns—468 of which were "highly diverse."[12] These are the genes that control other genes and determine when and if proteins in the cell are modified. Clearly these genes showed marked differences and were key to controlling regions in the genome for brain cell activity.

What does all this serious study mean? Simply this: There are profound genetic differences between humans and apes—such profound differences that there is no logical connection between the two types of creatures. These cutting-edge studies fit closely with the biblical message that you are not a "monkey's uncle."

All kidding aside, we may chuckle at the antics of the chimps and orang-utans we see in the zoo, but most of us are aware that the creatures we see are far removed from us—if by no other observation than the simple behavioral and anatomical distinctions. Popular scientific shows like *Nova* and *Discover* may present stunning photography of animal behavior in the wild with professional voice-overs that ascribe human behavior and thought to those animals, but empirical, testable, repeatable science does not bear out those documentaries.

Science demonstrates a vast difference. Science insists that humans are not chimpanzees. Science confirms what the Bible teaches. You and I are created in the image of God and bear the responsibility to care for the planet and the animals that share its resources with us.

What Difference Does It Make?

Over the last 30 years, the acceptance of this evolutionary story has influenced just about every form of sociological thinking. This is particularly true among the various disciplines that impact how we think about ourselves and our "fellow animals," the nonhumans. I hope that sounds a bit foolish to you, but it is absolutely no joke. As far as the overwhelming majority of the academic, legal, political, philosophical, and scientific world is concerned, you are an animal and you share this planet with fellow life forms that deserve, in some cases, better treatment than humans.

Dr. Peter Singer is an Australian philosopher who is currently a professor of bioethics at Princeton University and a Laureate Professor at the Centre for Applied Philosophy and Public Ethics at the University of Melbourne. He is most well-known for his 1975 book *Animal Liberation*, frequently referred to as a "canonical text" on animal rights and animal liberation theory. That book and subsequent publications have formed something of the core beliefs for the People for the Ethical Treatment of Animals, better known as PETA.

In one of Professor Singer's more widely read articles, "All Animals Are Equal" from the 1989 anthology *Animal Rights and Human Obligations*, he wrote, "I am urging that we extend to other species the basic principle of equality that most of us recognize should be extended to all members of our own species."[13] That platform has become the basic philosophical justification for many strange bedfellows.

PETA founder Ingrid Newkirk flaunts the position that animals are other nations, not slaves, hamburgers, handbags, cheap toys, and test tubes with whiskers. Today, Newkirk insists "that although our newspapers are full of stories of sophisticated communication in the animal world, and no one doubts that the other animals—we being just one—experience maternal love, pain, joy, loneliness, and fear, we dismiss those feelings as inconsequential...A full-grown horse or dog is beyond comparison a more rational as well as a more conversable animal than an infant of a day or a week or even a month old."[14] She and Peter Singer agree: Killing a human infant or deformed human baby—or even a "useless" elderly person—is no different from putting an animal to sleep.

Those earlier 1980s and 1990s efforts gave birth to the Nonhuman Rights Project, formed in 2007 after a decade of ceaseless lecturing and posturing by the various antireligious and pro-animal rights movements. According to Steven M. Wise, president of the Nonhuman Rights Project, Inc., their mission is as follows:

> Through education and litigation, to change the common law status of at least some nonhuman animals from mere "things," which lack the capacity to possess any legal right, to "persons," who possess such fundamental rights as bodily integrity and bodily liberty, and those other legal rights to which evolving standards of morality, scientific discovery, and human experience entitle them...[Dr. Wise] teaches "Animal Rights Jurisprudence" at several law schools and is the author of...*Rattling the Cage—Toward Legal Rights for Animals*; [and] *Drawing the Line—Science and the Case for Animal Rights*.[15]

All of the above is included to make you aware of two things: One, due to the impact of evolutionary theory, the majority of modern science is convinced that you are an animal—highly evolved, but an animal nonetheless. And two, the social movements among activist political and legal circles are inexorably moving toward legalizing animal rights—to the detriment and potential exclusion of human uniqueness and value.

You, as far as the majority of world thinkers are concerned, are an animal.

You Are Unique

There is a passage in C.S. Lewis's second chronicle of Narnia, *Prince Caspian*, where Aslan, the lion who represents the Lord Jesus in the allegory, tells young Caspian, "You come of the Lord Adam and the Lady Eve...And that is both honor enough to erect the head of the poorest beggar, and shame enough to bow the shoulders of the greatest emperor on earth. Be content."[16]

Good counsel.

We all go through various episodes during which we feel like we are not worth much—and conversely have occasions when we are sure that we are superior to others. Neither evaluation is right. No one is insignificant, and no one is irreplaceable. You are, indeed, unique! No one else is just like you, and no one else can *be* you. Be content!

Recombination

You probably remember that humans have 23 pairs of chromosomes, for a total of 46. Twenty-two of those look pretty much the same in all humans, but in women the smallest pair consists of two X chromosomes, while in men the pair consists of one X and one Y chromosome. Those are the genetic instructions that make the biggest difference!

Within those 46 chromosomes are some 20,000 to 30,000 genes, each "written" with the four DNA base pairs of A, T, G, and C (the nucleotides adenine, thymine, guanine, and cytosine) in the human genome. Nobody is really sure how many genes the human genome has because these three-billion-plus "instructions" are responsible for growing you during 9 months in the womb and then for keeping the trillions of cells of your body working and percolating over the course of your lifetime!

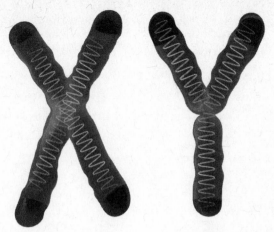

Figure 3.6—X and Y Sex Chromosome

By the way, grape plants have about 30,000 genes, and chickens have around 17,000. The *number* of genes isn't as important as what the genes and their genetic regulators "say." And it's that which makes you unique!

When you were conceived, one-half of the genetic instructions from your mom and one-half from your dad came together in an absolutely unique combination. The math on this is incredible. No one has been able to calculate the odds of what transpires at conception, but it is surely accurate to say there is no human being in all of history or the future who will have precisely the same information in their genome as you (or me). This is true even for identical twins, where one fertilized egg (zygote) splits and forms two embryos. Even though they share the same initial information, when the zygote splits, modifications to the use of the DNA sequence make identical twins unique individuals.

Becoming You

Dr. Randy Guliuzza is an engineer and medical doctor with a master's degree in public health from Harvard University. He joined ICR as a national lecturer after retiring as a Lieutenant Colonel from the US Air Force, where he served as flight surgeon and chief of aerospace medicine. One of Dr. Guliuzza's specialties, as you might imagine, is the stunning wonder and design of the human body. His writings and lectures on the development of a new person in the womb are especially enlightening.

Here is some of what Dr. Guliuzza writes about the way you and I began.

> The real star of the show, however, is the developing baby, who was once viewed as a passive object being built by the mother's body. Nothing could be further from the truth. In terms of guiding implantation into the uterus all the way to breastfeeding, it is the baby/placenta unit that is the dynamic force in the orchestration of its own destiny.

> The baby is a completely new individual, with unique genetic material that expresses foreign markers on his cells that are not recognized as "self" by the mother. The mother's immune system should destroy the new baby's first cells within just a few cell divisions, but substances secreted by the placenta and baby promote a complex suppression of the maternal immune response only within the implantation site of the uterus...

> The mother's body is now under the control of a new person...hormones produced by the baby induce adaptations in the mother's body that are absolutely necessary for the baby's survival...So it is the mother who is essentially passive, responding to signals emanating from the baby—even at times to her own detriment. Scientific research has shown that while the woman's reproductive organs and body are indispensable, they are not enough; it takes a baby to make a baby.[17]

There's a lot more to "you" that Dr. Guliuzza describes in his book *Made in His Image: Examining the Complexities of the Human Body*. If you would like to gain an appreciation of how "fearfully and wonderfully made" you are (Psalm 139:14), you might want to get a copy of that book from the Institute for Creation Research online store. You really are unique!

CHAPTER 4

The Fossils

1. Geospiza magnirostris.
3. Geospiza parvula.

2. Geospiza fortis.
4. Certhidea olivasea.

Figure 4.1—Darwin's Finches

When asked for evidence of any kind of evolutionary change happening in our observable world today, most secular scientists will point to adaptive changes within various types of animals—like the beak lengths of Darwin's famous finches. The reasoning is that because we can see these small changes occurring within species over just a few generations, then we can justifiably conclude that larger changes will come about over longer spans of time.

One of the more famous quotes of the secular faith in the importance of time was generated by evolutionary biologist George Wald, who later became a Nobel laureate:

> Given enough time it will almost certainly happen at least once...Time is in fact the hero of the plot...Given so much time, the "impossible" becomes possible, the possible probable, and the probable virtually certain. One has only to wait; time itself performs the miracles.[1]

However, it is becoming increasingly clear that the small modifications that develop as various animals adapt to changes in their environment do not produce permanent changes at all. The beaks of the finches change back! And, of course, the finches do not become pelicans or seagulls or robins. *Stasis* is the clearly observable principle. That is, creatures stay the same over time. The overarching axiom of observable biology is *conservation*!

Remember the two most fundamental laws of all empirical science. The First Law of Thermodynamics states that energy is always conserved; it cannot be created or destroyed. The Second Law of Thermodynamics states that when energy is transferred, there will be less energy available at the end of the transfer process than at the beginning.

These laws operate throughout the universe. There is some speculation that "somewhere out there" these laws are operating differently or are suspended from time to time. We are sure, however, that we have not found any place or anything in the universe that does not operate according to these laws. And small, adaptive changes notwithstanding, there is absolutely no upward change in complexity being observed. Mutational changes to the information systems (DNA) do not add novel information—rather, they take away information. All the evidence—everything that we can observe, analyze, test, see in the laboratory—demonstrates that upward evolutionary change is *not* happening in our universe today.

Since we do not observe genuine evolutionary changes in the kinds of animals we can see today (like from a dog to a cat), the secular story should expect to be able to find evidence of these transitional creatures buried in the sedimentary rocks of the earth's crust. The fossils should tell us the "real" story of the past when, presumably, different energy laws were functioning, allowing reversals of the laws of conservation and entropy. These swings in the operational function of the First and Second Laws appear to have been either some form of unseen and mysterious background pressure (since it would have pushed against the First and Second Laws), or reversals would have been like an "eruption" of organizational information, providing new information and extra energies that could have temporarily overcome stasis and entropy.

If life sprang into being from nonlife, and if that life, once generated, changed over time into more and more complex systems, then those events must have happened outside of our current environment—since it is not only not happening now, but the current laws forbid it from happening. Thus, if the evolution of life happened naturalistically in the ancient past, it must have been recorded in the vast tombs of the rock strata lying across the surface of the planet.

Simply put, because we do not find evidence in the present, we must find it somewhere in the fossil record preserved for us in the planet's sedimentary deposits.

What Makes a Fossil?

The question of what and how an animal or a plant becomes a fossil is an important one. These remains of organisms that lived in the past are the only hard evidence we have of a previous era. Some of these fossils represent creatures that are no longer alive—which makes fossils even more critical to our understanding of the past.

Just how, then, did these specimens become fossilized? Without trying to be too simplistic, here are the main features of all fossils.

1. **Fossils are dead animals and plants.** That may be obvious, but fossils are not alive. The creatures have been killed, many of them in a most horrible way, with the bulk of the larger animals torn apart and their pieces spread across large areas. There are fossil graveyards that contain thousands of bones of mixed animals all pushed and jumbled together in an enormous "cemetery" of horribly broken and mangled critters.

2. **Fossils are buried in water-deposited sediment**. There are a
   few fossils that are preserved in amber and some in volcanic dust,
   but the overwhelming majority of fossils are buried in mudrock,
   sandstone, shale, limestone, etc., and bio-rich deposits like
   coal. These animals did not die and slowly become covered with
   mud. They were suddenly and catastrophically buried in moving
   water-deposited sediment with no time to decay or be eaten by
   scavengers.

Figure 4.2—Fossil Trilobite

3. **Fossils are found all over the planet.** Some sedimentary deposits
   are thousands of feet thick. Some deposits are more shallow, but
   the fossil-bearing strata are on the tops of the highest mountains
   and down in the deepest parts of the earth's crust. Fossils are found
   on every continent on the planet!

4. **Fossils are mostly marine invertebrates**. Most places that are
   above water have fossil deposits in them. Some deposits are rich
   in certain types (fish, plants, insects), but most areas contain
   marine invertebrates (clams, sea stars, coral, etc.). Paleontologists
   recognize that the majority of fossils are marine invertebrates—
   ocean-bottom-dwelling creatures.

5. **Fossils most often become mineralized.** Once an animal is buried, the softer parts are quickly sloughed off or dissolved by the chemicals in the sediments. Then the biological material of the harder parts, like teeth, bones, and shells are replaced by the minerals in the water-deposited sediment so that the hard parts become mineralized, leaving behind a "rock" that is shaped like the bones or other hard parts of the animal.

6. **Fossils sometimes leave a cast of their shape**. Occasionally, an animal does not contain any hard parts (jellyfish, slugs, earthworms, leeches, etc.) and only the shape of the animal is preserved. This also happens, rarely, with footprints when the indentations are filled in quickly and preserved in a way that will allow the paleontologist to take careful measurements of the tracks.

7. **Fossils may preserve internal soft tissue.** Sometimes conditions are such that internal soft parts are preserved either by getting replaced with minerals (mineralization) or by mummifying. This is most often observed within larger bones (femurs, etc.) where the outside material has been mineralized but the internal core (such as bone marrow) is preserved so that the scientist is able to analyze the original tissue of the animal. The number of soft-tissue finds have increased dramatically during the early part of the twenty-first century, giving scientists exciting opportunities to study the molecular parts of long-extinct animals.

Evolution Defined

Evolution is a rather slippery term. The word is used in popular and ordinary language to cover almost every sense of the word *change*. For example, the newest model of an automobile is said to have evolved from previous models when it is presented to the public. Various politicians evolve in their thinking, as do artists and businesses and societies. In scientific and academic circles, however, the term is clearly more specific. Here are a few carefully worded statements about evolution by various organizations that have reason to be precise.

Society for the Study of Evolution

"Evolution" refers both to a set of scientific facts and to a theory explaining such facts. "Evolution" refers to the scientific fact that biological organisms have changed through time, and that all life, including humanity, has descended with modification from common ancestors. Evolution is as well documented as are other currently accepted scientific facts. The theory of evolution is a comprehensive and well-established scientific explanation, based on natural processes, of the fact of biological evolution.[2]

National Science Teachers Association

The National Science Teachers Association (NSTA) strongly supports the position that evolution is a major unifying concept in science and should be emphasized in K–12 science education frameworks and curricula...

Evolution in the broadest sense leads to an understanding that the natural world has a history and that cumulative change through time has occurred and continues to occur. If we look today at the galaxies, stars, the planet Earth, and the life on planet Earth, we see that the natural world today is different than in the past: galaxies, stars, planets, and life forms have evolved. Biological evolution refers to the scientific theory that living things share ancestors from which they have diverged; it is sometimes called "descent with modification." Biological evolution also encompasses a range of mechanisms that cause populations to change and diverge over time, and include natural selection, migration, and genetic drift. There is abundant and consistent evidence from astronomy, physics, biochemistry, geochronology, geology, biology, anthropology, and other sciences that evolution has taken place.[3]

National Association of Biology Teachers

The principle of biological evolution states that all living things have arisen from common ancestors. Some lineages diverge while others go extinct as a result of natural selection, mutation, genetic drift and other well-studied mechanisms. The patterns of similarity and diversity in extant and fossil organisms, combined with evidence and explanations provided by molecular biology, developmental biology, systematics, and geology provide extensive examples of and powerful support for evolution. Even as biologists continue to study and consider evolution, they agree that all living things share common ancestors and that the process of evolutionary change through time is driven by natural mechanisms. [4]

The Paleontological Society

Evolution is an elegant theory that explains the history of life through geologic time; the diversity of living organisms, including their genetic, molecular, and physical similarities and differences; and the geographic distribution of organisms. Evolutionary principles are the foundation of all basic and applied biology and paleontology, from biodiversity studies to studies on the control of emerging diseases. [5]

As indicated in the above position statements from four very well-known and prestigious scientific organizations, the secular and academic majority insists that evolution is an all-encompassing fact of science and philosophy that unifies how one must approach the understanding of all related data. It is indeed a worldview—a belief system that sets the stage on which all facts must be interpreted.

The biblical message is diametrically opposed to evolution. The fossils are evidence that can be evaluated and analyzed and can help us understand something about a past event. At first glance, all would agree that these enormous deposits speak of a vast catastrophe—a water catastrophe that inundated the entire planet. The Bible tells us that such a planet-covering water catastrophe did take place and that it was designed to destroy "the world that then existed" (2 Peter 3:6).

Those who refuse to accept that biblical record must, of necessity, deny that such a flood ever took place and attempt to describe processes and conditions that would, over time, produce the worldwide deposits of sedimentary rock and the billions of fossils they contain. Working from a secular viewpoint, which attempts to explain all data by natural phenomena, the evolutionary paleontologist must rely on the fossil evidence to "tell" the story of gradual evolution.

Fossils Are the Key Evidence for Evolution

This chapter attempts to "unlock" the enormous storehouse of information contained in the fossils that are preserved in the sedimentary layers of Earth's crust. Indeed, because the evidence for evolution is not observable in the present, the fossil record becomes all the more important.

> The fossil record is the primary factual evidence for evolution in times past, and evolution is well documented by further evidence from other scientific disciplines, including comparative anatomy, biogeography, genetics, molecular biology, and studies of viral and bacterial diseases.[6]

> Although the comparative study of living animals and plants may give very convincing circumstantial evidence, fossils provide the only historical, documentary evidence that life has evolved from simpler to more and more complex forms.[7]

Transitional Creatures Are Required by Evolution

One of the absolutes of the evolutionary idea is that life has changed from simple to complex over "deep time." That is, after life itself came into existence (a puzzle that still has not been solved by any evolutionary experiments), living creatures developed more and more complex structures as they diverged from the common ancestor.

There is a good bit of debate among evolutionary thinkers about how that development took place, but all agree that "somehow" the single-celled ancestor began to become an early form of a marine invertebrate. That transitional process must have continued over eons and various eras in order to evolve the different life forms that now exist. And as has been noted before, since the present and observable processes of today are *not* producing any kind of transitional forms, the record of the past *must* demonstrate that those major changes did indeed occur in the past.

Paleontology is the academic discipline responsible for finding and interpreting the fossil data. Although fossils were known for some time before Darwin published his famous book in 1859, the information was spotty and mostly confined to Europe. Darwin himself lamented that there was not enough fossil evidence to prove his theory, but expressed confidence that the evidence would be uncovered in the future as more and more qualified scientists continue to dig into the problem.

And there has been a good bit of digging! Universities and museums all over the world display the finds. However, the perception that many would gain from visiting these displays belies the reality of the fossil data. Most fossils are marine invertebrates—sea-bottom creatures like clams, coral, and trilobites. Fossils of sponges, jellyfish, marine worms, and crustaceans are everywhere! There really is an "explosion" of life preserved in the sedimentary layers of Earth.

In fact, these marine organisms are so common among the fossil strata that some of them have been selected as "index fossils"—fossils that are used to date the strata in which other animals and plants are found. While this practice is long established, the circular reasoning seems to escape those who use it. Simply put, sedimentary rock material is too mixed to make it possible to directly obtain a reliable date by chemical or mineral analysis. So when certain types of marine invertebrates are found within a location, secular researchers use these index fossils as evidence to date that fossil-bearing stratum for the rest of the fossils within it. These index fossils have already been assigned a date by evolutionary researchers based on their belief of how long ago that fossil evolved. In practice, fossils are dated by the layer in which they are found, but that layer is itself already dated by the index fossils.

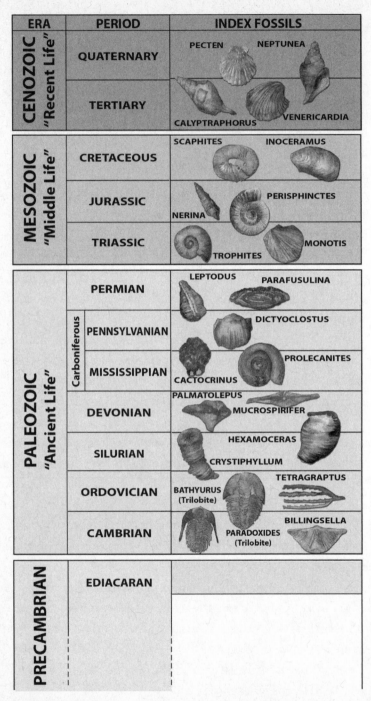

ERA	PERIOD	INDEX FOSSILS
CENOZOIC "Recent Life"	QUATERNARY	PECTEN NEPTUNEA CALYPTRAPHORUS VENERICARDIA
	TERTIARY	
MESOZOIC "Middle Life"	CRETACEOUS	SCAPHITES INOCERAMUS
	JURASSIC	NERINA PERISPHINCTES
	TRIASSIC	TROPHITES MONOTIS
PALEOZOIC "Ancient Life"	PERMIAN	LEPTODUS PARAFUSULINA
	Carboniferous PENNSYLVANIAN	DICTYOCLOSTUS
	Carboniferous MISSISSIPPIAN	CACTOCRINUS PROLECANITES
	DEVONIAN	PALMATOLEPUS MUCROSPIRIFER
	SILURIAN	HEXAMOCERAS CRYSTIPHYLLUM
	ORDOVICIAN	BATHYURUS (Trilobite) TETRAGRAPTUS
	CAMBRIAN	PARADOXIDES (Trilobite) BILLINGSELLA
PRECAMBRIAN	EDIACARAN	

Figure 4.3—Index Fossils

All of this raises several questions. These marine invertebrates are in Earth's sedimentary deposits all over the world's continents. If they are supposed to be the oldest and simplest of all the evolutionary life forms, then why do they appear in every layer, from the bottom of the seabeds to the tops of the mountains—and still live today essentially unchanged? If, indeed, they are the oldest and simplest life forms, why are these fossils not confined to the oldest layers of the earth's sedimentary deposits?

In evolution, the rocks date the fossils, and the fossils date the rocks!

Figure 4.4—Circular Reasoning

These fossils are supposed to represent the first life. Why, then, are they *still* marine invertebrates? Why, if they are the first life, are they the index for phyla throughout the so-called geologic column? The assumptions and circular deduction required to make all of this fit an evolutionary story is staggering. One wonders why this rather incredible cosmology is embraced by so many otherwise sensible people.

Could it be that "the god of this age has blinded [the minds of those] who do not believe, lest the light of the gospel of the glory of Christ, who is the image of God, should shine on them" (2 Corinthians 4:4)? Is it because "wide is the gate and broad is the way that leads to destruction, and there are many who go in by it" (Matthew 7:13)? The apostle Peter insisted that the facts of creation were so well-known that those who rejected them were willingly ignorant (2 Peter 3:5).

Perhaps no other major professor during the twentieth century expressed this open defiance against the evidence of creation more arrogantly than Dr. Richard Lewontin, a Harvard University geneticist, biologist, and social commentator who wrote an article in *The New York Review of Books* titled "Billions and Billions of Demons." He said,

> Our willingness to accept scientific claims that are against common sense is the key to an understanding of the real struggle between science and the supernatural. We take the side of science *in spite* of the patent absurdity of some of its constructs, *in spite* of its failure to fulfill many of its extravagant promises of health and life, *in spite* of the tolerance of the scientific community for unsubstantiated just-so stories, because we have a prior commitment, a commitment to materialism.[8]

Please note that Professor Lewontin admits that his colleagues have a "willingness" to accept various scientific claims that are "against common sense." Also please note the several "in spite of" admissions and that he and his colleagues have a "prior commitment to materialism." Dr. Lewontin continues:

> It is not that the methods and institutions of science somehow compel us to accept a material explanation of the phenomenal world, but, on the contrary, that we are forced by our *a priori* adherence to material causes to create an apparatus of investigation and a set of concepts that produce material explanations, no matter how counter-intuitive, no matter how mystifying to the uninitiated. Moreover that materialism is absolute, for we cannot allow a Divine Foot in the door.[9]

That last section is amazing. Dr. Lewontin insists that he and his colleagues are not "compelled" to arrive at material conclusions, but "on the contrary" they are "forced" because of their "*a priori* adherence" to the worldview of naturalistic and nonsupernatural causes "to create" the investigative apparatus and models that will "produce material explanations."

Stunning!

As the apostle Peter said, they are willingly ignorant. They know the truth. They can "clearly" see (as Paul insisted in Romans 1:20). These doctors of evolutionary philosophy are not "compelled" toward truth. They must produce an end product that is materialistic. Their commitment to a nontheistic explanation is absolute because Dr. Lewontin and his colleagues "cannot allow a Divine Foot in the door."

But There Is a Problem

An evolutionary scientist has admitted:

> Despite the bright promise that paleontology provides a means of "seeing" evolution, it has presented some nasty difficulties for evolutionists, the most notorious of which is the presence of "gaps" in the fossil record.[10]

The transitions between life forms—the necessary step-by-step developments over time from a common ancestor—have eluded the fossil hunter since such an idea was proposed. Darwin famously said: "If it could be demonstrated that any complex organ existed, which could not possibly have been formed by numerous, successive, slight modifications, my theory would absolutely break down."[11]

Yet here we are, after nearly two centuries during which thousands of evolutionary scientists have been searching and experimenting and drawing textbook ideas and sculpting dioramas with no evidence to back up their stories.

What Do the Fossils Show?

The evidence for single-celled life is sparse at best. There are a few supposed algae cells in the Precambrian layer, but there is no agreement on if they were alive, if they were merely viral cells, or—well, there is no agreement on what or if they were. But this is absolutely agreed on: There was *nothing* alive prior to those few things. No evidence of nonlife evolving into life. None!

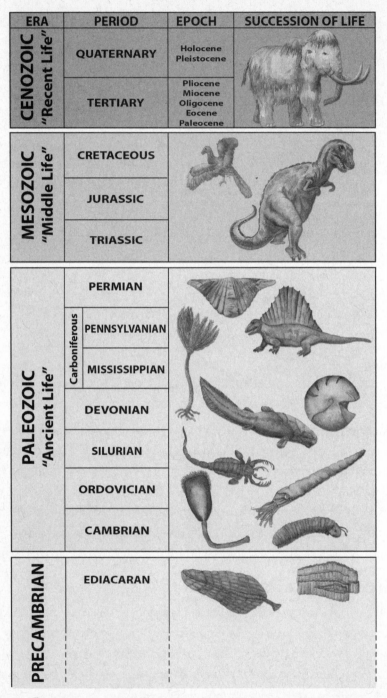

ERA	PERIOD	EPOCH	SUCCESSION OF LIFE
CENOZOIC "Recent Life"	QUATERNARY	Holocene Pleistocene	
	TERTIARY	Pliocene Miocene Oligocene Eocene Paleocene	
MESOZOIC "Middle Life"	CRETACEOUS		
	JURASSIC		
	TRIASSIC		
PALEOZOIC "Ancient Life"	PERMIAN		
	Carboniferous — PENNSYLVANIAN		
	Carboniferous — MISSISSIPPIAN		
	DEVONIAN		
	SILURIAN		
	ORDOVICIAN		
	CAMBRIAN		
PRECAMBRIAN	EDIACARAN		

Figure 4.5—Evolutionary Geologic Timescale

And then there is the Cambrian Explosion. And *explosion* is a very good term for what is found. Life in a myriad of forms. Life fully developed, fully functional, and completely unique. There is absolutely no evidence of anything evolving from a single cell into the majestically complex marine invertebrates that dominate the fossil record. Some are extinct. Many more are almost exactly the same as the forms still functioning happily in the oceans of the world today.

Some of them are much bigger than modern forms. That's a puzzlement! Oh, there are theories aplenty why that is, but nobody knows. Some clams are enormous, as are other creatures—trilobites and cuttlefish and ammonites and—well, fill in the blank. These animals either lived much longer or had relatives that were just plain huge. Nothing in their anatomy would suggest that they were anything else than a regular clam or ammonites, but their fossil remains include some giants.

Again, there is nothing in between. Nothing that was evolving into a squid from anything else. No part-clam, part-trilobite. Nothing that was half-jellyfish and half-coral. Nothing. They just appear in the fossil record as they appear today, fully formed, fully functional. An evolutionary geologist stated:

> Their high degree of organization clearly indicates that a long period of evolution preceded their appearance in the record. However, when we turn to examine the Precambrian rocks for the forerunners of these Early Cambrian fossils, they are nowhere to be found. [12]

Invertebrates to Fish

The fossil record entombs billions of fish. That would fit some form of watery catastrophe. But unlike marine invertebrates, the skeletons of these animals are on the inside rather than the outside (think crabs).

Unless you are totally unfamiliar with anatomy, it should be apparent that such a change is very significant! Although there are many varieties of invertebrates from the clam and the crustaceans to the cuttlefish and jellyfish, the shift from support systems that are on the outside to supporting bones on the inside indicates an enormous information change in the DNA. Yes, DNA is composed of the same four chemical "letters" that are hooked together in a chain of "words." But the way those words are hooked together tell a clam to produce a shell and a sardine to produce an internal backbone as each creature develops from an embryo.

Here's the problem: Again, there is absolutely nothing in the fossil record that gives any evidence of any kind of clam (or any other marine invertebrate) evolving into a fish. Nothing! There are no clamishes! Zero.

> In sediments of late Silurian and early Devonian age, numerous fishlike vertebrates of varied types are present, and it is obvious that a long evolutionary history had taken place before that time. But of that history we are mainly ignorant.[13]

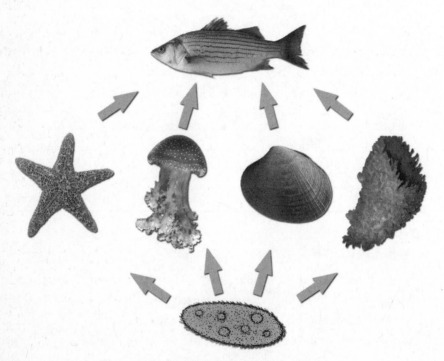

Figure 4.6—Invertebrates to Vertebrates

Fish to Amphibians

The next stage of evolution is supposed to be a time when the water-based creatures began to crawl out onto the land surfaces. The logic is that some fish began to develop connections between the bones in their fins and the ribs in their backbones so that the animal could eventually carry its body weight on land.

Once again, the informational change required for such a shift in design is huge. Much novel data would have to be developed in order for a set of "floating" hard parts (not yet bone) to change into leg bones, connect to a pelvic structure (that was not there previously), and over the same time period turn the gills into lungs. Amazing! One could almost use the word *miraculous* (except there are no miracles in evolution—just random events happening over long periods of time by chance).

Ah, but here's that problem again. No evidence! There are absolutely no indisputable cases of these transitional forms in the fossil record. Occasionally, one can find a story and various artistic renderings of how a coelacanth (a type of lungfish) that supposedly went extinct around 66 million years ago evolved into an amphibian. The trouble is that some folks found a thriving community of coelacanth fish living off the coast of South Africa. Explorers continue to find more. It looks exactly like its supposedly 66-million-year-old cousin.

Evolutionists once taught that the coelacanth's lobed fins were legs-in-the-making. Ironically, their deep-ocean habitats are farther from land than almost anywhere else on Earth. Those lobed fins have always been used for swimming. In spite of all the academic speculations to the contrary, it's still a fish!

Plants and Insects

Scattered throughout the fossil strata are large beds composed mostly of plant material. The bulk of these layers are found in deposits ranging from 40–350 million years old, according to the standard evolutionary dates. These region-wide sediments contain fossils of many different types of familiar plants like ferns, palm trees, coconuts, etc. The overwhelming consensus is that these carbon-based materials have been compressed under the pressures of the layers above, ultimately forming the fossil fuel that we commonly refer to as coal.

Remains of insects are sprinkled throughout the coal deposits, including wings from cockroaches (one of the more prolific living fossils of today). The mystery of the origin and demise of the plants and insects found all over the world has puzzled scientists for a long time. Once again, although we do find extinct forms of both plants and insects, many are precisely the same type as those that exist today—except that some of them were really big. Fossil remains of a dragonfly-like insect with a wingspan of 28 inches have been found, as well as the *Euphoberia*, an insect like the modern centipede that was over three feet long!

I'm glad some of these have become extinct.

And, just like the invertebrates, fish, and amphibians, all of these fossils appear abruptly in the sedimentary deposits fully formed and fully functional without any hint of transitional ancestors of any kind.

Carbon-14

Here's another puzzle for those who ignore the biblical data. Since these animals and plants are all carbon-based, it is relatively easy to date their remains for evidence of carbon-14, a radioactive isotope of carbon. Essentially, carbon-14 is formed in the atmosphere, absorbed into plants, and the plants are eaten by living things. The heavier carbon-14 decays rather rapidly, with a half-life of 5730 years. As long as the plants are functioning and the living animals are eating the plants, the ratio between the stable carbon element carbon-12 and the radioisotope of carbon-14 stays pretty much the same. However, once the plant ceases to function or the animal dies, the carbon-14 begins to decay into nitrogen-14.

Under normal conditions, one-half of the carbon-14 would decay over 5730 years. Another half would disappear over the next 5730 years, and still another half would disperse in the next 5730 years, and so on until there is not enough carbon-14 left to measure. After 18 of these half-life sessions of 5730 years (a cumulative total of about 100,000 years), the miniscule number of heavy carbon molecules remaining would be so small that, for all practical purposes, the amount would be zero.

That would mean that all of the coal and insect fossils should not show any carbon-14 in their remains at all—since they are millions of years old, according to the standard dating of the various eras in which their deposits are found.

But—and this is a big but—all of these deposits do show a rather significant amount of carbon-14! This is not a new find. These anomalies (as they are wont to be called) have appeared in the scientific literature for several years. Typically, these data are dismissed as being the result of contamination by groundwater or some other external factor. However, the anomaly has been documented by laboratories from coal deposits all around the world. That seems to stretch the idea of contamination a bit far.

The Institute for Creation Research conducted a multiyear study on issues relating to radioisotope dating.[14] During that study, ten carefully registered and documented coal samples from three major coal seams ranging from the youngest to the oldest deposits were sent to a world-class laboratory to analyze for the presence of carbon-14. All of the samples registered the presence of significant carbon-14. Even with the possible error-bar potential, the remaining carbon-14 indicated that these coal samples were all about the same age—even though their evolutionary age assignments differed by more than 100 million years!

More Missing Links
The Cambrian Explosion

What is clearly true with the Cambrian Explosion and the following layers with fish, amphibians, plants, and insects is also true for the more spectacular of the fossils, such as *Elasmosaurus, Ichthyosaurus, Archelon,* and *Kronosaurus*—all rather enormous and scary, but all fully formed and with no transitional evidence or ancestor found.

> The abrupt appearance of pterodactyls and other flying reptiles is stunning. Reconstructing the ancestry of a clan like the pterodactyls remains an especially difficult challenge. Flying dragons seem to burst into the world like Athena from the mind of Zeus, fully formed. Even the earliest skeletons of pterodactyls already

display fully developed wings and the specialized torso and hips so characteristic of the entire order...As of today, no fossils have been discovered to show how the pterodactyl's forelimbs became transformed into wings.[15]

The same is true for reptiles—they seemed to come out of nowhere. These creatures capture our imagination more than many others. They seem to represent a time when puny humans did not exist—and if they did, they would have been nothing more than a snack for the mighty *T. rex*! The problem is that they appear in the fossil record fully formed, fully functional, and completely without any hard evidence for an ancestor. They just existed at some time in Earth's past with no record of where they came from.

And the list goes on. Every time a new kind of creature is discovered in the fossil record, there is no undisputed evidence for any transitional form, let alone a common ancestor that is traceable (except on the pages of *Time* magazine, the walls of major museums, and various textbooks).

> The regular absence of transitional forms is not confined to mammals, but is an almost universal phenomenon, as has long been noted by paleontologists.[16]

> The known fossil record is not, and never has been, in accord with gradualism...Few modern paleontologists seem to have recognized that in the past century, as the biological historian William Coleman has recently written, "The majority of paleontologists felt their evidence simply contradicted Darwin's stress on minute, slow, and cumulative changes leading to species transformation."[17]

> Ironically, we have even fewer examples of evolutionary transition than we had in Darwin's time. By this I mean that some of the classic cases of Darwinian change in the fossil record, such as the evolution of the horse in North America, have had to be discarded or modified as a result of more detailed information.[18]

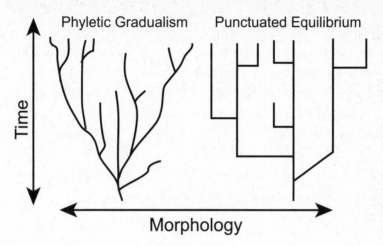

Figure 4.7—Punctuated Equilibrium

Punctuated Equilibrium

Because of the continued absence of missing links—that is, an absence of evidence for evolution—in the fossil record, Drs. Stephen Jay Gould, Niles Eldredge, Steven Stanley, and others proposed a modification of uniformitarian evolution back in the early 1970s that they called *punctuated equilibrium*. Essentially, they suggested that nature would continue in stasis for millions of years, then suddenly burst into a short period that "punctuated" the "equilibrium" with novel mutations that produced new creatures so rapidly that the process did not allow enough time for fossils to be captured and preserved.

Obviously, that theory left something of a hole in basic logic, but it has become more and more popular since its inception, mainly because the paleontological world is still looking for the transitional evidence. Yes, theories abound and are well-presented and widely accepted—because the only alternative is creation! If there is no evidence for gradual evolution from one kind of animal to another, if there is no empirical (observable, testable, repeatable) evidence for such upward movement from very simple life forms to the wide variety of complex plants and animals that abound today, then the alternative idea ultimately lies in a faith-based worldview like creation.

Assessing the Evidence

Dr. Douglas Futuyma is one of the more well-known and widely published evolutionary biologists of the twentieth century. He is a distinguished professor in the Department of Ecology and Evolution at Stony Brook University in Stony Brook, New York, and a research associate on staff at the American Museum of Natural History in New York City. Far from being a creationist, Dr. Futuyma has published several textbooks advocating the "fact" of evolution and is active in opposing any compromise toward a creationist perspective. Yet he is quite honest in his evaluation of the alternatives:

> Organisms either appeared on the earth fully developed or they did not. If they did not, they must have developed from preexisting species by some process of modification. If they did appear in a fully developed state, they must indeed have been created by some omnipotent intelligence.[19]

The point that the creationists keep making is exactly the same as Dr. Futuyma's conclusion: All the evidence seems to point to organisms appearing "on the earth fully developed." There is absolutely no evidence in the present world—and, so far, there is no evidence in the fossil record—of any kind of common ancestor or missing link.

One wonders how long the scientific world must wait for evidence to prove even the possibility of evolution.

The Missing Evidence

No evolution presently taking place—no new kinds
No known mechanism of evolution
No worldwide order
No transitional forms
No evidence that evolution is possible
No mathematical model for probability

The Observed Evidence

Biological stasis for all phyla

DNA mutations take away genetic information

Life always comes from life

Unbridgeable gaps between reproducing biological kinds

No evolutionary development of new body plans (dog to cat)

Mutation accumulation prohibits a million-year time frame in species

CHAPTER 5

Noah's Flood

The first six chapters of Genesis contain a very select set of data. The time that elapsed was 1656 years from creation to the Flood of Noah. There are several events listed that give us a chronology from which we can gain the overall picture.

For instance, the birth of Adam's son, Seth, is cited in Genesis 5:3 as taking place 130 years after Adam was created. Seth was certainly not the third child born, but his birth was a significant event since he was the "replacement" son for Abel, whom Cain had murdered. Several such key events (important births, major desecrations) are given to enable us to understand the beginning of the onslaught of the Flood destruction.

The record of the great Flood covers three chapters and contains specific historical information about the time, events, and nature of this worldwide catastrophe. One of the main reasons many do not like to accept the biblical record of the Flood as presented is that it expresses the awful wrath of the Creator God on those who would dare to rebel against His grace and provision.

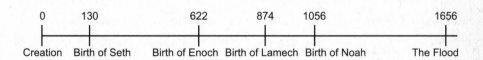

Figure 5.1—Creation to Flood Timeline

The Opening Chapters of Genesis

It is worth noting that the early chapters of Genesis, while covering a sequential period of time, are not to be understood as happening right after each other. Chapters 1 and 2 provide data about the creation week. The first chapter gives a short and carefully worded record of the main activity of each day, and chapter 2 gives us Adam's own insight about what transpired with him during some portion of the sixth day.

Chapter 3 covers only a few hours but gives specifics about man's awful rebellion against his Creator and God's subsequent judgment on the serpent, the woman, and on Earth itself because of Adam's sin. Were it not for the very intense and precise wordings, we would have little understanding about the significance of the gospel message that is the core of the rest of Scripture.

Chapter 4 leaps forward at least a century, probably to a period of time just before Seth's conception and birth at 130 years after the creation week. In this chapter we are told of the event that precipitated the murder of Abel. Not much detail is given, but the choice of words indicates that the sacrificial ceremony at which Cain brought his unacceptable offering was a regular event and that the subsequent rejection of Cain's sacrifice was not unexpected. The resultant rage, murder, and interchange between God and Cain emphasize the ongoing relationship between the Creator Redeemer and humanity and His agelong effort to bring about reconciliation.

Seemingly without pause, chapter 4 leaps forward to the seventh generation of Cain's descendants to describe Lamech and his family. Lamech is cited for his boastful song about his murder of a young man who wounded him in some way. He also married two wives—perhaps in open rebellion against the implied restriction of the one-man, one-woman relationship established at the time of creation.

Three sons of Lamech are identified as successful purveyors of major commerce or artistry. Jabal was the father of nomadic farming and ranching. Jubal was a prominent musician. Tubal-Cain was famous as a metalsmith. Whatever is implied by their success, the picture is of a population that has developed from the descendants of Cain, with cities, agriculture, entertainment, and significant craftsmanship in metallurgy. Given the later comments by God that the whole earth was filled with violence, it is at least plausible that the implements of warfare were being developed during these midcenturies after creation.

Chapter 5 gives us a list of the main descendants of Seth through the various heads of each generation until the life of Noah. Enoch, in sharp contrast to Cain's descendant Lamech, was humble and obedient. He was known as a righteous man rather than a murderous polygamist. His son Methuselah became the longest-lived person in that age prior to the great Flood. Enoch is also one of two persons in the Scriptures said to have been "translated" without dying (Genesis 5:24), Elijah being the other human so named (2 Kings 2:11).

Chapter 6 opens with a description of the sons of God who began an effort to rule the world through the selective breeding of giants. The evil condition of the entire planet caused God to decree the ultimate destruction and elimination of all air-breathing life. While the sparse information given is not sufficient to draw a full conclusion, evidently what has transpired is a deterioration of social order into such evil that "the wickedness of man was great in the earth, and that every intent of the thoughts of his heart was only evil continually" (Genesis 6:5). Twice, the Bible declares that the whole earth was "filled with violence" (Genesis 6:11, 13), and God is so angry that He will bring "floodwaters on the earth, to destroy from under heaven all flesh in which is the breath of life; everything that is on the earth shall die" (Genesis 6:17).

God intended to destroy all air-breathing life on the planet:

> The earth also was corrupt before God, and the earth was filled with violence. So God looked upon the earth, and indeed it was corrupt; for all flesh had corrupted their way on the earth. And God said to Noah, "The end of all flesh has come before Me, for the earth is filled with violence through them; and behold, I will destroy them with the earth" (Genesis 6:11-13).

> And all flesh died that moved on the earth: birds and cattle and beasts and every creeping thing that creeps on the earth, and every man. All in whose nostrils was the breath of the spirit of

life, all that was on the dry land, died. So He destroyed all living
things which were on the face of the ground: both man and cattle, creeping thing and bird of the air. They were destroyed from
the earth (Genesis 7:21-23).

Expressions of totality occur more than 30 times in Genesis 6 through 9. I
am not sure if there is any other way to phrase the extent of such destruction
with any more clarity. God intended to destroy all the life that was on the planet.
Even the Hebrew language has a special term for this phenomenon. The word
is *mabuwl*, and is used uniquely of the Genesis Flood 12 times in Genesis 6–11.

In the six hundredth year of Noah's life, in the second month, the
seventeenth day of the month, on that day all the fountains of
the great deep were broken up, and the windows of heaven were
opened (Genesis 7:11).

The language of these three key chapters is so carefully worded that it is hard
to get any impression other than that they were designed to record a historical event. For instance, the record specifies that the Flood started on the seventeenth day of the month Iyar, the second month in the Hebrew year that cor-
responds to our April/May. We are specifically told that Noah was 600 years
old and that the physical causes of the Flood were all initiated on that very day.

Genesis 7:11 is remarkable evidence that the biblical record is to be taken
as factual history.

The Fountains of the Great Deep

It is a common misconception that the Flood happened because it rained
for 40 days and 40 nights. It did indeed do so, but that rain was almost an additive to the major sources of water that covered the planet's surface.

Whatever is being referred to by the phrase "fountains of the great deep,"
it certainly includes some form of enormous reservoirs of water. Some who
have studied the potential causes of Noah's Flood have suggested that "the
great deep" refers to the oceans of the first world. The "fountains" refers to the
source of the deep and may well involve some form of subterranean reservoir

that contained the bulk of the waters God divided on Day Three of the creation week.

There is also an enigmatic reference to a mist that "went up from the earth and watered the whole face of the ground" (Genesis 2:6). That mist was apparently sufficient to keep the ground watered, since "the LORD God had not caused it to rain on the earth" (Genesis 2:5). That underground "sprinkler system" would fit the implied difference between the hydrological cycle of the pre-Flood world and the normal evaporation-precipitation-evaporation cycle we know today.

Any cursory look at the topography of ocean bottoms will show enormous rifts running up and down and sideways. Much of the earth shows huge pockmarks from enormous volcanic eruptions, and the surface is buried in water-deposited mud, sand, shale, and sediment, sometimes to the depth of thousands of feet. Whatever happened was a water catastrophe that was never before seen nor has occurred since.

The subterranean reservoirs of water broke open, likely as steam mixed with magma. Ocean floors erupted and gaped open. Land-based sources split and spewed in a worldwide cataclysm that occurred on the seventeenth day of the Hebrew month Iyar, when Noah was 600 years old. Water surged up and out. Land surfaces collapsed. Continental shelving was broken and sucked down into the widening maw of the ocean deep, and tsunamis began to heave back and forth across the land surfaces. Such geological energies would have triggered magma rents, and volcanic pressures would have exploded into enormous fire blooms of such intensity that anything in their paths would have been incinerated.

Such explosive energies would have pulverized the land surfaces and blown them into the highest reaches of Earth's atmosphere. The "windows of heaven" would have begun to collapse in a deluge that would make a summer thunderstorm seem like a spring sprinkle. No one knows for sure how the "waters above" were contained. The Bible merely hints at columns and foundations and beams. Something that God did during the second day of the creation week positioned some enormous volume of water above the planet. Now, with the fountains of the great deep exploding all over the globe, the upper reservoirs would begin to coalesce around the tiny land-based particles that were rocketing skyward, resulting in a 40-day inundation so rapid and awful that catching a mouthful of air would have been almost impossible.

Billions of creatures died during that year. The fossil record is the result of that terrible Flood. Some could swim, waddle, run, flee, and ride out the horror for a time, but ultimately "all flesh died" (Genesis 7:21).

Much More Than Rain

The water got deeper and deeper for 150 days:

> Now the flood was on the earth forty days. The waters *increased* and lifted up the ark, and it *rose high* above the earth. The waters *prevailed* and *greatly increased* on the earth, and the ark moved about on the surface of the waters. And the waters *prevailed exceedingly* on the earth, and all the high hills under the whole heaven were covered. The waters *prevailed* fifteen cubits upward, and the mountains were covered (Genesis 7:17-20).

The italicized words give a small sense of how intense this Flood really was. It did not just rain; the entire surface of Earth was covered. All the time the rain was coming down, the 40 days, the fountains of the great deep were spewing out their liquid horror and the entire earth was convulsing with explosions, tsunamis, sinkholes, earthquakes, and mountain eruptions.

> And *all flesh died* that moved on the earth: *birds* and *cattle* and *beasts* and every *creeping thing* that creeps on the earth, and *every man*. All in whose nostrils was the breath of the spirit of life, *all that was on the dry land, died*. So He destroyed *all living things* which were on the face of the ground: both man and cattle, creeping thing and bird of the air. They were *destroyed from the earth*. Only Noah and those who were with him in the ark remained alive. And the waters prevailed on the earth one hundred and fifty days (Genesis 7:21-24).

Did you catch that? Everything that had breath—everything that lived on the dry land—died except for the animals and the eight people God protected on board the Ark. Not only that, the waters prevailed for 150 days. Whatever is being described here is not some local or tranquil event. This horrific, world-wide, planet-destroying cataclysm *got worse* for 150 days!

The Wind-Down

That much water and upheaval doesn't just go away. When we work from the seventeenth of Iyar (the beginning) to the end—"the second month, on the twenty-seventh day of the month" over a year later (Genesis 8:14)—the Flood lasted 370 days! There has never been anything like that before or since.

Noah was 600 when the Flood started and 601 when Earth dried. The rain lasted 40 days, which are included in the 150 days the waters prevailed (Genesis 7:11, 24). The bottom of the Ark rested on the mountains of Ararat (Genesis 8:4), then it took another 74 days (from the seventeenth day of the seventh month to the first day of the tenth) for the waters to decrease enough for the tops of the mountains to show (verse 5). Noah waited 40 days after he saw the mountaintops before he sent out a raven (verses 6-7). He then waited 7 days before he sent out a dove (verse 8), another 7 before sending it out a second time (verse 10), and an additional 7 before he sent it out the third time, after which it didn't return (verse 12). (The fact that the raven and dove were not sent at the same time is indicated by the phrase it was "yet another seven days" before the dove was sent again.) It took another 29 days for the earth to reach its first stage of dryness (on the first day of the first month of the new year—verse 13), and a final 56 days until the land was completely dry enough to disembark. On the twenty-seventh day of the second month (verse 14), they left the Ark and entered the new world—and the new age!

Add it up: 150 + 74 + 40 + 7 + 7 + 7 + 29 + 56 = 370 days.

Chronology of the Flood	
Event	Days
Waters prevailed	150 (rain fell for 40)
Ark rested on Ararat, waters decreased	74
Noah waited, then sent out raven	40
Waited, sent out dove	7
Waited, sent out dove a second time	7
Waited, sent out dove a third time	7
Earth dried	85
Total	370

Figure 5.2—Chronology of the Flood

These calculations, which use the language of the biblical record, appear to follow the assumption of a 360-day year. Although there is no concrete proof that such a solar orbit was in place prior to the Flood of Noah's day, the only sufficient cause to slow the planet's orbit to its present 365.25-day cycle would have been the enormous forces involved as the planet erupted, exploded, and convulsed during the year-long cataclysm. Some earlier writers on this subject record a 371-day period. That additional day would include the very day on which the Flood started.

Quick Summary

The great Flood began with a worldwide explosion of the fountains of the great deep. That certainly included the fountains (sources) of the great ocean basins and the sources of the land-surface misting systems. This all occurred on one day—the seventeenth day of the second month of the year Noah was 600 years old.

The Flood would have included these kinds of geological and hydrological phenomena:

- Volcanic eruptions that blew the earth's crust into the atmosphere
- Magma flows, inundating the land surface
- Unimaginable waves of water flooding the surface
- Tsunamis hundreds of feet high
- Eruptions (explosions) of water
- Sinkholes thousands of feet across
- Landslides across large regions

Figure 5.3—Phenomena

These enormous explosions caused a collapse of the waters that were above the earth, causing a rain that lasted for 40 days—a condition that would not be possible under the evaporation-precipitation-evaporation cycle as we know it. It is not possible today for Earth's atmosphere to contain enough water vapor to allow for a continuous 40-day precipitation. That suffocating torrent then— plus the huge waves of water surging from the ocean and land reservoirs— ultimately covered all the mountains to a depth of at least 22.5 feet ("fifteen cubits," Genesis 7:20).

- Waters "increased" (Genesis 7:17)
- Waters "prevailed" (Genesis 7:18)
- Waters "greatly increased" (Genesis 7:18)
- Waters "prevailed exceedingly" (Genesis 7:19)
- It covered "all the high hills" (Genesis 7:19)
- All flesh died on the earth (Genesis 7:21)
- Only Noah and his family and the animals on the Ark remained alive (Genesis 7:23)
- The water got deeper for 150 days after the start of the Flood (Genesis 7:24)

Figure 5.4—Waters

Then the flow of water from above and the surging from under the surface was stopped and the waters began to subside. There was still an enormous back-and-forth movement as the tsunamis sloshed to and fro as if in a giant bathtub. Land surfaces were building and subsiding. Enormous geological energies shifted the still-unconsolidated sedimentary deposits into mountain ranges.

This went on for five months, finally allowing the Ark to settle on a solid surface seven months after the Flood began.

After ten months inside the huge Ark, Noah opened the "window" of the Ark and began to look out at what must have been a terrifying sight. The world of wonder and majesty—the beautiful good creation, marred no doubt by the violence that had dominated the later centuries of that first age—was now empty, disfigured, and inhospitable. The prospects were truly intimidating.

But God had promised to preserve life. Soon, after Noah's family had unloaded sufficient material to begin their new life, Noah built an altar and offered one of the precious animals as a sacrifice (as he had been instructed, no doubt), and God responded.

> The LORD said in His heart, "I will never again curse the ground for man's sake, although the imagination of man's heart is evil from his youth; nor will I again destroy every living thing as I have done. While the earth remains, seedtime and harvest, cold and heat, winter and summer, and day and night shall not cease" (Genesis 8:21-22).

If the Genesis Flood Is True, What Would We Expect to Find?

If anything like the details given in Genesis 6 through 9 actually occurred, there should be literally mountains of evidence that such a catastrophe did happen. That would explain why so much of the opposition over the past several hundred years has been focused against the idea of a planet-covering flood. If that event happened, then the geological and hydrological phenomena would forever alter the surface of Earth and undermine the entire concept of millions of years of slow and gradual development. If, indeed, such an event took place, what would we who are on this side of the cataclysm expect to find? We would expect to find just what we do find:

- The remains of bottom-dwelling marine life in every conceivable environment on the planet.
- Preservation of every kind of animal, in every conceivable

condition—broken, mangled, disarticulated, lumped together, as well as sorted by size and type and distributed over the entire surface of the earth.

- Vast graveyards of fossil deposits with creatures of every type and from every environment, violently killed, washed together, buried together, and fossilized rapidly.

- The abrupt and distinctive appearance of every kind of animal, with clear differences between the types.

- No physical evidence of time boundaries between rock layers; all types of rocks (shale, limestone, granite, etc.) throughout all the spectrum of deposits, with no worldwide sequence or unconformity. "Old" rocks and "young" rocks in every formation with no physical characteristics to indicate age.

- Worldwide evidence of recent water bodies in existing desert areas; worldwide occurrences of raised shorelines and river terraces; valleys much too large for the present rivers and streams; clear traces of rapid rises and drops in sea levels.

The Physical Evidences of the Flood Are in the Rock Layers

The nature of this evidence requires pictures. Some are included in this book, but there are many, many more available either in other publications by ICR authors or on our website, www.icr.org. There are, however, a few distinctions that can be recalled and visualized rather easily.

Pancake layers are laid down by water on a regional scale all across the globe. If the biblical Flood laid down the rocks and fossils, there were no geologic ages. The fossils are almost entirely contained in water-deposited mud. There are billions of dead things, all covered in mud, all laid down by water, all over the earth!

- ~95 percent of all fossils are marine invertebrates, primarily shellfish

- ~95 percent of the remaining 5 percent are plants

- ~95 percent of the rest are fish

- Most of what is left are insects
- Much less than 1 percent are land vertebrates, and those usually consist of a very few disarticulated bones

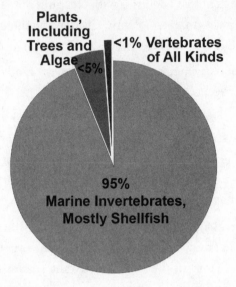

Figure 5.5—Marine Fossils

Science is what you can observe and test. Written records go back about 5000 years; the rest is speculation. All evidence points to an enormous water catastrophe that inundated the entire planet, causing rapid deposition. The geological studies of ICR have long been published, and the evidence is widely available. Summaries of that information are available on ICR's website.

Majestic Mercy, Open Rebellion

Of all the controversial issues regarding the early chapters of Genesis, the description of a worldwide flood seems to top the chart. It is obvious that the existence of an omnipotent and omniscient Creator God is a faith-based matter. It is certainly not possible to prove that God exists. The creation of God's image and likeness in two human beings named Adam and Eve is likewise an unprovable matter.

It is possible to give a strong, logical answer for the truth of God, and there are biological studies that demonstrate the plausibility of a common mother among the genetic data that are rapidly accumulating today. But it is very difficult to provide empirical proof of these belief systems—so they remain mostly that, belief systems.

In an attempt to bring about some agreement between the scientific-sounding philosophy of naturalism and the historical record of the early chapters of Genesis, Christian scholars and theologians have devised several hybrid theories to rationalize and try to harmonize the structure of evolutionary development with the precise information of the creation account. In those attempts, the record of the Flood provided in Genesis 6 through 8 is simply ignored or relegated to mythological tradition. These several theories are still taught today. A quick review of the more popular of them is helpful when trying to understand why the clear record of Scripture is so strongly resisted.

Hybrid Theories

It is interesting to note that many past civilizations have legends of a worldwide flood. The details vary somewhat, but almost all of them speak of a boat of some sort that carried a family of humans and certain specimens of plants and categories of land and air animals on board to preserve life on the earth. A majority of them even speak of eight people and of enormous rain and flooding from beneath the earth. The stories are remarkably similar to the biblical account, as well as noting that the flood was a punishment for disobedience to the god of the universe. Interesting, to say the least.[1]

Hybrid Theories	
Theistic Evolution	God directed natural processes.
Day-Age Theory	Each creation day represents a vast age of time.
Progressive Creation	Each creation day represents sudden creation acts.
Gap Theory	Genesis 1:1-2 and the fossil record represent a former world that was destroyed.

Figure 5.6—Hybrid Theories

But over the past three centuries, as the intellectual elite of Europe began to question the biblical account of a recent creation and a planet-destroying flood, various theories began to surface among religious leaders who attempted to accommodate the stories of Genesis with the growing science of naturalism, as evolution was then called.

Theistic Evolution

One of the more popular early efforts was an attempt to allegorize the creation record and attribute the processes of naturalism to the God of the Bible. This theory wasn't very well received among the churches but found a fertile ground in the academic institutions of the Enlightenment.

The major objection voiced against this idea was that it required God to be the originator of death and destruction, as well as the very messy process of random evolution over a long period of time. Even though Adam and Eve were considered real people, it was thought they must have evolved from subhuman creatures that were soulless.

The Flood of Noah's day was either dismissed as merely a legend or was seen as a tranquil flooding of the Mesopotamian Valley where civilization was thought to have developed. This hybrid theory wasn't taken very seriously until the late 1800s and has waxed and waned in popularity over the decades since.

The teachers of theistic evolution believe that creation came about through evolution. The only practical difference between this theory and the atheistic presumptions of the naturalist is merely that God uses evolution as a "creative" force. Most mainline Christian schools and universities espouse theistic evolution. Secular schools, colleges, and universities teach only naturalism and strongly exclude any idea of the supernatural. Some who embrace the overall idea of theistic evolution will allow for a providential involvement in the overall scheme of the process, but all of the evolutionary processes are presumed to be the mechanism by which God brought the universe, Earth, and life into existence. Like the deist, to them God is distant, disinterested, and disconnected from our reality.

They think the Bible may contain the message of God, but the concept of an inerrant and inspired written text from God is not accepted. The book of Genesis, especially, is considered to be a collection of myths or legends, similar to the mythologies of ancient Babylon, Greece, and other pagan religions.

Thus, all those who believe in theistic evolution would date the creation of the universe by evolutionary processes between 13 to 14 billion years ago.

The Day-Age Theory

The major difference between the day-age theory and theistic evolution is that the former attempts to follow the biblical sequence of the seven days outlined in Genesis 1. That is, each day represents a series of developments, overseen by God, in which the creative acts are intermingled with naturalistic processes. Some would suggest God's intervention is more evident during the development of life, but the biblical information is seen as merely an allegory meant to teach us that God exists and was somehow involved in the early origins.

Day One could represent the earliest eons of the expansion and coalescing of dust and gases as they stretched out after the Big Bang. Day Two might be the way God expressed the formation of the early earth's sphere and the organizational separation of the early elements. Days Three, Four, Five, and Six each demonstrate the continued development of the universe, with a special emphasis on Earth. God is active in a passive sort of way, and He monitors and ensures that everything will be good in the end. There are some very obvious disagreements with the evolutionary model of progression and the biblical text, however.

Theistic evolutionists do not attempt to equate the language of the Bible with the evolutionary theory, even though most of them would insist they believe in a real God. The day-age proponents, in contrast, try to draw direct analogies with the information given about each day as recorded in Genesis. Once again, the deep time required by evolution is embraced, as well as the procedural development of the evolutionary model. Thus, the universe began between 13 to 14 billion years ago, and Earth became an identifiable planet around 4.5 billion years ago.

Progressive Creation

While similar to the day-age theory, the various modifications of progressive creation are somewhat more biblical and, therefore, more acceptable to evangelical theologians, scholars, and pastors. Essentially, those who promote the idea of progressive creation would insist that God was directly involved in several specific stages of creation throughout the long ages. For instance, God created the energy speck that exploded in the Big Bang (or the Big Bang is the result of God's initial creation).

But God then allowed the natural forces to develop over the course of eons until certain "making" events were called for. There are many variations on this, of course, but all progressive creationists appear to agree that God had to create the first life. Several other events were necessary for God's intervention. Some suggest that the huge change from nonliving chemicals to single-celled life and the development of marine invertebrates would require God's creative power. Other events like the transition from fish to amphibians, various interventions or guidance for reptiles, mammals, hominids (soulless, manlike creatures), and finally man are considered creative acts.

Many progressive creationists believe that Adam and Eve were real, historical humans, created uniquely by God around 10,000 years ago. Others who hold to progressive creation (mainly within the broad Intelligent Design Movement) would not be as firm about the special nature of man but think that sometime recently, soulless hominids developed into what we now classify as *Homo sapiens*, and a pair (Adam and Eve) were singled out to receive God's special attention.

Though progressive creation theorists vary widely in their views, the common denominators appear to be that development (via evolutionary processes) is natural, and that God uses the natural laws that science has uncovered as His means of development. All proponents would insist that physical death is an integral part of the universe from the earliest functioning of replicating life. Those who would incorporate a biblical background for their model are more conservative and thus more often embraced by evangelical Christianity.

However, all who embrace the concept of progressive creation hold to an old-earth viewpoint, thus endorsing the idea of a 13.2-billion-year-old universe and a 4.5-billion-year-old Earth.

The Gap Theory

In the past, the most widely accepted hybrid theory among conservative churches was the teaching that there had been an earlier world that was destroyed when Lucifer fell from heaven in his rebellion against the Creator. That pre-Adamic age lasted for an unknown number of eons but accounts for the billions of years prior to the world's re-creation after Satan's fall. To accommodate this lost history, a gap is inserted in Genesis 1 between verses one and two.

> In the beginning God created the heavens and the earth. [Implied gap] The earth was without form, and void; and darkness was on the face of the deep. And the Spirit of God was hovering over the face of the waters (Genesis 1:1-2).

In the text, the earth is described as being without form and void. Proponents of the gap theory usually translate these terms as "ruined" and "desolate," suggesting something bad had happened previously. In essence, the theory is that God indeed created the heavens and the earth, but a cataclysmic event occurred after the initial creation—an event that demanded the judgment of God, thus ruining the earth and leaving it desolate. The terms "without form, and void," however, are more commonly understood in the Bible as formless and empty or uninhabited.

The apparent reading of the text would be that God created the heavens and the earth in their basic elemental components (space and matter), which were without form and empty, waiting to be developed by God. Some among those who still retain a belief in the gap theory teach that there was a race of pre-Adamic men, similar to the giants mentioned in Genesis 6. While this version of the gap theory is somewhat controversial, the common teaching among all proponents is that an older world grew more and more evil over time and was ultimately destroyed.

Made popular by the Scofield Bible of the early 1900s, this "ruin and recon-struction" idea is supposed to be further verified by the fossil record. The various gigantic fossils (dinosaurs, etc.) are assumed to be additional evidence of a pre-Adamic time that lasted for eons under the rule of Satan. Some suggest that since there are few verified human fossils, the race that inhabited Earth back then was some sort of hybrid of mammals and demons. Some even suggest that the so-called cavemen (hominid fossils) relate to that pre-Adamic time.

However, this gap between Genesis 1:1 and 1:2 is not linguistically, grammatically, or doctrinally required in any sense. It doesn't even hold up to basic logic. A cataclysm sufficiently powerful to leave the earth "without form, and void" would destroy any physical evidence of that event (such as fossils) and would do away with the place where the billions of years were supposed to have accrued. Furthermore, God's ultimate pronouncement of good on "everything that He had made" (Genesis 1:31) would be meaningless if there had been ages of wickedness prior to God's final evaluation of His work. For obvious reasons, no evolutionist accepts the gap theory.

Common Problems Among the Hybrids

Except for the gap theory, all of the various hybrid theories require that naturalistic evolution be a normal part of how God involves Himself in the creation process. The only practical reason to accept long ages is to allow for an evolutionary scheme to fit into the Bible, since the philosophical foundation of evolutionary theory is deep time—billions of years.

However, evolution in any form charges God with waste and cruelty. God must be either ignorant or impotent, since He must experiment and use trial and error to bring about the "most fit." Also, over the long ages of natural development, God would have to consciously choose the most inefficient, cruel, and wasteful process to create. Those factors would make death the device of God to produce this "best" over time. Death becomes good, even though the Bible calls it the last enemy to be defeated (1 Corinthians 15:26).

These various attempts to harmonize the text of Scripture with the "proofs" of modern science necessitate that God is the Evolver (theistic evolution), or the Guide or Experimenter (day-age and progressive creation), or the Reconstructionist (the gap theory). Each of these hybrids require that one must either reject the text (theistic evolution), allegorize the text (day-age), deconstruct the words of the text (progressive creation), or insert a "catchall" theory into the clear reading of the text (the gap theory).

All of these hybrid theories are attempts to accommodate the ages of evolutionary development. Each of them, in one way or another, makes God the author of some 4.5 billion years of death and confusion. Romans 5:12 proclaims that death is the result of sin, a fact that is either openly ignored or reinterpreted by these hybrids. First Corinthians 14:33 clearly states that God does not author confusion—but confusion and random processes lie at the very core of the evolutionary theory. All of these various accommodations to evolutionary naturalism fly in the face of biblical revelation and the attributes of God.

Exodus 20:11 states the reason for the fourth commandment to remember the Sabbath (God worked six days and rested one day). Those words, inscribed twice with the finger of God, cannot be taken in any sense as ages during which we are to work and rest. We, who are His created stewards, are to follow His example.

There is not much going for any of these theories from a biblical perspective, and none of them curry favor with the evolutionists whom they were devised to appease.

Final Thoughts

The Bible teaches a worldwide, planet-covering, life-destroying flood.

The empirical evidence supports the biblical account.

Those who reject that message and evidence do so for personal reasons.

The Bible also teaches that the Creator God entered this world some 2000 years ago to offer Himself as a sacrifice for our sins and make possible our salvation. Perhaps the difficulty in believing the historicity of the great Flood lies in the thought that the loving Creator Redeemer could become so angry at sin that He destroyed the very world and living creatures He had brought into existence.

God's wrath is a terrible thing to see!

Fortunately, just as the message of judgment is displayed in the horrific destruction of the Flood, so is the grace of our Creator displayed in His simple statement about Noah: "Noah found grace in the eyes of the LORD" (Genesis 6:8).

God's grace is also part of the Flood epic. For in the judgment was the possibility of rescue in the Ark. That Ark was in preparation for a long time, with Noah serving as a "preacher of righteousness" for those many years (2 Peter 2:5). All had the chance to believe the word of God that judgment was coming. All had the opportunity to believe the word of the preacher and enter into the Ark. Right up until the day Noah embarked, the opportunity was still open.

CHAPTER 6

The Age of Earth

All the questions about *how* and *what* regarding the origin of our universe revolve around age. The Bible clearly speaks of a recent creation, in contrast to the billions of years often touted as the assumed age of our universe. But in terms of real history, thousands is pretty old! None of us can trace our family origins back past a few hundred years with any certainty.

Biblical Chronology

The First World

In 2 Peter chapter 3, the apostle Peter identified three ages within God's overall plan for the universe. First was the world that existed prior to the Flood, which is described in Genesis 6 through 8—a world that was brought into existence "by the word of God."

> ...that by the word of God the heavens were of old, and the earth standing out of water and in the water, by which the world that then existed perished, being flooded with water (2 Peter 3:5-6).

That world was destroyed by "being flooded with water." It is no longer accessible to us. The geological evidence discussed in the previous chapter testifies to a horrific cataclysm in the past. There is evidence in those geological records of a very different world with vastly different topography and climate. Peter alluded to that when he spoke of an earth that was "standing out of water and in the water," clearly a reference to the second day of the creation week when God divided the waters, placing some amount of those waters above the planet itself.

Whatever cosmological structure was put in place on that second day, it was evidently significant enough for Peter to mention it as the unique feature of that first world. Since we cannot reach back to evaluate such a phenomenon, we are left merely with the record itself, the obvious collapse of an enormous reservoir of water in a 40-day rain at the time of Noah and the fossil residue of that world entombed in the sedimentary rocks of our planet. Those fossils speak loudly of a different world.

Much of the fossil record was discussed in chapter 4. The obvious world-wide distribution of those once-living creatures tells us that the world's climate was far more regionally temperate than it is today. Not only are fossilized animals spread across every continent, with many of them recognizable as requiring a warm climate, but the plant remains (mostly in coal beds) contain fossil ferns, palm trees, and flora that are only able to survive in tropical or wet climates. For instance, one of the largest coal deposits on the globe is in the continent of Antarctica, indicating an abundance of plants and organic material not at all possible in today's world.

Here is the main chronology from creation through the start of the Flood.

Event	Age at Occurrence	Reference	Total Time
Creation	In the beginning	Genesis 2:1-4	7 days
Birth of Seth	Adam was 130	Genesis 5:3	130 years
Birth of Enosh	Seth was 105	Genesis 5:6	235 years
Birth of Cainan	Enosh was 90	Genesis 5:9	325 years
Birth of Mahalalel	Cainan was 70	Genesis 5:12	395 years
Birth of Jared	Mahalalel was 65	Genesis 5:15	460 years
Birth of Enoch	Jared was 162	Genesis 5:18	622 years
Birth of Methuselah	Enoch was 65	Genesis 5:21	687 years
Birth of Lamech	Methuselah was 187	Genesis 5:25	874 years
Birth of Noah	Lamech was 182	Genesis 5:28	1056 years
Birth of Shem, Ham, and Japheth	Noah was 500	Genesis 5:32	1556 years
Start of the Flood	Noah was 600	Genesis 7:11	1656 years

Figure 6.1—Total Time Chart

Something was radically different about that first age. The biblical record indicates the world was both civilized and evil. The historical records and various legends that have passed down through the millennia echo such a past age but contain very little that is verifiable from a scientific perspective. But we do have a rather detailed account of the major events of that time recorded in Genesis 4 through 8. Those chapters list the heads of two family lines—the descendants of Cain, the brother and murderer of Abel, and Seth, the son born to Adam and Eve after Abel's death.

It should be emphasized that these records are not intended to portray each of the named sons as the firstborn, but rather, that they became the noteworthy heads of the family in each generation. The Bible often gives specific instances where the firstborn is not chosen to lead the family—especially where spiritual commitment is concerned. Perhaps you remember God's sovereign choice of Jacob over Esau:

> Not only this, but when Rebecca also had conceived by one man, even by our father Isaac (for the children not yet being born, nor having done any good or evil, that the purpose of God according to election might stand, not of works but of Him who calls), it was said to her, "The older shall serve the younger." As it is written, "Jacob I have loved, but Esau I have hated" (Romans 9:10-13).

There is no linguistic reason to suggest that the ages of the various fathers should be allegorized or spiritualized in any way. The most common rebuttal is that these years are really months and that the initial records were distorted or improperly translated. If that were so, then the entire record is meaningless.

The recorded ages of these men listed in the first chapters of Genesis average 912 years. On the surface it might appear possible that those years could be understood as months, since if you divide the number of cited years by 12, then an average of 912 years would have equaled 76 years. That seems comparable with today's ages. However, if you use that approach, then the rest of the documentation would have many of the heads of the families producing children before puberty.

- Genesis 5:6—Seth at 105 would have been 9
- Genesis 5:9—Enosh at 90 would have been 7½
- Genesis 5:12—Cainan at 70 would have been not yet 6
- Genesis 5:15—Mahalalel at 65 would have been not quite 5½
- Genesis 5:18—Jared at 162 would have been not yet 14
- Genesis 5:21—Enoch at 65 would have been not quite 5½
- Genesis 5:25—Methuselah at 187 could have produced a child at 15½

All these records would seem ludicrous if we arbitrarily change the meaning of basic words that are used the same way throughout the entire Old Testament. We appear to be stuck. Either we take the record at face value, or we reject it.

The Second World

After describing the first age, Peter wrote about the second:

> The heavens and the earth which are now preserved by the same word, are reserved for fire until the day of judgment and perdition of ungodly men (2 Peter 3:7).

From God's perspective, there was one cosmos (age-world) that existed from its original creation until it was destroyed by the great Flood during the days of Noah. That world was both supernaturally created and supernaturally destroyed. Then there is "the heavens and earth which are now" (2 Peter 3:7). Then there will be yet another world, a "new heavens and a new earth" (2 Peter 3:13), that will be brought into existence at the end of our current world, which began with Noah and his three sons and their wives.

> Now the sons of Noah who went out of the ark were Shem, Ham, and Japheth. And Ham was the father of Canaan. These three were the sons of Noah, and from these the whole earth was populated (Genesis 9:18-19).

Since the Bible has given us a rather clear and tight chronology of the time of the first world, it would follow that the subsequent accounts would also establish a chain of records to help us identify and sequence the progression of family, tribe, and national entities that would bring us into sync with modern dates and calendars. And, indeed, that is just what we find, beginning with Genesis 8 and 9, recorded by Noah's sons and listing the major heads of the families well into the time of Abraham, of whom there is more than adequate information to connect the records in time.

Event	Age at Occurrence	Reference	Elapsed Time
Start of the Flood	Noah was 600	Genesis 7:11	1656 years
Duration of the Flood	370 days	Genesis 8:14	1657 years
Birth of Arphaxad	2 years after the Flood	Genesis 11:10	1659 years
Birth of Salah	Arphaxad was 35	Genesis 11:12	1694 years
Birth of Eber	Salah was 30	Genesis 11:14	1724 years
Birth of Peleg	Eber was 34	Genesis 11:16	1758 years
Birth of Reu	Peleg was 30	Genesis 11:18	1788 years
Birth of Serug	Reu was 32	Genesis 11:20	1820 years
Birth of Nahor	Serug was 30	Genesis 11:22	1850 years
Birth of Terah	Nahor was 29	Genesis 11:24	1879 years
Birth of Abram	Terah was 70	Genesis 11:26	1949 years
Abram to Canaan	Abram was 75	Genesis 12:4	2024 years

Figure 6.2—Elapsed Time Chart

All the biblical data through Abraham seems to be both consistent and tight. That is, there is no indication of any kind of gaps in the record. Yes, there are a couple of names in subsequent genealogies in other sections of the Old Testament and in the early chapters of the gospel accounts, but these names are not additions in the sense of more years but merely additional names that have been cited by the later historians as being of significance in the family lines.

Please remember that the primary purpose of the genealogies is to identify the family heads of each generation, not just to list the sequence of firstborn children. In most of the cases, it would appear that the named heads of the families were not the firstborn but were rather the sovereign selection of the Creator as He preserved the godly line from Seth through Noah to Shem to Abraham, Isaac, Jacob, Judah, and each godly heir to David, then ultimately to Jesus of Nazareth, the Messiah.

The biblical data contain a genealogy from Adam to Jesus. The opening chapter of the Gospel of Matthew and the companion view from Luke provide the clear Messianic line, citing these family heads. The basic message is this: God has been in charge since the beginning, creating, protecting, selecting, and preserving His servants through whom the ultimate Servant would come.

> "Behold! My Servant whom I uphold, My Elect One in whom My soul delights! I have put My Spirit upon Him; He will bring forth justice to the Gentiles."...Thus says God the LORD, who created the heavens and stretched them out, who spread forth the earth and that which comes from it, who gives breath to the people on it, and spirit to those who walk on it: "I, the LORD, have called You in righteousness, and will hold Your hand; I will keep You and give You as a covenant to the people, as a light to the Gentiles, to open blind eyes, to bring out prisoners from the prison, those who sit in darkness from the prison house. I am the LORD, that is My name; and My glory I will not give to another, nor My praise to carved images (Isaiah 42:1, 5-8).

It is this very passage that the Lord Jesus read when He entered a synagogue in Nazareth very early after He had begun His public ministry. After reading from the Isaiah scroll, Jesus said: "Today this Scripture is fulfilled in your hearing" (Luke 4:21). The "fullness of the time had come" (Galatians 4:4), and the long human history of 4000 years had been consummated. The seed of the woman had arrived to "bruise" the head of the serpent (Genesis 3:15).

Faithful Simeon, who had served in the Temple in Jerusalem all of his adult life and was nearing death, was privileged to see the infant Jesus when Joseph and Mary brought Him to be circumcised. As the child was presented for the official rite of all Jewish males, Simeon burst into joyful praise, referring to the same passage in Isaiah:

Lord, now You are letting Your servant depart in peace, according to Your word; for my eyes have seen Your salvation which You have prepared before the face of all peoples, a light to bring revelation to the Gentiles, and the glory of Your people Israel (Luke 2:29-32).

The record was complete. The family line had been protected and preserved. The Messiah had come, and the last days of the second world were being ushered in.

Correlation of Secular and Biblical History

Obviously, billions of years of supposed Earth history do not correlate at all with the biblical data. What are we to make of this? How, indeed, can we rebut the majority of scientists and academic experts who have amassed such a volume of information insisting that planet Earth is more than likely 4.5 billion years old? Nothing like that is even hinted at in Scripture.

The birth of the stars and planets in our universe is supposed to have happened well over 13 billion years ago in some sort of cosmic explosion, causing enormous and random forces to slowly organize into stars, galaxies, planets—and ultimately, life on this planet.

How do we deal with this discrepancy?

Historical Records on Earth

The life of Abraham is fairly well established in secular history. There are debates on the date of his birth, and there are some questions about his time in Ur of the Chaldees and the length of his stay in Haran, but all the estimates vary by only a few decades. Some of the more antibiblical scholarship would try to insert another century either before or after the biblical dates, but those years are less than 3 percent of recorded history—let alone any significant percentage of the billions of years of evolution's supposed history.

Most secular paleontologists would insist that man (*Homo sapiens*) has been around at least 100,000 years, and others suggest that early man was here nearly one million years ago. Those dates are quite divergent! Yet the debate is not over substance or empirical data or historical records. The debate is philosophical—a belief system over interpreted information. The actual human records, records that are verifiable and trustworthy, go back only a few thousand years. And the further back they go, the less trustworthy and verifiable they become.

Most of the confirmable historical records place Abraham at or near 2000 BC. Some think his birth can be verified at 2100 BC. Others suggest that his known life would sync with a period of around 1900 BC. That's a span of 200 years, hardly anything like thousands or millions or billions. Everything else is either speculation based on the philosophical commitment of the academic or, well, the Bible.

And, of course, that is not acceptable to a secularist!

Just a quick thought: If we pick a mid-range date from secular history on the birth of Abraham (2000 BC) and add the 1949 years that the Bible records from the creation of Earth to the birth of Abraham, we arrive at something like 3950 years from creation to the birth of Christ. It is interesting to note that the Jewish calendar cites creation as taking place about 3760 years before the Common Era (what most of us would call BC).

Yes, there are some differences, but not much—and certainly not anything like many thousands of years' difference. The basic secular data compare pretty well to the religious data of the two largest monotheistic religions of the world, Christianity and Judaism. As for the third largest monotheistic religion, Islam, when we ask Islamic academics and historians about their reckoning on the creation of the world, we are not given a specific date but are assured that the Koran teaches a recent creation and does not support any kind of random evolutionary development over billions of years.

Interesting. The three monotheistic religions of the world all embrace a supernatural creation by an omnipotent and omniscient Creator not very long ago. However, I would hasten to add that all three religions now resist and sometimes openly reject their historical position on a recent creation, with the academics and clerics of these religions now embracing some form of hybrid compromise that would allow for deep time and evolutionary development during those ages.

Most of the other major religions of the world teach some form of a creation story as well as a flood story. Some of them do not attempt to date those events, but those that do all give dates in the low thousands of years. The exceptions would be the Egyptian, Assyrian, and Babylonian mythologies, along with our Western cultures of Greek and Roman mythologies that sprang from those same sources.

Dating Processes

Human science is based on at least two fundamental assumptions: first, that the universe is ordered, and second, that the order is comprehensible to the mind. Biblical data confirm those assumptions in that God's revelation is verified by observation (i.e., what is revealed in Scripture is easily observed in nature). Everywhere we look, whether in our telescopes or our microscopes, the ingenuity and elegance of design is "clearly seen," as the apostle Paul so eloquently noted in Romans 1:20.

But in spite of the obvious, in spite of the correlation of historical records with the biblical record, the vast majority of the academic world insists on enormous amounts of unfathomable time over the course of which evolution happened.

Why is time such an issue? Permit me to suggest several reasons.

Incomprehensible ages make evolution seem possible. In billions of years, seemingly anything can happen. That kind of time cannot be tested but allows the construction of a story and a mathematical model that appear credible. But if the earth is young, then the whole idea of evolution is impossible! The Bible clearly teaches a much younger earth, created supernaturally by an omnipotent, omniscient, and transcendent Being.

> In six days the LORD made the heavens and the earth, the sea, and
> all that is in them, and rested the seventh day. Therefore the LORD
> blessed the Sabbath day and hallowed it (Exodus 20:11).

If one destroys the Bible's credibility, then it is easy to deny the Bible's Creator.

This conflict is not new. The arguments from earlier mythology, although pantheistic and polytheistic, were all immersed in the idea of eternal matter in some form or other. As our intellectual world began to replace pagan myths about the forces of nature with science, "deep time" was the baby that was kept as the bathwater of mythology was thrown out.

> Given so much time, the "impossible" becomes possible, the possible probable, and the probable virtually certain.[1]

> The secrets of evolution are death and time—the deaths of enormous numbers of lifeforms that were imperfectly adapted to the environment; and time for a long succession of small mutations that were by accident adaptive, time for the slow accumulation of patterns of favorable mutations.[2]

Where Is the Evidence for Time?

The evidence for deep time is not in the sedimentary rocks spread all over the planet. Enormous layers of water-deposited rock show unconformities, usually seen as a line that shows where another layer was deposited. Those unconformities mark where time has passed but not how *much* time. Radiometric dating is not possible in sedimentary rock because the material is so mixed that a sample of the necessary material cannot be obtained. What is done, however, is to locate a nearby sill or dyke of some igneous rock (a heat-related formation) and gain a sample from that for laboratory analysis.

Most of the unconformities or nonconformities show absolutely no evidence of time elapsing between the deposits. There is little or no erosion, no evidence of movement (except in very obvious thrusts and faults), and several places have massive layers that are bent and folded like taffy on a scale that stuns our minds. Energy companies worldwide have drilled and cored just about everywhere looking for oil, gas, or coal, and their recordings have identified continent-wide slurries and mudflows that left deposits of the same material covering most of North America, Europe, and Africa like a huge pancake.

Figure 6.3—Bent Strata/Split Mountain

The amount of time that passed between the creation of these layers is theorized, not evidenced.

The evidence is not in the fossils contained in sedimentary rocks. Much of this was discussed in chapter 4. Essentially, the standard interpretation of the fossil data is that there is a generalized order from simple life forms to more complex life forms observed in the sedimentary strata of Earth. The lower or deeper the fossils are buried, the older and simpler those fossils are assumed to be.

Actually, all of the phyla are represented in the lowest layer, the Cambrian deposits—often called the Cambrian Explosion. Each of those creatures, along with plants, is found up and down the so-called geologic column, with the dominant fossils throughout being marine invertebrates. As was mentioned earlier, around 95 percent of the fossil record is composed of marine invertebrates (clams, coral, trilobites, sponges, and jellyfish). Most of the rest are plants (largely in coal deposits), insects, and fish. Less than 1 percent of the entire fossil deposits are larger vertebrates like dinosaurs.

The evidence is not in present-day life forms either. Any natural selection is conservative, not innovative. Whatever is involved with environmental adaptation among living things comes from within the design of the creatures themselves—not from the external activity of nature. Even the most ardent Darwinist is beginning to understand that nature is not a being and it does not select anything. Creatures do adapt, sometimes rapidly, sometimes over several generations. But the ability to change shape or color or structure requires *informational* changes. That, of course, is within the DNA, and nature can only exclude; it cannot and does not add information.

Living mechanisms are short processes that deteriorate rapidly. Ecosystems are fragile. Extinction is an alarming phenomenon. There is absolutely no evidence for any kind of *macro* (upward) evolution. Humans may indeed select and breed animals for desired traits, but no amount of selection can breed a cat out of a dog or a tulip out of a rose. It just does not happen!

Here is a quick look at a few worldwide processes and their ages.[3]

Measured Process	Estimated Age
Accumulation of calcareous ooze on the sea floor	~5,000,000 years
Decay of Earth's magnetic field	~10,000 years
Decay of natural plutonium	~80,000,000 years
Deceleration of Earth by tidal friction	~500,000,000 years
Efflux of helium-4 into the atmosphere	~1750 to 175,000 years
Erosion of sediment from the continents	~14,000,000 years
Influx of calcium to the oceans via rivers	~1,000,000 years
Influx of chlorine to the oceans via rivers	~164,000,000 years
Influx of copper to the oceans via rivers	~50,000 years
Influx of juvenile water to oceans	~340,000,000 years
Influx of lithium to the oceans via rivers	~20,000,000 years
Influx of magma from the mantle to form Earth's crust	~500,000,000 years
Influx of magnesium to the oceans via rivers	~45,000,000 years
Influx of potassium to the oceans via rivers	~11,000,000 years
Influx of radiocarbon to the earth system	~10,000 years
Influx of sediment to the ocean via rivers	~30,000,000 years
Influx of silicon to the oceans via rivers	~8000 years
Influx of zinc to the oceans via rivers	~180,000 years
Leaching of calcium from the continents	~12,000,000 years
Leaching of chlorine from the continents	~1,000,000 years

Figure 6.4—Measured Process

The evidence for deep time is not found in worldwide phenomena. There are many processes that occur on a global basis. Measurements have been made often and precisely of most of these processes for many decades, some for well over a century. Applying even the most linear extrapolations and the full evolutionary assumptions to these processes often gives ages in the millions of years—but those millions are too short for any evolutionary model to use.

These are but a sampling of processes that occur all across our planet on a daily basis. These calculations have been made using the standard formulas still in common use today by scientists at laboratories and academic institutions all over the world. As can easily be seen, the results vary widely. And even though these processes are indicative of the age of Earth, they are seldom acknowledged in the textbooks—because the yield is far too young for any evolution to take place.

Radioisotope Dating

The evolutionary requirement of deep time cannot be supported by evidence in the sedimentary rock layers, evidence from the fossils contained in those layers, evidence from existing life forms, or even evidence from the measurement of worldwide processes. The question then arises: Where does the scientific and academic confidence come from that undergirds the majority view? How can these significant claims about billions of years be perpetuated, given the scarcity of empirical evidence?

Their confidence comes from two main sources: mathematical models and extrapolations that are based on radioisotope decay rate measurements. Even though both sources are hypothetical and based on assumptions that have long been critiqued by the very scientists who use the models, radioisotope dating is now considered a hard science. That is, the models and processes have been in place and have been accepted long enough (about 100 years) that the published results are taken for granted as accurate and proven.

Here are the main assumptions behind the mathematical models.

A Closed System

All the models start with the assumption of a closed system. Essentially, this requirement assumes that every decay process is protected from any outside influence and that internal forces have not caused leakage of the decaying or already decayed material from or into the rock sample. This assumption forbids any change in the process. For instance, one of the more well-known processes is the decay of uranium-238 into lead-206. Uranium-238 is water-soluble and groundwater is a constant source of dissolution of that uranium. Furthermore, amounts and temperatures of ancient groundwater cannot be known. The closed-system assumption ignores the possibility that any uranium might have been dissolved by natural groundwater. Ironically, radiodating experts call on ancient, unknown episodes of groundwater transportation to explain mismatching age assignments for the same rock sample.

Stable Decay Rates

All the models demand stable decay rates for all of the different processes. While the measurement techniques and equipment used today are quite good at counting accurate amounts of decaying or decayed atoms, in order for the calculations to be useful it is assumed that these rates do not ever change. Remember, we are supposedly dealing with billions of years. This assumption enormously stretches credibility! To suggest that absolutely nothing varies within the closed system for thousands of millions of years is requiring an awful lot of faith in random processes, to say the least. It is known, of course, that decay rates can and do change—especially under anything like catastrophic conditions (heat, solar flares, floods, explosions, etc.).

Known Initial Conditions

As igneous rocks are formed, atomic elements are trapped in crystalline structures. Some of these elements are unstable (radioactive) and begin to change from one product (the parent) to another (the daughter). All the age-dating models require that one assume the initial conditions (the amount of parent and daughter elements) are specified at "time zero." Picture an hourglass or an egg timer that uses the movement of sand from the top of the container to the bottom. As sand passes through the neck, an accurate count is made of the grains. If one knows the total number of grains and the rate (speed) at which the grains pass through the neck, then it is entirely possible to "clock" and predict the process for the sand to move from one position to the other. But herein lies the problem. No human being (or measuring device) was present at the formation of the particular source material being tested by the dating model, so the initial conditions cannot be known.

Radioisotope Modeling

As our technical instrumentation has improved, more and more precise measurement has become possible. Some processes, even though worldwide in scope, have proven to generate ages (rates of formation or development) that are deemed too young for evolutionary theory to be plausible. After all, the ages of the various layers of the geologic column have been published in scientific literature since the postulations of Charles Lyell, the British lawyer and geologist who authored *Principles of Geology* in 1830.

With the discovery of radioactive materials in the late 1800s, scientists began efforts to analyze the processes. By the second decade of the 1900s, many of the more famous of those processes were publicized and applied to the evolutionary timescales postulated by Lyell. Early on, however, it was discovered that the ages obtained by the laboratory analysis varied widely, bringing about a peer-review rejection of discordant results and the publication of those ages that fit the already-assumed age of the particular strata or the fossils within the strata.

That problem still exists today—with the added burden of the increasing accuracy and precision of the equipment that is used to date the process. Simply put, the more accurate the equipment, the more challenging it became to weed out the wrong dates and agree upon the right date because the rock under scrutiny ought to produce the same age no matter what radioisotope ratio was being analyzed. The "clock" ought to "tick" at the same rate for the same rock—no matter what kind of clock is being watched! This is one reason why radioisotope-based age assignments are constantly amended.

Different Radioisotope Ages

The four major radioisotope dating methods used on rocks are:

- potassium-40 (parent) >argon-40 (daughter)
- rubidium-87 (parent) >strontium-87 (daughter)
- uranium-235/238 (parents) >lead-207/206 (daughters)
- samarium-147 (parent) >neodymium-143 (daughter)

Geologists normally use only one or two of these radioisotope methods on the same rock samples because they assume all methods would ideally yield the same age for the same rock. In a study that concluded in 2005, the Institute for Creation Research tested all four methods on samples of known rock formations in the Grand Canyon. This ICR team also used the superior isochron technique, which involves analyzing five or more samples and/or minerals in a sample.

Here is the summary information of those studies.[4]

Bass Rapids diabase sill, Grand Canyon

potassium-argon isochron age of 841.5 million years
lead-lead isochron age of 1250 million years
samarium-neodymium isochron age of 1379 million years

Cardenas Basalt lavas, Grand Canyon

potassium-argon isochron age of 516 million years
rubidium-strontium isochron age of 1111 million years
samarium-neodymium isochron age of 1588 million years

Brahma amphibolites (metamorphosed basalts), Grand Canyon

rubidium-strontium isochron age of 1240 million years
lead-lead isochron age of 1883 million years
samarium-neodymium isochron age of 1655 million years

Elves Chasm Granodiorite, Grand Canyon

rubidium-strontium isochron age of 1512 million years
lead-lead isochron age of 1933 million years
samarium-neodymium isochron age of 1664 million years

Figure 6.5—Grand Canyon Layers

These test data were sent to one of the most prestigious laboratories in the country under conditions that met or exceeded the most rigorous standards required by the top universities in the world. There could be no question of sample contamination, information "interpretation," or miscommunication. Each of these rock samples was captured using pristine conditions from areas that have been proven to be a unique (once only) geologic event: the formation of a sill; the volcanic eruption of lavas; the metamorphism of lavas; and the crystallization of granite.

If these radioisotope "clocks" were accurate, always "ticking" at the same rates as measured today, each clock should have given the same age for each rock unit. However, even when all four major radioisotope clocks were used to date the same samples from the same rock unit, they invariably yield different ages.

Radioisotope measurements are very accurate, but the dates disagree. Something thus must be very wrong with the assumptions used to convert amounts into "ages"!

Carbon-14

While most of us are not very familiar with the terminology of long-age radioisotope processes, almost everyone has heard about carbon-14 (C-14). Often that information is not sufficient to understand how important the actual process is to the dating of the age of Earth. Perhaps a short discussion of carbon dating would be helpful.

Carbon-14 (a "heavy" form of carbon-12) is formed in the atmosphere when cosmic rays (mainly high-energy protons) trigger a process that changes nitrogen into C-14, which is unstable and eventually decays back into nitrogen. That heavy form of carbon "sinks" down onto Earth and is captured through the photosynthesis process of plants. Animals eat plants, and we eat the plants and the animals, absorbing some of that C-14 into our molecules. As long as the plant or the animal is alive, the balance between the normal (and stable) carbon-12 and the radioactive (and unstable) C-14 stays the same.

However, C-14 is unstable (radioactive), and the atom decays and changes back into nitrogen. That decay rate can be measured. Normally, the rate is expressed in terms of a half-life, the amount of time required to change half of the C-14 back into nitrogen. Simply stated, after one half-life, 50 percent of the original C-14 atoms will remain in the sample. After two half-lives, 25 percent will be left, and so on. It takes 5730 years for one half-life to occur. Thus, after 11,460 years (two half-lives), only 25 percent of the original sample would remain, and after 17,190 years (three half-lives) only 12.5 percent of the initial C-14 would be left. Because of this relatively rapid decay process, the amount of C-14 left after 18 half-lives (103,140 years) would measure as zero.

Elapsed Radiocarbon Half-lives	% Modern ^{14}C/C Ratio (pMC)	Calculated Years Before Present (YBP)
0	00.000000000	0
1	50.000000000	5730
2	25.000000000	11,460
3	12.500000000	17,190
4	6.250000000	22,920
5	3.125000000	28,650
6	1.562500000	34,380
7	0.781250000	40,110
8	0.390625000	45,840
9	0.195312500	51,570
10	0.097656250	57,300
11	0.048828125	63,030
12	0.024414063	68,760
13	0.012207031	74,490
14	0.006103516	80,220
15	0.003051758	85,950
16	0.001525879	91,680
17	0.000762939	97,410
18	0.000381470	103,140

After 18 radiocarbon half-lives, the ^{14}C/C ratio has definitely dropped below the AMS detection threshold of 0.001 pMC, as can easily be verified with a pocket calculator.

Figure 6.6—C-14 Rates

Since carbon atoms are such a vital part of biological material, this C-14 ratio is a very clear method to determine the age of a biological sample once it has ceased functioning. In other words, when a creature dies, the C-14 in its remains progressively transforms back to nitrogen via radioactive decay. Simply put, the fraction of the original C-14 remaining in a fossil (assumed to have been the same as today's C-14 levels) can help give us the age of that creature.

But here's the problem: The vast majority of fossils are supposed to be hundreds of thousands or millions of years old—and C-14 decays so rapidly that there should be no detectable trace of it in anything older than 103,140 years. Finding C-14 in fossil material supposedly one million or 10 million or 100 million or 300 million years old is unthinkable!

Astonishing Discovery

However, C-14 is present in most fossil organic material that has been tested.

Over the past 20 years, technical experts have developed a highly accurate system called the accelerator mass spectrometer (AMS) method. This AMS method is widely used and has documented significant and repeatable levels of C-14 in organic samples from every portion of the fossil record. These recorded findings have not been secret at all, but they have been ignored or relegated to tiny-print footnotes because they do not fit the evolutionary story. Yet the standard scientific peer-reviewed radiocarbon literature has indeed exposed that these fossil samples are not millions of years old, but only thousands.

ICR Analysis of Coal and Fossil Samples

ICR's scientific team selected ten samples from the US Department of Energy Coal Sample Bank maintained at Penn State University.[5] The team wanted to obtain a good representation of the location and the depth of coal deposits in the geologic record. The ten samples included three from Eocene strata (dated at approximately 30 to 50 million years old), three from the Cretaceous Era (supposedly 65 to 145 million years old), and four samples from Pennsylvanian coal layers (identified by standard evolutionary age suppositions as between 290 and 325 million years old).

Again, because of the rapid decay (the half-life) of C-14, there should be absolutely no measurable C-14 remaining in any organic material older than about 100,000 years. Each of these ten samples was sent off to one of the top AMS laboratories in the world, and measurements were performed using the AMS equipment and methods to ensure precision.

ICR asked the laboratory to do four tests on each sample. Every one of these ten samples displayed significant levels of C-14.

These coal samples spanned a large portion of the fossil record (from 30 million to 300 million years in evolutionary age). Statistically, there was no difference in the C-14 levels from the youngest to the oldest samples. This suggests the plants comprising these separate coal deposits all grew on Earth at the same time and were buried at the same time.

The same could be said of a variety of fossil bones and wood, all of which showed easily measurable amounts of radiocarbon. Even though some of these fossils were assigned ages of over 100 million years, they had radiocarbon in them as though they were only thousands of years old.[6]

Well, So What?

This chapter has presented a lot of relatively complex and technical data. What does all of it mean? Simply this: The supposed age of our planet is based on a scientifically shaky process that is full of unprovable assumptions.

The vast layers of water-deposited sediments and mud do not show evidence of long spans of elapsed time but, to the contrary, appear to be laid right on top of one another just like a stack of enormous pancakes. Entombed in those huge layers are billions of fossils that do not show any empirical evidence of evolutionary transition at all. In vivid contrast, these fossil remains appear fully formed, highly complex, and in many cases are ancient relatives of the same creatures alive today.

Indeed, the plants and animals that exist today show absolutely no possibility of evolving from one kind of animal or plant into another. It is easy to observe the complexity and adaptability of the biological flora and fauna around us. But nowhere do we see evidence of change from a catfish to a cat or a turnip to a tulip.

Our Earth is dynamic. Worldwide processes abound, and those processes have been analyzed and measured often and long. Many of those processes give ages far too young for any evolutionary scheme to happen. Most are ignored. A few—a scarce few discovered in the last 100 years or so—have radioisotope decay processes that yield "long" ages to those who search for them. But the radioactive carbon molecules that are embedded in all organic material (plants, animals, and humans), plus many other processes, demonstrate a very recent origin.

Essentially, all the observable, testable, and repeatable information available to any and all of us is shouting that Earth is not billions of years old but only thousands—just like the Bible says!

CHAPTER 7

Dinosaurs

Figure 7.1—T. rex

Dinosaurs fascinate people of all ages. Ever since British paleontologist and anatomist Sir Richard Owen coined the word *Dinosauria* in an address to the British Association for the Advancement of Science in 1841, the idea of fierce creatures dominating the world of the past has captivated the scientific community. Sir Owen did not agree with Darwin's idea of evolutionary development and fought rather public battles with the thinkers of the day about his "fearfully great lizards." He teamed up with Benjamin Waterhouse Hawkins, a well-known sculptor, to build a huge model of an *Iguanodon*—and held a dinner for prominent scientists *inside* the model to promote his ideas!

It's the big ones that grab our attention. Although there are between 300 to 500 different kinds of dinosaurs (depending on who is doing the sorting) and some 700 to more than 1000 species (again, depending on who is telling the story), most of us remember only the *T. rex* or the *Triceratops* or maybe the *Stegosaurus*. Perhaps, if you are a movie buff, you are convinced that the only monster worth knowing is Godzilla! Well, maybe you can remember the group of little *Compsognathus* that ate the bad guy in the movie *Jurassic Park*.

All kidding aside, dinosaurs *are* fascinating. Part of that fascination is related to the fact that they are extinct and we don't find any specimens in our local zoo. What we do have, of course, are their bones and teeth, some imprints of their feet, a few places where their eggs have been fossilized, and scientists have even found a mummy. Yes, a mummified fossilized skeleton of a duck-billed dinosaur was found in Montana in the year 2000 and was named Leonardo.[1] He was a teenager (in dinosaur years) when he died, and the skeleton was covered in soft tissue impressions showing scales, muscle forms, foot pads, and even remnants of the last meal still in his stomach.

Remarkable!

What Do We Know?

Putting stories and movies aside, what does science really know about dinosaurs? What can we verify (observe, test, repeat) about these extinct creatures? Actually, not too much. The biggest problem is that dinosaurs are extinct. That means we are unable to observe their behavior and must infer (make a sophisticated guess) about their relationships. Many of the species that have been named by various scientists are quite probably the same kind of dinosaur but just in a different stage of development. Some have been named twice.

Initially, dinosaurs were divided into two types based on their hip styles. British paleontologist Harry Seeley, who lived in the late 1800s, named dinosaurs with hip structures resembling those of birds "Ornithischia," and those with hips similar to lizards "Saurischia." As more fossils were uncovered and analyzed, it became clear that even though the pelvic bones of the lizard-hipped dinosaurs resembled those of lizards, the hip sockets still enabled them to walk upright. Within those two major classes (bird-hipped and lizard-hipped), most creation biologists identify 5 suborders, 13 infraorders, and some 60 families of dinosaurs. Each of the 60 families would approximate a created biblical kind of dinosaur.

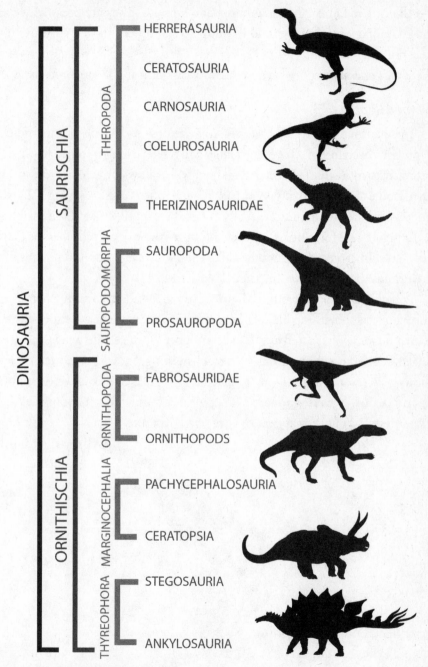

Figure 7.2—Dino Suborders

All of these kinds of dinosaurs are land animals. They are the ones we are most familiar with, but we tend to lump several other unusual creatures that were not really dinosaurs—like extinct marine reptiles and flying reptiles—into the same general category because their fossils occur in the same rock layers.

Winged Reptiles

These animals are usually referred to as pterosaurs. Fossils of their descendants have been found all over the planet and range in length from a few inches (bat-size) to more than 40 feet. All of them had hollow bones like birds, streamlined bodies built for flying, and had large, strong wings. A few of the fossil impressions are said to indicate that some of these reptiles had fur on their bodies (a bit strange for reptiles). Others interpret these fossilized fibers as partly decayed skin. Some flying reptiles, like the *Pteranodon*, had pointy crests on their heads that may have functioned like a rudder.

This unusual group of animals had leathery membranes covering their wings. The wing was something like a strange hand with long fingers—especially the fourth finger, which acted as the main support for the entire wing. The other fingers sported claws at various points on the wing, and all connected back to the legs. Pterosaurs were different indeed than regular birds and were definitely not dinosaurs. Because they are extinct we don't know much about their habits or lifestyles, but they appear to have flown just fine.

Figure 7.3—Pterosaur

The North American Indians appear to have known these creatures. Stories have been told and drawings have been found depicting creatures very similar to the fossils we know about. Those stories and pictures assign different names to the events in which they interfaced with the Indians, but one of the more familiar legends is that of the thunderbird. The descriptions all speak of a large birdlike animal that made a sound like that of thunder when its wings flapped, with supernatural light (or fire) coming from its eyes or body. Some of the stories state that the animal was multicolored, with horns and teeth in its beak.

Indonesian island natives tell of a cliff-dwelling flying reptile that they call a *ropen*. The legendary dragon that killed Beowulf on a cliffside had two names: ligdraga, meaning "light dragon," and wydfloga, meaning "wide (long-range) flyer." The fifth-century accounts speak of an animal that bears similarities to a pterosaur of some kind in the area that is now known as Denmark. Even the Bible contains references to a "fiery flying serpent" recorded by the prophet Isaiah in the eighth century BC (Isaiah 14:29 and 30:6). While stories tend to grow more fanciful over time, the pictographs and totems tend to keep the main elements intact. What has survived across time and culture is the insistence that creatures like the *Pteranodon* and pterosaurs really did exist—and not so very long ago.

Marine Reptiles

The first appearance of a word that translates to "dragon" is found in the Bible in Genesis 1:21. There we read about God creating the great *tanniym*—"dragon" or "sea monster." Unfortunately, in English, it is often translated "whale." Apparently the first "sea monster" was brought into existence at the same time as other ocean creatures, and modern paleontologists do find several monsters entombed in the sedimentary deposits of Earth.

In 1821, an early specimen of the plesiosaur was found. It had a broad, flat body, a short tail, and a long neck. Its four long and prominent flippers were attached to bony plates at the shoulder and pelvis. Since that initial find, hundreds of additional plesiosaurs have been found that have given more insight into their basic place in the oceans of the world. They were air-breathing (like whales and dolphins), bore their young alive, and appear to have been warm-blooded. Some plesiosaur were smaller, around 14 feet in length, while others grew as long as 45 feet.

The well-known story of the Loch Ness Monster has tenaciously hung on for many, many decades. The true believers among those who still search for this monster think it is some sort of plesiosaur. And in 1977, off the coast of New Zealand, a Japanese fishing boat dredged up a horribly decomposed body that looked suspiciously like that of a plesiosaur. Japan even issued a stamp commemorating the event, although subsequent evaluation of the pictured evidence may favor it having been the remains of a basking shark.

Figure 7.4—Japanese Plesiosaur Stamp

As far as we know, none of them have survived into modern times, so we are unable to study their habits and lifestyles carefully.

The pliosaurs were somewhat similar to plesiosaurs but were more sturdy and with a more pronounced head and mouth. These were not fish or dinosaurs but marine reptiles. One of the larger fossil finds of a pliosaur was named *Kronosaurus*, which had an overall body length of around 30 feet. The head was quite large, placed on a short neck, and attached to a chunky body with the four flippers common to the plesiosaurs. And the mouth was full of sharp, conical teeth.

Ichthyosaurs were fish- or dolphin-shaped reptiles. Fossil remains of these animals vary from a rather small 3 feet to more than 50 feet long. One fossil was found in which the ichthyosaur was actually giving birth to its young when it was suddenly buried by a fast mudflow. That obviously tells us that ichthyosaurs bore their young alive rather than laying eggs.

Figure 7.5—Kronosaurus

Like the pliosaur, these animals were stocky rather than slim, had flippers like the plesiosaur, and pointed noses and mouths full of small, sharp teeth. The ichthyosaur had large, round eyes mounted high on its head, a stiff neck, and a trunk that ended in a larger tail fin. Even though these animals lived in the ocean, they had nostril holes in their skulls, indicating they were air-breathing like the plesiosaur, pliosaur, and many of the marine mammals we are familiar with today.

Figure 7.6—Ichthyosaur Giving Birth

An even more common monster of the ocean was the mosasaur. They are found in just about every area of the world and seem to be well-known by all fossil hunters. They were much like their more rare cousins the pliosaur and ichthyosaur in that they were air-breathing, bore their young alive, and appear to have been an "eating machine." On display at ICR is the skull of a mosasaur that was unearthed in Morocco. It is a little over four feet from the tip of its snout to the back of its head, and nearly 20 inches wide at the bridge of the skull. The attached vertebrae are of such a size that the paleontologist who studied the fossil suggested the animal might have been about 40 feet long. One mosasaur fossil housed in the Canadian Fossil Discovery Centre in Morden, Manitoba, is 13 meters long (about 43 feet).

The mosasaur mouth has two sets of wicked-looking teeth. One row is on both the upper and lower jaws, and another set rests near the throat. Whoever happened to get near those jaws was in for a very painful bite! This animal really looks the way most of us picture a dragon. And as with many of the other marine reptiles, their remains indicate they were air-breathing. That would mean that while they were good swimmers well-adapted to an ocean environment, they needed to surface regularly, which made then readily observable by the ancient seafarers who wrote about them.

Figure 7.7—Mosasaur Skull and Mosasaur Drawing

Basic Dinosaur Facts

With the popularity of dinosaur legends, museum dioramas, and TV specials documenting the imagination of storytellers, as well as modern movies clouding much of our understanding, it may be worth a few moments to review the basic facts we know about dinosaurs.

Modern large land reptiles like the monitor lizard and the crocodile have low-slung bodies with legs that stick out and down. By contrast, the land dinosaurs, both the bird-hipped and the lizard-hipped kinds, had legs that were like pillars that went straight down from their bodies to support their weight and gave them the ability to walk and run rather than waddle. Of the some 60 families of dinosaurs, many were smaller, with a median size approaching that of an adult bison. The few that were larger were really big!

The marine reptiles that we often call marine dinosaurs were all somewhat similar. Their bodies were shaped for life in the water but varied in size and length from a few feet to some that approached 50 feet. All of them appear to have borne their young alive rather than by depositing eggs like many fish, turtles, and other marine creatures do. Though these fearsome creatures are extinct, we have found many of their fossilized remains all over the world, which has helped give us a fairly good idea of their structure and habitats. Unfortunately, because none of these animals survived into the modern era, we do not have the opportunity to study their behavior.

Flying reptiles are not dinosaurs—nor are they birds. Because they lived most of their life as airborne creatures, they do not have the features of a land-based animal. Like birds, when they were on the ground, they either hopped or flapped from place to place. Their grace and majesty were displayed in the air. But unlike birds, they did not have feathers. Their wings were leathery membranes supported by elongated, hollow finger bones unique to their own kind, the pterosaurs. Like the dinosaurs and the marine reptiles, these extinct creatures appear in the fossil record fully formed, with no evidence whatsoever that they descended from anything else.

Apparently they were all created at the same time, just as they appear in the record.

Biblical Information

As was mentioned earlier, the Bible introduces the Hebrew word *tanniyn* in Genesis 1:21, where we are informed that "God created great sea creatures and every living thing that moves, with which the waters abounded, according to their kind, and every winged bird according to its kind. And God saw that it was good." This was on the fifth day of the creation week, and the narrative tells us the Creator concentrated on the air and water animals that day. The *tanniyn* were, obviously, one of the water creatures.

That word appears 28 times in the Hebrew section of the Bible. It is translated in the King James Version as "dragon" 21 times, "serpent" three times, "whale" once, and "sea monster" three times. The more recent Bible versions do not use "whale" but most frequently use "sea monster" or "dragon," depending on whether the context is speaking of a water animal or a land animal. Whatever was meant by the early writers, the overwhelming sense of the context where the word appears suggests that the animal in view was big and awesome—perhaps even dangerous.

The Book of Job

You may be familiar with the epic poem that constitutes the biblical book of Job. The book tells the story of a righteous man who was caught in an awful contest between the devil and the Creator. God pointed out Job's righteous behavior to Satan as an example of how God intended for man to live. Satan responded that Job was righteous only because God had blessed him. If God would just let Satan have him for a time, God would see how quickly Job would turn against Him.

God allowed Satan to do his worst to Job (except for physically killing him), and tragedy after tragedy befell Job in a matter of hours so that all his children were killed and his agricultural wealth stolen or destroyed. Job staggered under all this calamity, as any of us would, but he remained true to his faith in God. Then Satan asked permission to destroy Job's health—and Job became covered in painful, seeping sores that must have been horrible to see and smell. Even Job's wife suggested that he should "curse God and die!" (Job 2:9).

Job did not, of course, but he was stunned by the awful situation in which he found himself. When some friends arrived, it took them several days to get over their horror at what they saw. Then they began a long series of diatribes, essentially telling Job that there must be some secret sin in his life that had caused God to punish him so severely. Finally, after 34 chapters of logical heresy from his friends (even if well-meaning), God Himself intervened and spoke in a conversation with Job.

He didn't offer one word about why Job was suffering. Not one word was stated about what had happened in the heavenly courts between God and Satan. Nor did He give a personal rebuke to any of the four "friends" who had been darkening "counsel by words without knowledge" (Job 38:2). Rather, God proceeded to deliver 77 rhetorical questions about creation! Job didn't respond until the end. There was no need to. Every question pointed to the fact that no one could do or did do or does do what God does.

After confronting Job with the wonders of the planet, the universe, and even the configuration of the stars, God called Job's attention to the animal creation and His care for them. Everyday details and observations that Job and his friends would be familiar with were laid out from the perspective of the Creator Himself, with every question pounding home the fact that each and every one of these events—from the rising of the sun and the movement of the stars to the feeding of the wild goats and the foolishness of the wild desert ostrich—was under the minute care and provision of the Creator.

Then, as Job acquiesced to the overwhelming evidence of God's omniscience and power, God mentioned two great creatures that He had "made along with [Job]" (Job 40:15). The first animal was the behemoth. The second was leviathan.

Behemoth

Look now at the behemoth, which I made along with you; he eats grass like an ox. See now, his strength is in his hips, and his power is in his stomach muscles. He moves his tail like a cedar; the sinews of his thighs are tightly knit. His bones are like beams of bronze, his ribs like bars of iron. He is the first of the ways of God; only He who made him can bring near His sword. Surely the mountains yield food for him, and all the beasts of the field play there. He lies under the lotus trees, in a covert of reeds and marsh. The lotus trees cover him with their shade; the willows by the brook surround him. Indeed the river may rage, yet he is not disturbed; he is confident, though the Jordan gushes into his mouth, though he takes it in his eyes, or one pierces his nose with a snare (Job 40:15-24).

Figure 7.8—Sauropod

Whatever this animal was, it was not small! The Hebrew word in this passage has merely been transliterated rather than translated. That is, an English-letter equivalent has been supplied for the Hebrew characters—תומהב (bᵉhemowth) is its name. Several lexicons have attempted to render the term, but because this particular form appears only in this specific passage in the book of Job, the translations and applications run the gamut from "cattle" to "hippopotamus." Some Bibles supply a note that suggests the writer of the book really meant an elephant, or fall back on the German liberal school's thought that the Hebrew word is derived from the Egyptian term for hippopotamus.

But the description given by God Himself does not depict an existing animal that you and I would be familiar with. Let's review the description:

- "Behemoth" was a land animal whose normal habitat was wetlands.

- The creature was a vegetarian, with grazing habits similar to those of an ox.

- This animal was very large, with strong hips and power in the stomach muscles.

- When the tail moved, it did so like a cedar tree.

- The bones were like "beams of bronze," and the ribs were like "bars of iron."

- Behemoth was so large and so placid a beast that a raging river or an attempt to pierce its nose did not rile it.

- God named behemoth the "first of the ways of God."

None of our modern-day animals fit this description. It cannot be an elephant or a hippopotamus, for they do not have a treelike tail. It is not likely to be some form of aggressive animal, since the description emphasizes its gentle, grazing, ox-like character. That this beast was described as the "chief" (first) of the ways of God suggests an animal that would express something of the immensity of God. This also indicates it was an animal Job and his friends would have been familiar with, for it was "made along with" humans on Day Six.

Several of the sauropod dinosaurs could fit the description of behemoth in Job. The *Apatosaurus* is a good bet. Those animals had a long neck and a long tail, with four pillar-like legs that held up an estimated 50 tons (more than 100,000 pounds). Several of their fossil finds reveal animals that averaged 75 feet long and could, with their extended necks, reach heights of up to 30 feet.

These were *big* creatures! Yet there is absolutely no evidence that they were car-nivorous or that other animals preyed on them. "Chief" of the ways, indeed!

However we may choose to identify the behemoth, that big creature was one Job would have known about, for the description would have been utterly worthless if Job had never seen the animal. Our museums are full of the bones and skeletons of some sauropod dinosaurs that are big and awesome, but we have absolutely no idea what they were like in real life. For the habitat and behavior of behemoth to mean anything to Job, he would have had to have seen or heard about the creatures in his day and within his experience. God was not referring to a pile of bones that had belonged to an extinct animal!

Job was a contemporary of Abraham (around 2000 BC). That means Job lived *after* the Flood of Noah. The specific behemoth God was referencing to Job would have been a descendant of the pair of behemoths carried on the Ark. And that means, of course, that land dinosaurs (at least two of every kind) were on board the Ark. Then they disembarked, foraged, found suit-able living environments, and reproduced enough descendants for God to show one to Job.

Leviathan

Within God's discourse to Job is an entire section devoted to the leviathan. Once again, the translators have decided not to attempt to identify this animal with a more contemporary English name, but have merely transliterated the Hebrew וְתִיוֹל (livyathan) with English characters.

Whatever this creature may have been, it is certain that it was mostly a water-based animal that could crawl up on the shore to leave marks in the mire, perhaps something like the *Spinosaurus*, an animal that was larger than the *Tyrannosaurus*. It is also clear that Job knew of this fearsome creature because he spoke of this animal earlier in the book: "May those curse it who curse the day, those who are ready to arouse Leviathan" (Job 3:8). A thousand years later, Asaph, one of King David's songwriters, composed a psalm with a mention of leviathan: "You broke the heads of Leviathan in pieces, and gave him as food to the people inhabiting the wilderness" (Psalm 74:14). In one of David's many praise songs, the name leviathan appears: "There the ships sail about; there is that Leviathan which You have made to play there" (Psalm 104:26).

As late as the eighth century BC, the prophet Isaiah described leviathan as he mentioned the future judgment of Earth by the Lord: "In that day the LORD with His severe sword, great and strong, will punish Leviathan the fleeing serpent, Leviathan that twisted serpent; and He will slay the reptile that is in the sea" (Isaiah 27:1).

In those passages are references to the life, character, and even the physical appearance of this wild and untamable "monster" of the deep. It is in Job 41, however, that we gain the most insight about this large and fierce marine animal:

> Can you draw out Leviathan with a hook, or snare his tongue with a line which you lower? Can you put a reed through his nose, or pierce his jaw with a hook? Will he make many supplications to you? Will he speak softly to you? Will he make a covenant with you? Will you take him as a servant forever? Will you play with him as with a bird, or will you leash him for your maidens? Will your companions make a banquet of him? Will they apportion him among the merchants? Can you fill his skin with harpoons, or his head with fishing spears? Lay your hand on him; remember the battle—never do it again! Indeed, any hope of overcoming him is false; shall one not be overwhelmed at the sight of him? No one is so fierce that he would dare stir him up. Who then is able to stand against Me? (Job 41:1-10).

These rhetorical questions are meant to be understood as reflecting the efforts of humanity to catch or tame this beast. Job did not need to answer with words. He was a very wealthy businessman, probably in the international trade business, and he would have heard about—if not actually experienced—this great sea serpent. No doubt many had tried to catch this monster. Stories about these efforts would have been rampant. But like all stories, the reality is often more awesome (and dangerous) than the "fish stories" of those who like to brag of their own bravery.

Figure 7.9—Leviathan could be Spinosaurus or Kronosaurus.

Leviathan may be the source of some dragon stories:

> Who has preceded Me, that I should pay him? Everything under heaven is Mine. I will not conceal his limbs, his mighty power, or his graceful proportions. Who can remove his outer coat? Who can approach him with a double bridle? Who can open the doors of his face, with his terrible teeth all around? His rows of scales are his pride, shut up tightly as with a seal; one is so near another that no air can come between them; they are joined one to another, they stick together and cannot be parted. His sneezings flash forth light, and his eyes are like the eyelids of the morning. Out of his mouth go burning lights; sparks of fire shoot out. Smoke goes out of his nostrils, as from a boiling pot and burning rushes. His breath kindles coals, and a flame goes out of his mouth (Job 41:11-21).

God Himself is describing this creature! It has limbs, power, and graceful proportions. Any one of the huge extinct marine animals listed earlier in this chapter would fit this description. When you add the "terrible teeth all around" in the "doors of his face," the description may be narrowed down somewhat to the ichthyosaur or the mosasaur, or perhaps the pliosaur might fit. But when you add the scales that are so tight that they seem to be put together "as with a seal"—so tight that "no air can come between them"—that begins to look more like the large *Kronosaurus*.

It is also possible that this enormous animal could have been the *Spinosaurus*. ICR's Dr. Tim Clarey favors this semiaquatic dinosaur over the *Kronosaurus*.[2] As more research is done, the biblical information resonates more precisely to the anatomy of the fossil data. Whatever this creature may have been, God Himself used it as an example of a real animal that Job would have known— either from his own personal experience or from the accounts of merchants and sailors who plied the waters and traveled the open routes of the ancient world.

Then there are the combustible "sneezings" that flash light. None of the reptiles alive today do anything like that, and because leviathan is extinct, we have no means of studying it. There are, of course, many legends and stories from the past about fire-breathing dragons. It is interesting to note that all the past references to these dragons of the sea and land mention some sort of fire that came from the mouth or nostrils of these ancient animals. What are we to make of that?

Although we cannot access the activities of these extinct reptiles, we can and do make comparisons between anatomical features that appear to have similar purposes among animals of the same kind. And we can and do notice features of existing creatures that may have similar functions to those of extinct life forms. Sometimes the structures of one form show remarkably similar functions to the structures of another form in a completely different animal.

Such is the case with the bombardier beetle. More than 500 species of these Carabidae have a defense mechanism in their abdomen that can eject a combination of hydroquinone and hydrogen peroxide that explodes in a noxious spray that can reach 100 degrees Celsius. Twin chambers store these volatile chemicals until the beetle feels threatened. Then it "sneezes" (squeezes appropriate muscles in its abdomen), simultaneously closing the valves into the beetle's internal organs and opening the valve on its backside, allowing the now rapidly expanding gases to explode with a loud pop into the face of its predator. Some species of these beetles can swivel the spray over a span of 270 degrees, pulsating at a rate of nearly 500 pulses per second, the explosion shooting out 70 pulses of its fire each time. Hot and noxious, this is "fire in the belly" indeed!

What's the point? While we cannot observe the "sneezing" of the leviathan, we can compare the structural mechanisms of the bombardier beetle with the mechanisms that may have been present in extinct marine reptiles. It is not plausible to identify for certain what might have been, but it is certainly plausible to infer from the observable fossil data that such mechanisms could have been present given the close resemblance of the habits and known anatomical features of these Carabidae insects.

Given what we know from the fossil data and what we know from the established behavior of beetles with "exploding" mechanisms, it is not at all beyond reason to suggest that the God who created all creatures actually knew what He was talking about!

Leviathan was unconquerable by man:

> Strength dwells in his neck, and sorrow dances before him. The folds of his flesh are joined together; they are firm on him and cannot be moved. His heart is as hard as stone, even as hard as the lower millstone. When he raises himself up, the mighty are afraid; because of his crashings they are beside themselves. Though the sword reaches him, it cannot avail; nor does spear, dart, or javelin. He regards iron as straw, and bronze as rotten wood. The arrow cannot make him flee; slingstones become like stubble to him. Darts are regarded as straw; he laughs at the threat of javelins. His undersides are like sharp potsherds; he spreads pointed marks in the mire. He makes the deep boil like a pot; he makes the sea like a pot of ointment. He leaves a shining wake behind him; one would think the deep had white hair. On earth there is

nothing like him, which is made without fear. He beholds every
high thing; he is king over all the children of pride (Job 41:22-34).

Please remember, this information was passed on to us by God Himself.
He was the One describing these events, and He was the One attempting to
help Job understand how small and insignificant he was when compared to
the majestic wild creatures on the one hand and the omniscient and omnipotent Creator on the other. The behemoth and the leviathan were prime examples of the inability of mere human creatures to cope with the strength that was
inherent in their natures. Yet God had given man the responsibility to rule over
every living thing on the planet! No wonder King David said, "What is man
that You are mindful of him?" (Psalm 8:4).

Job 41 described leviathan as a creature that "laughs" at the weaponry of
humanity. Yes, today we could probably slaughter such an animal with our
more advanced weapons, but until the sophistication of modern warfare, the
"spear, dart, or javelin" were the killing tools of the day. In fact, the arrow was the
ultimate in weaponry during the millennia of the advancement of civilization
from Moses' time until the arrival of the cannon. Slingshots were the favored
weapon of armies. You may remember that young David killed the giant Goli-
ath with such a weapon.

Leviathan ignored all of that. Nothing man could do would bring this creature under control. This great marine monster was designed to bring fear into
the heart of man. And maybe, just maybe, that was why God used it as an illustration to Job. It seems behemoth was cited to convey immensity and patience
in spite of circumstance—and perhaps something of the mercy and majesty of
God. Leviathan seems to be displayed as fierce and unconquerable, especially
when attacked. Perhaps God wanted Job to get the two "bookends" of God's
attributes, the sides to God's character that would impact humanity the most—
mercy and patience as far as salvation is concerned, and implacable justice and
punishment as far as rebellion is concerned.

Just a thought.

Ask the Beasts

> Now ask the beasts, and they will teach you; and the birds of the
> air, and they will tell you; or speak to the earth, and it will teach
> you; and the fish of the sea will explain to you. Who among all
> these does not know that the hand of the LORD has done this, in
> whose hand is the life of every living thing, and the breath of all
> mankind? Does not the ear test words and the mouth taste its
> food? (Job 12:7-11).

Even Job's rather uninformed friends knew enough to learn from the creatures God had created. The beasts and the birds would tell us if we would but
listen to what they have to say. The great mystery of life shouts for a Creator.
Everything we know, everything we can observe, everything we can test and
reproduce in a laboratory tells us that living creatures (the beasts, the birds, and
the fish of the sea) teach us that "the hand of the LORD has done this."

Even the hard evidence of the fossils buried all over the planet in water-
deposited sediments and mud shouts of creation. Evolution requires transitional forms of animals. Nothing like that exists in the fossil record, let alone
in real life. All true science demands that what we observe and can evaluate by
testing—then repeat the tests and get the same answer—verify that these living beasts, birds, and fish of the sea have been brought into existence by Someone or some Cause that is both all-knowing and all-powerful.

Random processes just won't cut it.

Speak to the Earth

In the opening chapter I attempted to present some rather obvious illustrations of the design prevalent throughout the universe. Unless there has been
an educated prejudice pounded into our thinking, it is simply impossible not
to see design in everything. Every system, every process, every functional relationship, certainly every living thing screams "design"! Yet those who would
write God and creation out of the story must—*must*—ignore and explain away
any attempt to point it out.

Job and his friends would not have known much about the majesty of the stars and galaxies—though they were familiar with the star configurations referenced as "Mazzaroth" in God's instruction (Job 38:32). But these men would have been very familiar with the wildlife and environment of the post-Flood world. Much of what the Creator declared to Job was the clear evidence of design all over the earth and in the life that flourished on it. Some of this you can grow to appreciate more when you get to chapter 11.

Design begs that a Designer must have designed it!

The Ice Age

While everybody knows there was an ice age, few know much about it—except for what they've seen in the *Ice Age* movie franchise that stars a mammoth named Manny, a giant sloth named Sid, and Diego, a saber-toothed tiger. In all the movies released so far, there is also a little saber-toothed squirrel named Scrat that carries the subplot. The movies do a pretty good job of telling the evolutionary perspective—and keep viewers pleasantly engaged as well.

But when you begin to look into the academic literature about the Ice Age, it turns out there is a range of opinions about it. Some suggest that there have been lots of ice ages. And, of course, they all happened long ago over a span of time covering hundreds of thousands—perhaps even millions—of years. That age thing just doesn't go away. It's part of the naturalistic story. If the various geological records that we can identify suggest there was a time in the past when the ice caps extended beyond the Canadian border into the United States, then it is assumed to have happened a long time ago.

The Majority Opinions

Obviously, the majority is made up of a *lot* of opinions! The academic pursuit of a rationale to fit the geological evidence has gone on for more than two centuries—and has waffled from one or two ice ages to dozens. However, during the past 50 years or so, most of the literature has stated that 4 to 5 major ice ages have occurred over the "ages" of the planet's evolution.

These ice ages have been named the Huronian, the Cryogenian, the Andean-Saharan, the Karoo Ice Age, and the Quaternary glaciation. The first one supposedly took place as long as two billion years ago, followed by a melt-back, reformation, remelt, etc., up until about 100,000 years ago, when the last ice age was "officially" here. And according to many, we are still in that last ice age.

Betwixt and between the ice ages were periods of cooler and warmer climates known as glacials and interglacials. During glacials, the bulk of the planet was both cooler and drier. It is in these periods that the ice grew to a maximum reach, while the open land areas shrank and the sea levels dropped. The interglacial times were periods of an overall warmer planet. The ice receded, and the land began to become visible again, with ice replaced by tundra, tundra by forests, etc. According to many naturalists, we are now in an interglacial interval called the Holocene that has persisted since the end of the Pleistocene about 11,700 years ago.

Then there are the proponents of global warming (aka climate change), who insist that one of the awful signs of pending doom is the melting of the world's glaciers. And since we humans are considered to be responsible for this disaster, we are told we need to stop using fossil fuels, flush refrigerants out of our lavish lifestyles, and stop generating such horrible carbon footprints, whatever those are.

I'm being a little facetious, but the more one tries to make sense out of the academic literature, the more confused and mistrustful one becomes. Even within the staunchly naturalistic community there is very vocal (sometimes vitriolic) disagreement on the facts, with many different interpretations all making for a widely divergent set of solutions—most of them either politically or monetarily motivated.

The Basic Facts and Features

Most of the evidence for a prior encroachment of glacial ice in the northern and southern hemispheres is found in several geological phenomena that are best explained by glacial advances and retreats.

Glaciers are not static sheets of ice. They grow and melt. They are also very big and very heavy. Scientists have been observing glacial behavior fairly intensely since the mid-1700s and have noticed and documented several common effects produced by them.

- Glaciers act like huge bulldozers. As they advance, they dig into the earth and rock of the surface over which they are traveling and begin pushing the debris forward in an ever-growing pile.

- They drag the scooped-out debris under and around them as they move forward. There are constantly moving piles of rubble that create scars along the sides and bottoms of the paths they carve. They include underground rivers of melting ice and leave behind mounds of scrapings that turn into features geologists can recognize even after the ice has melted away.

- The enormity of the ice packs affects the nature of the climate and the kinds of plants and animals that live near, on, and around them. All of these nongeological phenomena leave traces and records that help us understand what has happened.

Here are a few of the most ordinary and observable features of glacial work.

Moraines

Figure 8.1—Glacial Moraines

When a glacier is moving, the fact the ice is so heavy makes the glacier like a large earth-moving machine that scrapes and gouges the terrain and pushes material along the front of the glacier's leading edge. All this activity leaves piles of moraines, jumbled rock and ground-up dirt and rock, along the front and sides of the glacier.

Sometimes these piles are enormous, sometimes not so much, but they all bear similar characteristics. The rocks and glacial flour (fine-grained, silt-sized particles of rock) all have the angular edges worn off by the movement of the glacier and tend to be rounded. They sometimes contain huge boulders much larger than anything else in the pile that seem to be "magically" placed in the mix.

The energies involved in a moving glacier approach a terrifying level. They do a significant amount of geological work as they grow and melt. For example, Half Dome, the famous formation in Yosemite Valley, California, was once fully round until an ancient glacier carved and transported away one-half of the solid granite dome.

Lateral Moraines

As a glacier moves, particularly if it began its life in a mountain valley, the moraines tend to form at the sides, being ground under the glacier and pushed sideways and up by the meandering of the ice, and leaving the piles of ground and broken rock in long lines of detritus. After the glacier melts back, these lateral moraines are easily seen and provide a marked trail to be studied.

Often the movement of a glacier can cause rocks and other materials to be deposited on top. The position on top of the ice tends to protect the glacier from melting in those specific areas and, at the same time, preserves the depositional nature of the lateral moraine when the glacier finally does melt away, leaving a rather pronounced high-ridge formation that is easily identified.

Ground Moraines and Till

Glaciers also produce ground moraines that manifest as lumpy hills, usually in mountain areas, that sometimes develop into gently rolling hills or high plains. More often than not, these ground moraines are found between two lateral moraines.

Much of the material in the ground moraines is called till, a mixture of unsorted sediment that has been ground out, eroded, or carried along by a moving glacier. This mixture looks like soft rock with chunks of rounded rock fragments on the surface of and mixed within the till. As the glacier plods along, it pushes and distributes the till. The result is an excellent farmland composed of soil, crushed and ground-up rock, various animal remains, and an occasional boulder for interest. Western Ohio is covered in till-rich plains left behind by a rather recent glacial period.

Glacial Striations

All of this movement by glacial ice ends up leaving marks on the solid rocks over which the glacier travels. The most obvious markings are the glacial striations (gouges, scratches, abrasions) caused by the glacier dragging bits and pieces of rock and ground debris over the surface of the earth. Some striations are quite pronounced, while others are more subtle and finely segregated. But all of them come to light only after the glacier has melted back enough to expose them.

Figure 8.2—Glacial Striations

These striations normally run in straight, parallel lines and appear in multiples. That is, they are usually made by several rock fragments embedded in the base of the glacier. These fragments become "cutting tools" on the ground surface as the glacier winds along its slow way. Along with the rock fragments, finer sediments tend to scour and polish the bedrock, forming a pavement under the glacier.

There are lots of categories for moraines. The scholars and geologists who study these phenomena find ways to identify unusual effects that can add to the knowledge of how glaciers impact our planet. Much of their work is helpful in understanding what has transpired, but the story behind the story often causes disagreement.

The Basic Science

Humans are pretty good at understanding present-day processes. The meteorologist on our favorite TV news program has gone through some pretty tough college training and has been given the tools to make fairly accurate short-term predictions about the behavior of our weather patterns—because observational science has done a good job of noting and recording the behavior of the hydrological cycle.

We have learned that when the ocean basins are warmer, evaporation increases. And when evaporation increases, the atmosphere becomes more laden with water moisture that ultimately falls back to Earth in the form of rain or snow. Intense weather phenomena like thunderstorms, tornadoes, hurricanes, etc. are unusual but are statistical variations of the same basic processes.

Glaciers are formed by heavy snowfall followed by a series of cold summers. The increase in snowfall is the result of greater evaporation caused by warmer oceans. The colder-than-normal summers allow the snowpack at the higher elevations to remain (not melt as much) so that when the next snowfall occurs, that snow is added to the remaining pack on the ground. As the snow accumulates over several years, the air in the snow below is squeezed out by the weight of the snow above, and ice is formed.

If the series of warm oceans, increased evaporation, greater snowfall, and cold summers continues for many years, a glacier can form at higher elevations and latitudes that begins to add its own "weather" to the sequence. When that occurs over a long-enough period with many glaciers, an ice age ensues.

Past Problems with Present Predictions

As mentioned earlier, scientists have a serious dilemma when it comes to understanding the past—especially a past during which there were no people around to observe and document what was happening. This is because science (the simple meaning of the word is "knowledge") is based on observation. The scientific method is a process of observing what is happening, trying to detail those processes, testing the observations under controlled conditions, and then repeating the testing often enough to be sure that what is thought to have occurred really did happen.

Here's the problem: Past events are different from current events that are observable and repeatable. They cannot be subjected to the same testing—unless you have a time machine.

So a type of science has developed called *forensic science* or *historical science*. Essentially this type of science makes careful observations of the existing or remaining data and attempts to construct a scenario of what might have happened in the past based on certain assumptions that appear to fit the observed facts.

A good example of forensic science is the process used by a police detective. After a crime has occurred, the detective carefully observes the clues left behind at the scene and then attempts to reconstruct what happened. With careful analysis and determination, the detective can sometimes determine the perpetrator of the crime and compare his observations against the actual crime. If the two fit, or at least are close enough to convince a judge and jury, the criminal is convicted and the crime is solved.

Two Basic Assumptions

Although there are variations on that theme, there are really only two basic contrasting assumptions about the undocumented distant past. One, that there is a Creator who brought everything into existence not so very long ago; and two, that there is no Creator, and everything that exists came about through natural processes over long ages.

These two assumptions are often called *worldviews* by philosophers. That is because they are foundational belief systems that form a thinking matrix that shapes the way reason is used to evaluate everything.

- The worldview with a Creator is often called *creationism* because it assumes there was a supernatural beginning to everything. Biblical creationists accept the Bible as actual history and depend on that revelation from the Creator to shape their thinking.

- The worldview without a Creator is often called *naturalism* because it assumes that everything has a natural explanation. Naturalists do not accept the Bible as history and usually depend on other naturalists to guide their explanations.

Clearly, these two assumptions are mutually exclusive. Although some people attempt to harmonize them into various hybrid theories, those hybrids break down very quickly under close scrutiny. Only one or the other is true; they cannot both be true.

Acceptance of one over the other impacts how the evidence is interpreted. That applies to everything. It applies to how we view our world. It applies to how we live. It applies to how we "do" science.

Ice Age Science

Written records, which are based on human observation, go back around 5000 years. Anything older than that is "ancient," and we have no documentation about the years prior, other than what we are told in the Bible. Yes, there are other stories about the ancient past, but most of them are wildly imaginative and tell such fanciful stories that they are considered myths or legends and are not taken as fact.

So what are we to do about the evidence left by glacial activity that occurred in Earth's history? How are we to evaluate what we know? What assumptions can we make that will assist us in determining what happened—and, for that matter, will help us understand how to use that information correctly?

- If the Bible is accurate history, then there has been only one Ice Age.
- If the planet is billions of years old, then there may have been many ice ages.
- If the Bible is true, then the cause of the Ice Age could have been catastrophic.
- If the processes over immense time have been uniform, then the causes of the many ice ages would be natural, and they would have taken ages to develop and recede.

It is those assumptions that are used to explain the moraines, till, and striations that show our planet was partially covered with ice sheets in the past.

Assumptions Behind the Assumptions

In the complex world of naturalistic explanations, the deeper one goes into the efforts to explain the evidence, the more difficult it becomes to explain the exceptions. Here are the foundational premises upon which naturalistic theories about many ice ages are built:

- The Bible is *not* true as far as ancient history is concerned.
- The planet is billions of years old.
- Uniform processes have always been in force since the universe began.

This worldview is often called *uniformitarianism*. Essentially, this assumption embraces the concept that natural processes, interacting randomly over eons with no supernatural intervention or direction, have produced everything that now exists. Whenever we observe phenomena that have occurred in the past that do not appear to be happening in the present, it is assumed that we can rely on present processes to give us enough information to extrapolate how those phenomena came about.

As far as ice ages are concerned, we observe glaciers today and know that those glaciers produce moraines, till, and striations. We are able to measure the rates at which those phenomena occur. Having measured those rates, we can calculate the time necessary for those glaciers to advance to the places on the continents where the geological evidence tells us they reached in the past.

Assuming that "all things continue as they were from the beginning of creation" (2 Peter 3:4), naturalists use the information of the present to extrapolate the time and conditions in the past that will explain the beginnings (and perhaps the many beginnings) of the Ice Age.

And, since all of the above is assumed to be true, there should be parallel data from several worldwide processes that demonstrate correlation between the assumptions. Here are the main sources of data that naturalists use to understand the formation of ice ages:

- Accumulation of seafloor sediments
- Layers of deposits obtained from ice cores
- Astronomical theory about the earth's axis

Let's take these one at a time and try to understand how they add to the naturalistic understanding of the Ice Age.

Seafloor Sediments

Given the assumption that the rates of anything we can measure today are the same as rates operating in the past, the accumulation of the sediments at the bottom of the oceans has been going on for a very long time. We can measure the rate at which "stuff" drops. That sediment accumulates slowly today—only a few centimeters every thousand years. Yet the sediment at the bottom of the oceans is hundreds of feet deep in places. If we discount the idea that there has been a planet-covering flood in the recent past—complete with historic erosion as the floodwaters raced off the continents and into today's relatively new ocean basins—then sediments have been dropping to the bottom of the ocean for millions of years!

Part of the seafloor sediment includes the shells of very tiny organisms called *foraminifera,* forams for short. When the forams are alive, they build their shells from calcium carbonate, which contains oxygen. Two forms of oxygen are used in the construction—oxygen-16 and oxygen-18. Oxygen-16 is much more common than oxygen-18. Since the ratio of those two types of oxygen can be measured in the fossil foram shells, the assumptions are that the differences in that ratio at different depths of the seafloor sediment give us a good idea of the climate conditions in the distant past.

So far so good, except that the seafloor oxygen-18 to oxygen-16 ratio has nothing to do with time, only with the differences in climate—and even that is speculative.

Ice Core Layers

As ice is formed, each annual snowfall leaves layers in the ice. The assumption is that layers mark annual events much like the rings in a tree mark growth from year to year. Tree rings show differences between climate from year to year, and the theory is that the layers in the ice show similar differences. Plus, it is possible to measure the same kind of oxygen-18 to oxygen-16 isotope ratio in the ice.

Scientists have drilled deep into the Greenland and Antarctica glaciers and brought up cores that have exposed depths of well over 8000 feet. Using the layers and the chemical ratios, it would seem plausible that one could count the layers and come up with a reasonable age for the ice accumulation. However, deeper layers cannot be seen in the Antarctic cores—and can only be seen in the upper halves of the Greenland cores. The weight of the ice above "squashes" the lower layers so much that they merge until they simply disappear. Even though secular scientists still hold on to the idea that there are many layers in that deeper blend, it is just about impossible to determine how many layers there are. That's why they resort to mathematical models of ice flow, not layer counting, to estimate ice core ages. And even those mathematical models are not enough!

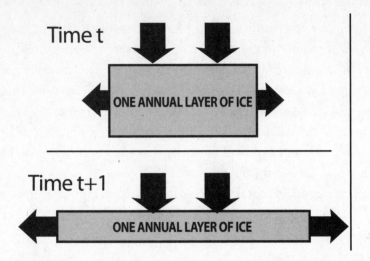

Figure 8.3—Because layers of ice become thinner at increasing depths within an ice sheet, mathematical flow models must be used to determine how much thinning is present at a given depth.

Time for another help to calculate ages.

The Astronomical Theory

Since both the seafloor oxygen ratios and the ice layers have significant correlation problems—particularly as it comes to relating the information to years—naturalists have come to rely on a specific interpretation of astronomical behavior as it relates to the ages of the glacial and interglacial periods of Earth.

Every 24 hours, the earth turns around an axis that is tilted at around 23.5 degrees. The tilt of this axis of rotation is decreasing very slowly. Assuming that this has been going on for millions of years, it can be calculated that the axis would change from 22.1 degrees to 24.5 degrees and back again every 41,000 years. Because the tilt of the earth's axis has an impact on climate, one can assume this "wobble" would cause cycles that could be recognized in the seafloor sediments and the ice layers.

Added to that information is the shape of the earth's orbit around the sun. The orbit is something of a squashed circle called an *ellipse*. This orbit is also slowly changing, becoming less squashed over time and drifting toward a more complete circle. Again, assuming deep time, the cycle of ellipse to circle repeats itself about every 100,000 years.

Then there is the cone-shaped motion that the earth's axis makes as it slowly wobbles about every 26,000 years—or would if it existed long enough—and the relationship of the earth's orbit to the background stars that cycles roughly every 22,000 years. These two motions produce a third cycle of about 23,000 years.

What does all of this have to do with the Ice Age, you might ask? About 70 years ago, an astronomer laid the groundwork for calculating the times of past ice ages. He postulated that those orbital changes would affect climate by varying the amount of summer sunlight in the northern high latitudes. That combination theory is known as the Milankovitch theory. Secular scientists now use this theory—which relies on the assumption that Earth has been around enough time to experience these cycles—to assign ages to the ice cores and seafloor sediments by baking it and its deep time into ice flow models.

Quick Review

The forams (little marine organisms) in the seafloor provide a chemical chart of likely climate changes over time by the ratio of oxygen-18 to oxygen-16. The "wiggles" in the chart are thought to provide insight to times in the earth's past when intense glacial periods occurred. But this requires ages to be assigned to the wiggles, and the secular scientists use the Milankovitch theory to do that.

Ice cores have layering that supposedly shows annual deposits of snow. The difficulty caused by the fact the lower layers are squashed over time was resolved by a mathematical flow model that predicted the number of expected ice layers—and any of the discrepancies in those flow models can be corrected by "tuning" them with the Milankovitch theory. So with the presumed climate changes recorded in the ice cores and the assigned ages of the wiggles from the seafloor sediments, the two sets of data should correspond nicely.

Just in case you had a bit of trouble following all of that, the data from the wiggles caused by the seafloor forams' changing oxygen ratios and the data from the ice core studies from the Antarctic and Greenland (extended and extrapolated by the "flow" models) are all corrected by tuning them with the Milankovitch astronomical theory.

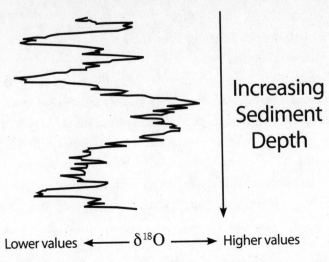

Figure 8.4—Secular scientist believe that "wiggles" in the chemistry of the seafloor sediments can yield information about past climates. For example, maximum values in a quantity call the oxygen isotope ratio ($\delta^{18}O$) are thought to indicate times of maximum glacial extent.

An interesting dance, to say the least, but this combination of disparate measurements and mathematical magic is far from empirical science, since it relies wholly on assuming deep time.

Other Problems

It is not within the scope of this chapter to go into the details of the difficulties of the naturalistic assumptions that underlie these various theories of past ice ages. However, it is worthwhile to list a few of the problems that the uniformitarian view must face and solve if the theories are to be accepted as historically accurate.

Please remember that the foundational assumption behind evolutionary ideas is that all processes and observational phenomena must be understood in terms of natural explanations with nothing supernatural at all in the answer. This applies to all questions under evaluation by the scientists and philosophers of our day. Nothing is to be understood as having originated from an omnipotent and omniscient being of any sort. Past, present, and future must be analyzed by the overriding presupposition that everything has come about by natural processes interacting randomly over vast undocumented and uncountable ages.

Here are a few of the problems with those assumptions regarding ice ages.

Circular Reasoning

The isotope ratio gained from forams is assumed to reflect major climate changes over the ages the seafloor sediment has been accumulating. The connection between the differences in the oxygen types is somewhat shaky, but even given that point, applying the data from seafloor sediment to ice layers is a bit of a stretch. Scientists may assume, for example, that the ocean temperature implied from the foram data has lasted for centuries. But in fact, the temperature may have lasted for only a few days or weeks. Likewise, they may assume that the foram inference in one location also applies to the whole ocean—but for all we know, it may be that only small pockets of water have held those temperatures.

The seafloor data are artificially synchronized to the layering data from the ice cores in Greenland and Antarctica. Those presumed annual layers are themselves interpreted by a mathematical flow model—that is, attuned to the data from the seafloor ratios. And both of them are tuned by the use of the Milankovitch speculations. That theory enables the dating of the seafloor sediments, which are then used to calibrate the ice flow models that are used to assign ages to the ice cores.

All of which is based on an unprovable assumption of long ages.

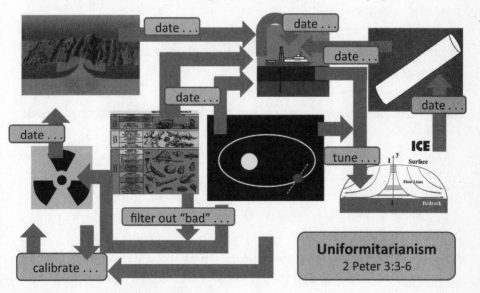

Figure 8.5—Circular Reasoning

Orbital Tuning

The wiggles displayed on the charts of the foram data are assumed to identify changes in climate. Those changes are assumed to be caused by changes in the astronomical functions of the earth's axis and orbit. Even though secular scientists know that the rate of deposition has not been perfectly constant, the differences are assumed to be resolved by the check against the astronomical theory. The calculations for the seafloor data are "proven" by the assumption that the ice ages would have occurred during the periods predicted by the astronomical formulas—seafloor ratios tuned by astronomical data.

Remember, the calculated regular cycles of the earth's axis and orbit changes are based on the assumption of long ages. The assumption of long ages is built into the reasoning behind the math. Small wonder that the answer is long ages.

Fossil Events

For the past 200 years or so, fossils buried in the earth's sedimentary layers have provided a snapshot of moments in time. To the creationist, they are a record of God's judgment on a world gone terribly wrong and not only tell us of God's righteous anger but also document the kinds of creatures living at the time of that great judgment.

To the secular naturalist, those same fossils are seen as a long history of the evolutionary development of life from the earliest marine organisms in the Cambrian Explosion to the more recent mammals and supposed humanoids in our supposed ancestry tree. These fossils have been placed in sequential eras and are identified by certain index fossils that are used to connect similar strata to assumed time periods throughout the planet.

These fossils are dated today by radioisotope measurements of nearby volcanic intrusions into the strata in which the fossils are embedded. Fossil events are more specific to a narrow time range than the broad categories of the eras that span hundreds of millions of years of supposed time. These events are particular to a specific type of fossil and are supposed to help identify that same specific time period throughout the planet wherever that particular index fossil is found.

However, multiple exceptions to these specific times are widely known and clearly documented in the academic journals. These exceptions are rarely publicized outside of the insider journals and are often ignored or brushed aside even in those studies. Basically, if the data don't fit the accepted model of long ages and progressive development, the information is considered irrelevant.

The concept of long ages is an article of faith, and any information that appears to contradict that faith is deemed unfit for discussion. ICR has been exposing these issues for decades. Many people have been helped by the information, but the scientific majority runs a tight "membership club" that keeps outsiders out.

Truth, however, has a way of coming to the surface.

The Biblical Answer

In contrast to the circular and convoluted reasoning of secular scientists, the Bible provides simple and satisfactory answers to the question of the Ice Age. From this author's perspective, the Bible stands true even if the proof is not easy to find. If God does exist, then such a being—as described in the pages of Scripture—could not lie or distort information in any way that would lead a person to a wrong conclusion.

The God of the Bible must reveal truth. He might not provide technical details about a given topic, but if He speaks to a principle of science, then that which is recorded must be accurately stated. It is often said that the Bible is not a textbook of science. That is certainly true, but if indeed God is the Creator of the universe, then whenever the Bible deals with "the things that are made" (Romans 1:20), those passages must be accurate.

What, then, does the Bible tell us about the Ice Age and the causes that would bring about such an unusual period?

Basic Requirements for an Ice Age

Creation scientists have dedicated much of their research to this issue. Dr. Michael Oard, Dr. Larry Vardiman, and Dr. Jake Hebert are three of the more well-known, but just about any evaluation of the causes for a period of glaciation would require four consistent source causes, which can be remembered by the acronym HEAT.[1]

- *Hot water*—The first element in the causal chain must be hot oceans. If the major water basins of our planet are cool, the possibility of an ice age is gone.

- *Evaporation*—Rain and snow cannot exist without a transfer of water from the ocean basins up into the atmosphere. Evaporation is that transfer process.

- *Aerosols*—Aerosols are tiny particles that become suspended in the atmosphere and reflect sunlight, producing cooler surface temperatures.

- *Time*—Sequential events over long periods of time undermine Ice Age models. These elements must be concentrated in a relatively short time period to have the additive effect necessary for an ice age.

The Biblical Flood

Although the Bible has few references to snow and ice (most of which are in the book of Job), it does have a lot to tell us about the catastrophic judgment the global Flood executed on Earth during the days of Noah. It is that event that provided the enormous energy necessary to start the processes that would initiate the climate changes and provide the conditions that would allow for a buildup of an ice age.

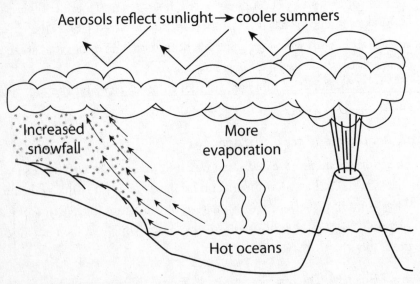

Figure 8.6—Ice Age by Heat

Hot Oceans

All agree that much warmer oceans would be necessary for an ice age to occur. But what could do that? The amount of temperature change needed for an El Niño or La Niña event is less than a few degrees Fahrenheit. Those events produce more or less rain, but nothing like the amounts necessary for a buildup of ice or the glaciation of half of a continent. What kind of energy source would be necessary to heat up the world's oceans to such a degree that rain and snow would continue for decades?

> In the six hundredth year of Noah's life, in the second month, the seventeenth day of the month, on that day all the fountains of the great deep were broken up, and the windows of heaven were opened (Genesis 7:11).

One of the more interesting features of the ocean floors are the rift valleys associated with underwater mountain ridges. Most have been mapped by satellites and sonar, and these valleys appear to develop as new seafloor is formed. Similar rift valleys are well-known across land surfaces; all appear to have been underwater at one time. Lots of speculation has gone into the processes by which they could have been formed, but because we are unable to see these processes today, the assumptions are based on nonsupernatural explanations.

The biblical story is less complicated, but it is supernatural. God brought about a worldwide explosion of all the underground geological systems. Just what these were is unknown, but the effects are rather easily understood. For the purpose of finding a source to heat up the oceans, these "fountains of the great deep" could hardly be more satisfactory. They would have opened up the earth's mantle, pouring out unimaginable waves of magma and intensifying the heat of the ocean water. The closest example we see of this today is the lava flows into the ocean off the coastlines of Hawaii.

The evidence for that is pretty convincing. Those underwater mountain ridges are all volcanic and were clearly formed underwater. The land ridges and rift valleys are less obvious, but most of them have the same indicators: quick formation, volcanic origins, unstable past, and current erratic behavior. All of that underscores the biblical imagery of the fountains of the great deep ripping open on one day in the not-so-distant past.

And such enormous changes would have had enormous consequences. Eruptions continued underwater, and the displacement of the ocean reservoirs caused an increase in tsunamis. The Bible notes that the water increased ("prevailed") for five months, and the surges across the land continued as well. Once heated, the oceans would retain that heat for many years. Go back to chapter 5 and review the evidence for the Flood.

Evaporation Episode

Those warm oceans would have increased evaporation to levels not seen before or since. Secular scientists simply ignore this phenomenon because they reject the entire idea of a global flood. However, the Bible's record is both precise and insistent. It is either accurate or preposterous. If it happened as described in Genesis 7 and 8, then the ensuing decades of evaporation would cause the ideal scenario for an atmospheric buildup of water vapor that must have colossally increased the snowfall at higher elevations.

Studies by Drs. Vardiman and Wesley Brewer have shown that the snowfall would have exceeded anything we are familiar with.[2]

Aerosols Abound

The volcanic activity on land would have continued for a long time after the eruptions of the fountains of the great deep. Evidence abounds that huge volcanoes devastated vast portions of the continents. Yellowstone National Park is one big caldera. Calderas and various "bathtub rings" scar every continent on Earth. Our planet has undergone immense eruptions in the past that spewed billions of tons of aerosols into the atmosphere.

Those particles would have created a blanket over the earth that would have abated sunlight and lowered the average temperature across the globe. The few big volcanic eruptions during the twentieth century have provided sufficient glimpses into that condition. Weather patterns changed. Aircraft had to be rerouted. Birds sought their nests, and sweaters were donned during summer. All of this was sufficient to initiate and maintain the cycles of increased snowfall and cooler summers needed to build an ice age.

Time Truncation

The biggest problem (although never addressed) for the long-age naturalist is the slow, sequenced advance of the supposed climate changes prior to and during the various ages of glaciation. El Niño conditions fall away fairly quickly. Evaporation is dependent on heat sources maintaining the energy. Aerosols fall out of the atmosphere within a couple of years—unless replenished regularly over time. None of this fits the observable data very well. But the energies dissipated during the great Flood of Noah's day are sufficient to start and prolong the conditions necessary for an ice age to build up and continue until the earth settled back into equilibrium.

The geological evidence insists that glaciers did indeed flow down into the middle of the northern and, to a lesser extent, the southern hemispheres. The moraines, glacial till, and striations are solid evidence—but they speak of one such period, not many. Evolutionists must postulate many such ages to fit the evolutionary story and to cover over the "missing" answers. Exceptions and speculations abound amid the assumptions in these theories. Perhaps these naturalistic scientists should recall Occam's Razor: Among competing hypotheses that predict equally well, the one with the fewest assumptions should be selected. Put another way, the fewer assumptions that are made, the better.

The Most Reasonable Conclusion

The Bible's message is clear, sufficient, and supported by the observable evidence with the fewest exceptions or assumptions. There was one Ice Age, and it happened after the Flood and because of the Flood. Yes, the whole of the biblical record is based on the assumption that an omnipotent and omniscient Creator exists. But that one assumption fits exactly what we see.

Once again, we are faced with a dichotomy of ideas. One or the other is true—not both.

CHAPTER 9

Ancient Civilizations

Our current world began shortly after Noah and his family stepped off the Ark. There was a world before that, a world with cities and sophisticated agriculture, metallurgy, and fine arts. All of that is mentioned in Genesis 4. Unfortunately, we don't have any direct access to that world. God destroyed it in His righteous anger. That world "was filled with violence" (Genesis 6:11) and humanity had reach a stage where "every intent of the thoughts of [man's] heart was only evil continually" (verse 5).

From time to time, however, anomalous fossils are uncovered in coal or amber that seem to give us a glimpse into that era. The various legends of Atlantis and other such stories tease us with ideas of a lost civilization. But God's view of those people is not good:

> The earth also was corrupt before God, and the earth was filled with violence. So God looked upon the earth, and indeed it was corrupt; for all flesh had corrupted their way on the earth (Genesis 6:11-12).

Ancient History

Our world—the world of historical records and tombs and archaeological digs—is a world that is not very old. Demonstrably accurate historical records go back only about 5000 years. Yes, some of those documents speak of times before them—like the book of Genesis itself. Moses is its historian, and he identifies 11 other records he had access to that helped him provide accurate information about the time before he led the nation of Israel out of Egypt.[1]

There were other ancient historians, like Herodotus (c. 484–425 BC), who is often called the father of history, and Ptolemy I Soter (c. 367–283 BC), a general of Alexander the Great and founder of the Ptolemaic dynasty in Egypt. But as you can easily see, these men lived long after Moses (c. 1400 BC).

Historian	Time Lived
Plutarch	AD 46–120
Julius Caesar, Gallic Wars	100–44 BC
Ptolemy I Soter	c. 367–283 BC
Manetho, Aegyptiaca *(History of Egypt)*	Third century BC
Herodotus	484–425 BC
Moses	**c. 1400 BC**

Figure 9.1—Historians

Manetho, an Egyptian priest thought to have lived in the third century BC, wrote the *Aegyptiaca* (*History of Egypt*). Julius Caesar (100–44 BC), whom many of us studied in high school and college, wrote about the Gallic and civil wars of Rome. Plutarch (AD 46–120) is well-known because he parallels much of Greek and Roman history that is of interest to Western civilizations. We also know about Flavius Josephus (AD 37–100) because he concentrated on Jewish history and is one of the few who wrote independently about Jesus of Nazareth.

Many scholars have struggled with the disparities between the accounts of Egyptian, Jewish, and Greek historians, who wrangled over which society deserves the honor of being named the oldest civilization, making arguments that seem a bit childish and throw the various dates into debate. But these historians and many more like them wrote about periods of history that were close to their own lifetimes and don't give us much more than hearsay about the early times around the start of the world's major civilizations.

Really Ancient History

The Bible is one of a precious few books that give insight into genuinely ancient history. There are other "bibles" that speak to beginnings. One of the more famous is the *Enuma Elish*, an early creation myth from Mesopotamia written on seven tablets. This story tells of the god Marduk, who battles the chaos goddess Tiamat and defeats her with superweapons. After Marduk becomes the leader of the gods, he makes heaven and earth out of Tiamat's body. Humanity is self-made from Marduk's blood and bone. Intriguing, to say the least—and the story has some shadows of the biblical account snuck in there.

By the way, Nimrod (Genesis 10) assumes the name Marduk as he writes his history—and all of this culminates in the *Enuma Elish* being written long before the reign of King Nebuchadnezzar of Babylon in the twelfth century BC.

The *Epic of Gilgamesh* is another story that came from ancient Mesopotamia. It is a bit older than the *Enuma Elish*—it was written on 12 tablets about 2100 BC, the time of Abraham. Again, the narrative theme throughout the poem seems to reflect an awareness of the biblical account, but the style of writing and development of the main characters is a far cry from what is in the Scripture.

There are other pieces of ancient writings of the beginnings of civilization. Most of them are preserved on stone or clay tablets, and many of them are located in areas around Egypt and Babylon. Since both of these empires conquered much of what we think of as the Middle East, we also find corresponding material in Syria, Turkey, Iran, and Iraq—not to mention Israel.

Modern Archaeology

Archaeology didn't become much of a science until the 1700s. Early efforts to unearth, locate, catalog, and eventually restore the sites and findings of ancient civilizations left much to be desired. Active sites were often burglarized, tombs looted, and artifacts either destroyed or sold on the black market to unscrupulous buyers who kept them for private hoards rather than make them available for study. The Indiana Jones movies are not far from the truth as far as the warring factions and "adventure" behaviors of some of the early explorers.

The surprise of archaeology—for everyone except those who trust the Bible—has been the confirmation of the biblical records. As the evolutionary mindset grew into the majority view among educators, the biblical accounts were disdained as either untrustworthy oral tradition or simply foolish mythology. In spite of the notorious mythology of some of the more famous epics, in spite of the blunders and bluster of the early days of archaeology, in spite of the anti-Christian academic bias of most secular scholars and universities, much has been discovered and accurately documented of the people and places of ancient civilizations.

The Value of History

Running through the centuries of history can seem a bit daunting, especially when trying to gain a quick overview of why we need to take the trouble to do this. Sometimes one wonders if it is even necessary to look backward—it is history, after all. You can't do anything about it, so why bother? Perhaps the best answer to that is the famous statement attributed to Edmund Burke: "Those who don't know history are doomed to repeat it."

But perhaps a more important reason is that what one believes will affect the way one thinks! History is the foundation for our belief system. If we do not have a reliable source for what happened in the past, then we are doomed to be the victims of those who are telling the story of the past. More to the point of this book, the beginning of our existence and the subsequent outworking of that beginning are the framework through which we view and live our lives.

What you believe directs how you think.
What you think dictates what you do.
What you do dominates your life.

Your knowledge of Genesis (the beginnings) is the basis for the way you think about yourself, the world around you, and the way you live your life. Take the time to wade through these few pages of history. It just may be that the knowledge gained will make a difference to you.

The Beginning of the Nations

Several of the nations mentioned in Genesis 10 are recognized throughout Scripture and play major roles in history. All of the people groups of today have come from the three sons of Noah.

> Now the sons of Noah who went out of the ark were Shem, Ham, and Japheth. And Ham was the father of Canaan. These three were the sons of Noah, and from these the whole earth was populated (Genesis 9:18-19).

> God, who made the world and everything in it, since He is Lord of heaven and earth, does not dwell in temples made with hands. Nor is He worshiped with men's hands, as though He needed anything, since He gives to all life, breath, and all things. And He has made from one blood every nation of men to dwell on all the face of the earth, and has determined their preappointed times and the boundaries of their dwellings (Acts 17:24-26).

Noahic Son	Lands Settled
Japheth	Europe
Shem	Middle East
Ham	Africa, Asia

Figure 9.2—Noahic Sons

The Nations of Japheth

Japheth was the eldest son of Noah. His seven sons recorded in Genesis 10 are Gomer, Magog, Madai, Javan, Tubal, Meshech, and Tiras. Many of their family groups moved north and west after the incident at the Tower of Babel. Japheth himself is frequently connected with the Iapheti, the commonly accepted ancestral name for the Greeks. That same name is also associated with the Aryans of India. Javan is connected with the Ionians, who are identified as early Greek peoples. Many scholars strongly suggest that the bulk of the Indo-European populations came from the Japhetic sons.

Herodotus, the noted Greek historian, insists that Japheth's son Gomer is the father of the Cimmerians, now extinct or integrated into other people groups. Crimea is located on the northern shores of the Black Sea today. Evidence indicates that some of these people later migrated into Germany and Wales. Gomer's brother Magog seems to have had his name settle in Georgia, one of the former Soviet territories. Etymologists tell us that Magog means "the place of Gog." Gog and Magog are mentioned frequently in Ezekiel and in the book of Revelation, along with Meshech and Tubal. The names of Meshech and Tubal surface early in southern Russia, apparently now preserved in the modern names of Moscow and Tobolsk. Tiras, the seventh son of Japheth, is probably the ancestor of the Thracians, who covered a large area of central and southeastern Europe

Ashkenaz was Gomer's son. This name has long been connected with German Jews. The Ashkenazi continue to use that title to describe themselves. Most of them settled in places like Bohemia, Hungary, Poland, Belarus, Lithuania, Russia, Ukraine, and Romania in Eastern Europe. William Albright, the famous archaeologist, identifies the Ashkenazi with the Scythians, while Josephus equates the Scythians with the Magogites.

Two other sons of Gomer are Riphath and Togarmah. Josephus writes that Riphath fathered the Paphlagonians, an ancient people group settling in the mountainous areas along the coasts of the Black Sea. Always mixing and mingling with the Greeks and later the Romans, these folks became assimilated into the Roman Empire and lost their identity. Togarmah may have followed his father Gomer into Germany. Some suggest that Togarmah's name is the source for the name Armenia, and that name seems to connect later to Turkey.

Elishah, Tarshish, Kittim, and Dodanim are Javan's sons. The Iliad mentions a people called the Eilesians, probably connected to Elishah. It is also likely that Elishah is preserved in the Hellespont group the Hellenists—the same as the Greeks. The name Tarshish is famous in the Bible as the city which Jonah fled toward to keep from going to Nineveh. (His trip was interrupted when he got swallowed by the great sea creature.) Tarshish is widely connected with seafaring peoples like the Phoenicians, the city of Carthage in North Africa, and Tartessus in Spain.

The book of Genesis lists these forebears so we will gain a clear perspective on what has happened in the past and understand where these many nations came from. If these names were not given to us, we would be without any source to identify where, from whom, and why there are so many nations today. Japheth was the genetic starting point for the bulk of the European people groups. Genesis provides the record that anchors the starting point.

The Nations of Shem

The biblical event at the Tower of Babel took place in the fifth generation after the Flood. Noah, Shem, and many of the others lived until the time of Abraham and Job. Shem was still living when Abraham died, some 467 years after the Flood ended. The recordkeeping of the time was not a scattered collection of notes and memories; the birth dates and people mentioned were personally related and well-known to those keeping the logs.

Shem identifies himself as "the father of all the children of Eber, the brother of Japheth the elder" (Genesis 10:21). Eber is known to have been the king of Ebla, a major city of that era located in northern Syria. Its remains have provided a wealth of information about the early centuries after ancient Babel. Eber is also connected with the term *Hebrew*; the "h" sound is a common linguistic addition over time. Therefore, "the children of Eber" would include Peleg and direct descendants down to Terah and Abram, the one whom God chose to begin the nation of Israel.

Abram later became Abraham, the "father of many nations." Abraham's son, Isaac, produced both Jacob and Esau. Jacob was the father of the 12 sons who became the tribes of the nation of Israel. Ishmael was the son of Abraham and Hagar, the bondwoman who belonged to Sarah, Abraham's wife. Abraham married Keturah after Sarah died, and that union produced six sons, and seven grandsons and three great-grandsons who are named in the Bible (Genesis 25:1-4). Thus, the families of Ishmael, Esau, and descendants of the prolific union with Keturah (all related to Abraham) produced most of the people groups that are thought of today as the Arab nations.

The Nations of Ham

The record in Genesis lists four sons of Ham: Cush, Mizraim, Phut, and Canaan. All of these sons founded well-known nations. Cush had at least six sons and two grandsons. Mizraim is recorded as having six sons, and Canaan is said to have had at least two sons—with nine "ites" being named as descending from his line (Genesis 10:6-18). The Canaanites, of course, were the nations that inhabited the area promised to Abraham, the area that has been the source of so many battles and political concern.

Cush's most famous son was Nimrod, who developed the complex of cities centered around Babel and Nineveh. Those who remained with Nimrod would later become known as the Sumerians, who became one of the great empires of the ancient world. Nimrod later conquered Ashur's city (later known as Assyria), called the "land of Nimrod" by Micah some 1200 years later (Micah 5:6). *Cush* is typically translated "Ethiopia," since it has been well established that it was settled by the Kashi, as the Cushites were called in the Tel el Amarna tablets.

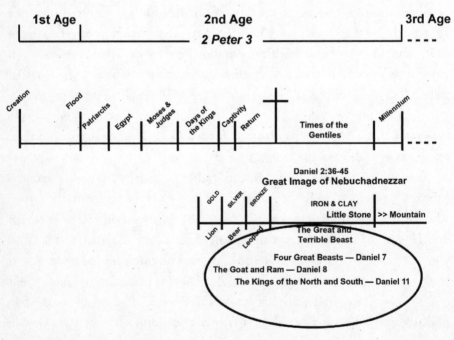

Figure 9.3a—Prophecy Chart

The Prophetic Ages Of Scripture

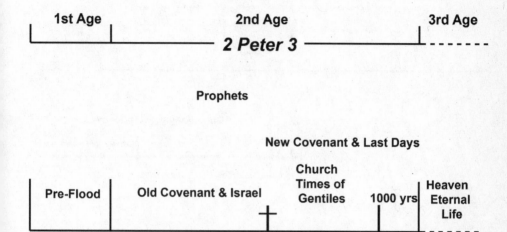

Sequence of World Empires

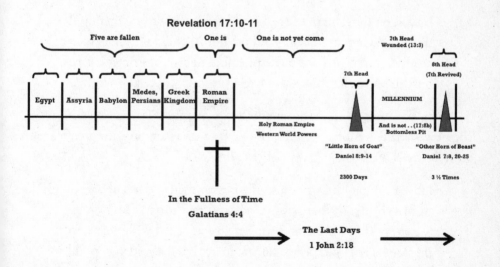

Figure 9.3b—Prophecy Chart

The Theological Debate on the Rapture

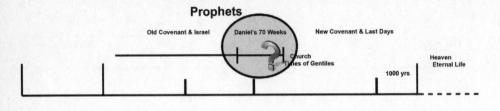

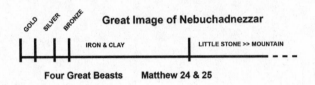

Figure 9.3c—Prophecy Chart

The Seven-Headed Dragon

The book of Revelation provides a prophetic look back at the way Satan has built and controlled the major nations of the world. The picture is of a seven-headed dragon empowered by "the dragon" that is clearly identified as Satan (Revelation 20:2).

> I stood on the sand of the sea. And I saw a beast rising up out of the sea, having seven heads and ten horns, and on his horns ten crowns, and on his heads a blasphemous name...The dragon gave him his power, his throne, and great authority (Revelation 13:1-2).

Later, the apostle John is given another picture of this beast engaged with the power structures of the world, ridden by a drunken prostitute, in league with the beast who is named as "Babylon the Great."

> I saw a woman sitting on a scarlet beast which was full of names of blasphemy, having seven heads and ten horns. The woman was arrayed in purple and scarlet, and adorned with gold and precious stones and pearls, having in her hand a golden cup full of abominations and the filthiness of her fornication. And on her forehead a name was written: MYSTERY, BABYLON THE

GREAT, THE MOTHER OF HARLOTS AND OF THE ABOMINATIONS OF THE EARTH. I saw the woman, drunk with the blood of the saints and with the blood of the martyrs of Jesus. And when I saw her, I marveled with great amazement (Revelation 17:3-6).

That this scarlet beast is the same as the seven-headed beast identified in Revelation 13 is made clear later in chapter 17. In the subsequent verses, John makes sure we are able to identify the imagery as a picture of the Satanic-controlled sequence of empires from the beginning of the second age that started after the great Flood of Noah's day.

> The beast that you saw was, and is not, and will ascend out of the bottomless pit and go to perdition. And those who dwell on the earth will marvel, whose names are not written in the Book of Life from the foundation of the world, when they see the beast that was, and is not, and yet is. Here is the mind which has wisdom: The seven heads are seven mountains on which the woman sits. There are also seven kings. Five have fallen, one is, and the other has not yet come (Revelation 17:8-10).

"Five have fallen, one is, and the other has not yet come." That is the key that locks together the data from Daniel's visions, the information in Revelation, and the records of history. The one active during John's time is clearly the Roman Empire. Five "heads" (kings, empires) had "fallen" previously. The angel Gabriel names three others to Daniel during three key incidents: Nebuchadnezzar's dream of the golden image (Daniel 2), the vision of the four great beasts (Daniel 7), and the vision of the ram and the goat (Daniel 8). In each of these, God verified the sequences of empires from Nebuchadnezzar (Babylon) to Media-Persia to Greece. The passages of Scripture are explicit. There can be no mistake.

Thus, we have a sequence: Babylon, Media-Persia, Greece, Rome. But that is only four of the six (the seventh is still future). History provides the easy identification of the empires prior to Babylon. Nebuchadnezzar conquered Assyria, the empire that took the ten northern tribes of Israel captive in 722 BC. Assyria was the empire that supplanted Egypt in power and influence. Therefore, the seven heads start with Egypt, then Assyria, then Babylon, then Media-Persia, then Greece, then Rome—then, yet to come, a seventh empire after Rome.

Egypt, the First World Empire

The Hebrew word *Mizraim* occurs at least 680 times in the Old Testament, 610 of which are translated "Egypt." Ham's son Mizraim was definitely the founder of Egypt. From a biblical perspective, Egypt was settled by his descendants beginning in the twenty-second century BC. Mizraim was most assuredly a major factor in the nations of history. It was to Egypt that Abram fled when he first arrived in Canaan (Genesis 12:10). It was in Egypt that the patriarch Joseph ruled and embraced the group of 70 souls who one day would become the nation of Israel (Exodus 1:5).

Figure 9.4—Court of Ancient Egypt/Temples of Luxor

One reason Egypt holds such fascination for the modern world is that famous discoveries like Tutankhamen's tomb held such fabulous wealth. Much of what is known about the development of Egypt comes from the tombs and temples that have survived the efforts of looters and black-market archaeologists. The artifacts that have been found in Egyptian tombs are astounding. The frescoes and sculptures on the walls of tombs and temples are magnificent, and the wealth and power they portray—even if incorrect by half—show a rise to power and prosperity that is both swift and difficult to imagine today. Modern engineers marvel at the pyramids of Giza. The precision of the construction and the placement of the foundations to align with astronomical phenomena still puzzle them.

If the depictions of the artwork and the sampling of the artifacts are any indication, Pharaoh's court would have struck awe into anyone. Perhaps the only record that can offer a comparison is the reaction of the Queen of Sheba when she visited Solomon's court.

> When the queen of Sheba had seen the wisdom of Solomon, the house that he had built, the food on his table, the seating of his servants, the service of his waiters and their apparel, his cupbearers and their apparel, and his entryway by which he went up to the house of the LORD, there was no more spirit in her. Then she said to the king: "It was a true report which I heard in my own land about your words and your wisdom. However I did not believe their words until I came and saw with my own eyes; and indeed the half of the greatness of your wisdom was not told me. You exceed the fame of which I heard" (2 Chronicles 9:3-6).

Pharaoh's Rule

The records in every dynasty insist that Pharaoh held absolute power in the empire. Although he implemented his authority through layers of bureaucracy, each of the various viziers, governors, treasurers, and so forth served totally at the pleasure of a pharaoh who could demote or execute them at a moment's whim. Some pharaohs were more benign, like the ruler who placed Joseph in power. Others, like the pharaoh who ruled Egypt when Moses approached the throne for Israel's release, were moody and capricious, ruling by fear rather than by wisdom.

Egypt's economic engine was agriculture. Population estimates of Egypt at the time of Abraham vary widely, but if the city of Ur had some 200,000 and Ebla in Syria had 250,000, it is not at all unreasonable to suggest that Egypt's population could have been in the millions. In order for a pharaoh to stay "favored" by the gods, he must feed his land. Many deities in the pantheon of gods were related in one way or another to the productivity of the land. Pharaoh, as the divine emanation of the greatest god, must control all things so that life was pleasant.

Thus, government was totally controlled by the brokers of power. All power flowed from the pharaoh to his vassals, who implemented the plan throughout the nation. Prosperity lay in the favor of the pharaoh. Punishment for disobedience was swift and terrible. Taxes were enormous, but cradle-to-the-grave provisions were the promise of government, and a docile or subject people was the labor that moved the engine of the economy. Laborers were paid in grain. Housing was assigned. Clothing reflected a person's station in life. Everything had its place, and every place had its purpose.

Court documents that survive from ancient Egypt do not demonstrate a defined legal code such as the Code of Hammurabi or the Ten Commandments. Rather, rules appear to be based on custom or some sense of fairness at the local level. Punishment involved fines for minor infractions, imprisonment for some offenses, but physical mutilation for property or personal crimes (theft, embezzlement, rape, murder). Punishment for crimes among the nobility—those that rose to the knowledge of Pharaoh—was both capricious and vicious. Recall the baker and the butler who served the pharaoh of Joseph's day. The baker was hung; the butler was restored. The closer one was to the person of Pharaoh, the more precarious was the position.

Pharaoh's Religion

The religious philosophy of Egypt was a curious mixture of ritual piety and flagrant polytheism. There was usually a supreme god. Ra (or Re, sometimes Amun-Ra) was the god normally associated with the sun and was, therefore, ruler of all things. This is the god most often associated with Pharaoh. However, other deities by the dozens ruled over various aspects of nature. Most of the major deities had cult temples that held the secrets of various rites to guarantee fertility, a good harvest, cure diseases, bring the annual flooding of the Nile, and many other needs and blessings.

Figure 9.5—Egyptian Sun God Ra

Sometimes, gods were combined. For instance, Amun-Ra was considered "the hidden one," an invisible creator deity with a cult temple in Thebes whose earthly manifestation was the sun. The priests of these many gods and goddesses held a mystical power over the populace and often vied for political power with the pharaohs. The influence of Nimrod's Babel is fairly obvious, with the distortion of the sovereignty of the triune Creator split among the personification of natural forces, luring many into demon worship and religious rites that would shame the face of perverts. It was in Egypt that God implemented the ten plagues that drove Pharaoh to let the people of Israel go. These plagues were directed specifically at the power of the main gods of the Egyptian pantheon.

Other Hamitic Nations

Phut (or Put), the third son of Ham, appears seven times in the Scripture and is translated by "Lybians," "Lybia," and "Lubim." That fits with other sources suggesting that the descendants of Phut settled somewhat west of the descendants of Mizraim. Others have suggested that at least some of the Phut peoples moved eastward toward Ethiopia and Somalia. Obviously, the bulk of the descendants of Mizraim and Phut moved around the Red Sea to settle North Africa and eastward toward the Horn of Africa.

Canaan appears to be the source of much of the biblical concerns relating to the interchange between Israel and the nations living south of Syria. Canaan is the ancestor of the Phoenicians and the Hittites. Canaan's firstborn son, Sidon, is named in a city in Lebanon. The companion city of Tyre formed the dual headquarters for that well-known nautical nation whose exploits are still being uncovered. Heth, Canaan's other named son, became the father of the Hittites. Through Sidon and Heth came the many other "'ite" nations known by Moses and Joshua collectively as the Canaanites.

The Hittites have been verified as having settled in Turkey. Herodotus makes mention of the famous King Midas as one of the peoples connected to the Hittites. The Sinites (Genesis 10:17) migrated from Ararat and Babel into parts of Asia. That migration may be the beginning of the Chinese nations. The term *Cathay* may have a linguistic connection to Khittae, used by the Hittites in some of their ancient monuments.

The Tower of Babel

History is a good teacher. Yet it can be disturbing if we struggle to fit the interpretations of secular historians within the framework of biblical information. If history has taught anything, it is that the majority is seldom right and that the majorities of all nations have chosen to move away from God rather than submit to His authority.

Figure 9.6—Ziggurat of Ur

There are some questions that arise purely because of the evolutionary story of long ages with slow and random development over eons. That is particularly true of the story that revolves around the history of man. According to evolutionary understandings, humanity has developed over millions of years from a common ancestor. That ancestor has yet to be found, but the idea of hominids and various links in the chain have been developed into a rather amazing tale, complete with PBS documentaries and Smithsonian exhibits.

Part of the evolutionary story is that man slowly evolved through various stages until the modern *Homo sapiens* came on the scene. Every museum of natural history has some diorama showing cavemen in long-armed, low-browed, stoop-shouldered stature, with animal-skin loincloths, huddled around a fire while drawing stick figures on the cave walls. These fanciful pieces are developed from tiny bits of fossilized material, some tools found near cave sites, cave pictures and pictographs discovered in a few locations around the world, and plenty of speculation to fill in the blanks.

Despite the impression given by these depictions, such discoveries are few, and they appear in a recognizable ring around the European continent, with just enough evidence to establish that there was a hunter-gatherer culture around those areas. There is no evidence of a long residence at the sites. There is also no evidence that these peoples were large groups; rather, they lived in a few shelters in a known area and then...disappeared!

Contrary to evolutionary pictures of primitive man, early civilizations obviously possessed great knowledge or they never could have built monuments like the pyramids or operated such sophisticated societies. But if early mankind was so knowledgeable, who were these "cavemen"?

The Bible suggests an answer in its account of the Tower of Babel. God divided humanity by language so that people could never again unite in total rebellion as they had at Babel (Genesis 11:5-9). That division separated mankind into genetically isolated groups, which caused the rapid development of differing physiological characteristics. That is just what one would expect if the event at Babel transpired as the Bible teaches.

Suddenly, the language of each family became gibberish to everyone else. The weaker and smaller families were either driven away by the stronger groups or chose to find another location. They had knowledge, since they were part of the group at Babel that was building a brick city and a worship tower. But when forced to find another place to live, they were driven into a short "hunting and gathering" subsistence while they migrated.

Even the people of the great nation of Egypt had to migrate from Mesopotamia after their language was separated from that of others. They had the knowledge to build the pyramids, but they then had to supply their people on a long march through uninhabited wilderness, surviving in natural shelters to start with and making use of minimal tools until the leadership began to shape and organize the new nation. Once they found a location and resources that could be developed for use, their knowledge came back into play.

Historical Records

Secular history is helpful. There are written records preserved in various forms that carry a student of history back some 5000 years—somewhere in the neighborhood of 3000 BC. However, historical records as they are normally written today began much later. Greek historian Herodotus, mentioned earlier, was born in the Persian Empire in the fifth century BC during the Persian Wars. Manetho, the third-century BC Egyptian priest, segregated the early kings of Egypt into dynasties and started the classification system that is still used today.

Josephus, who is often cited by biblical scholars, lived and wrote during the first century AD. Much of that material has been assembled since the 1700s.

The ancient records from secular history are difficult to trust. The difficulty is twofold. First, early kings and pharaohs tended to view themselves as god-like viceroys of the deities their culture worshiped. Thus, the stories of their rule were colored by assumed heavenly authority. Many of their inscriptions were dedicatory citations with flowery language about the opening of a canal or the victory of a certain battle. Completion of a palace or temple is couched in religious tones, praising the ruler and the god(s) they represented. Hunting expeditions are noted with nearly the same level of honor as a military campaign. Selective history, to be sure.

Second, the day-to-day recordings of business transactions, property transfers, and wholesale mercantile purchases do not add much to the broad picture of history. They are interesting insights into the daily life of those early cultures, but they seem oddly out of place with the "heavenly" decisions of the kings. These mundane transactions number in the thousands, preserved mainly on clay tablets. They rarely make the news when found and are often relegated to the arcane musings of scholars. Coupling the two ends together often produces a historical novel, but the truth of those days remains elusive.

Yet some facts worth noting emerge.

Ur of the Chaldees

For many years during the height of the school of higher criticism, Ur was considered a mythical city. Then in the mid-1800s, John G. Taylor began excavations in what is now known as Tell al-Muqayyar, halfway between the Iraqi capital of Baghdad and the northern shores of the Persian Gulf. Later, in the early 1900s, the British Museum funded an extensive effort under the leadership of Reginald C. Thompson and H.R.H. Hall. Layers of remains were uncovered that indicated the city developed from a small farming community in its early days into a thriving urban center of nearly 200,000 at its peak. During the several excavations, it was discovered that the Persian Gulf had extended much farther during the time of Ur, and it is very likely that Ur was one of the major port cities of the Sumerian Empire for a century or more. Now the ruins are much farther inland.

Perhaps the more significant discovery by Taylor was the uncovering of the famous ziggurat at Ur. In that temple site, he found cuneiform cylinders, several of which identified the city as Ur of the Chaldeans. The biblical name was confirmed, and the disdain of the evolutionary scholars who had insisted such a city never existed exposed them for the biased professors they were. In fact, until those cylinders were found, it had been the position of such scholars that writing had not yet been invented that early in man's history, and Abraham, if he existed, could have been nothing more than a wandering illiterate goatherder.

Much more was discovered, of course, and the Tell al-Muqayyar became one of the most valuable sites of antiquity. Sir Leonard Woolley found more than 1800 gravesites, with 16 sites known to be tombs of royalty. Those royal bodies were dated by the scholars as having been buried prior to the birth of Abraham. The more famous of the royal burial sites, that of Queen Puabi, had not been looted and yielded quite a cache of art and valuable personal items. Her tomb, along with the attendants who were buried with her, gave a clearer picture of her life and the practices of that culture.

Sir Woolley surmised that this stunning tomb was a "death pit." The bodies were in formal dress and positioned in careful rows, indicating they willingly died with the king and queen they served. The king was buried first (and was looted), the queen on top of him, and the 74 bodies of 6 men and 68 women followed in sequence on top of the queen. The bodies of the men were warriors or royal guards buried with their weapons near the entrance to the pit. Most of the women were in four rows across one corner of the tomb. Six other women were under a canopy in the opposite corner. Another six were near the southeast wall. Almost all of them wore fragile headdresses of gold, silver, and lapis, mimicking the headdress of Queen Puabi.

> Shell, used for cosmetics cases, pouring vessels, and cylinder seals, came from the Persian Gulf. Carnelian, a semi-precious stone used extensively for beads, came from eastern Iran and/or Gujarat

in India. Lapis lazuli was used for jewelry, cylinder seals, and inlays, and came from northeastern Afghanistan. Mentioned in Mesopotamian myths and hymns as a material worthy of kings and gods, lapis would arrive in small, unfinished chunks to be worked locally into beads, cylinder seals, or inlays. Similar beads of agate and jasper came from Iran's mountains and plateau.[2]

The site has not been further excavated since Sir Woolley ended his work in 1934. Suffice it to say, however, Ur of the Chaldees was not a myth but a vibrant, bustling, pagan port city by the time Abraham was born. It is likely that Job had commercial interchange with Ur, although he lived a considerable distance to the west. Whether Job and Abraham ever met is purely speculative, but the differences in their cultures were significant. Ur was most certainly connected to the culture of Babel and its polytheistic worship. The biblical information about Job and his friends indicates they were still keeping faith in Jehovah.

Haran

Haran was a pagan city much like Ur of the Chaldees. The commercialism of the trade routes would have emphasized secular behavior, but the astrology of Nimrod and Babel were strongly practiced in both Ur and Haran. There are several attempts by various authors to trace the Babylonian worship of astrology throughout the centuries. The most notable is *The Two Babylons* by Presbyterian theologian Alexander Hislop in 1853.

Like Ur, Haran was a thriving trade city, heavily influenced by the pagan worship started under Nimrod. Terah moved his family and probably a family-owned business to Haran. When Abraham left Haran, he was 75 years old, a wealthy and well-established businessman.

Canaan

Much of the archaeological information about the Canaanites comes from the excavations of the city of Ebla in northwest Syria. Eventually, nearly 20,000 tablets were uncovered from a building next to the royal palace. At its peak, Ebla held more than 250,000 people. Many of the biblical city names are verified by these records, along with their geographical locations. Sodom and Gomorrah were repeatedly noted as important trading partners to the south of Ebla. The many names and transactions help date the city to the time of Abraham.

The Hittites were also present. Abraham purchased a cave and its associated plot of land from Ephron the Hittite (Genesis 23:10-16). Ephron was "among the sons of Heth" (verse 10), one of the sons of Canaan, son of Ham, son of Noah (Genesis 10:15). Recall that this period is barely 400 years after the Flood—perhaps around 2000 BC or a bit earlier. By this time, the sons of Heth (the early Hittites) recognize Abraham as "a mighty prince among us" (Genesis 23:6). It is unfortunate that many of the depictions of Abraham and the many "ites" of that day give the impression of nomadic bedouins who wander from place to place eking out a bare existence from the open range. As was the case of Ur and Haran, the major cities of the Canaanites were large, sophisticated, and wicked.

Helpful Thoughts

The Bible is a book of history and has been remarkably corroborated by archaeology. God's purpose for telling us this history is twofold:

1. He has set all of this in motion and controls history (Acts 17:26).
2. He has allowed humanity to continue to allow time so more can be redeemed (2 Peter 3:9).

Human history has been a constant story of wicked rebellion against God. The hope of all humanity lies in the gospel of Jesus Christ (Hebrews 6:17-19). The "new heavens and a new earth" toward which everything is moving is absolutely guaranteed to come about (2 Peter 3:10-13). At that point, all history from this cursed world will be wrapped up, and everything will function under the perfect holiness and flawless design of the Creator.

CHAPTER 10

Origin of the Universe

The Bible insists that the physical universe of space, time, and mass-energy has not always existed but was supernaturally created by a transcendent personal Creator who alone has existed from eternity. The laws of science demonstrate that mass and energy were created to last. Our place in the universe is perfectly balanced for life.

The Universe Demands a Designer

The universe looks designed. To begin with, it is absolutely beautiful! Beauty is hardly a random circumstance but is rather the result of a magnificent mind with unusual imaginative abilities that produces the art for the rest of us to enjoy.

Naturalists want to explain the universe as a necessary outcome of physical laws and initial conditions. The Big Bang theory, its attendant inflation theory, and the search for structure in the cosmic background radiation are all part of this effort. The design argument took on renewed urgency in the 1930s when quantum physicists realized that certain constants, like the force of gravity and the charge on the electron, might just as well have taken on arbitrary values. The problem was, of course, most values would never produce a universe with atoms, stars, planets, or observers. Lots of technical savvy has gone into trying to understand what happens in our universe—but when the technical people are stuck with a "no miracles" rule, the problem of "How did it get here?" really gets gnarled.

One early escape from the design inference was the so-called anthropic principle. Essentially, that principle states that observations about the universe must be compatible with the conscious and intelligent life that is doing the observing. Most naturalists dismissed such speculation as metaphysical fluff. However, in 1996, something was discovered that brought cosmologists kicking and screaming back to the anthropic principle.

The careful study of the universe has demonstrated that it is not only expanding, it's actually accelerating. This acceleration value, or what is called the cosmological constant, appears to be so finely tuned (nearly zero, but slightly positive) that almost any other value would prohibit the formation of stars and galaxies—assuming they formed naturally and not supernaturally.

Previous theoretical predictions were off by 120 orders of magnitude.

Theories to account for this began to pour out of academic inner circles. Some hoped that superstring theory would come to the rescue, but its champions found that their equations permit 10,500 different sets of initial conditions—most of them life-prohibiting. The only way our universe could be explained, therefore, was either by a Designer who chose the right values or by luck among untold numbers of alternate universes with random values.

This presented a series of scientific conundrums. The more complex the problem, and the more complex the solutions to the complex problem, the more problems cropped up. That's why most scientists keep coming back to one of the basic axioms in science: Occam's Razor. In its simplest form, Occam's Razor states that one should make no more assumptions than are needed. That keep-it-simple principle would surely prefer a single Designer to uncountable universes.

Everything we see and know shows careful design by an omnipotent and omniscient Designer who planned and purposed everything to function together. The exceptions are breakdowns in the system. The Bible explains them as the result of man's sin (Genesis 3:17-19). That death sentence impacts the entire universe (Romans 8:20-22).

Just the Facts

A famous detective on an old TV show purportedly used to say, "Just the facts, ma'am." So, in the interest of "just the facts," here is a quick overview of what all scientists know about our universe—although some of the information is so stunning it might seem to approach the fantastic. Every time we discover something more about the immensity of the universe or the enormous variety of stars, our language becomes rather inadequate. Much of the difficulty astronomers face is how to tell the story—because the story tends to change as our scientific tools uncover more information.

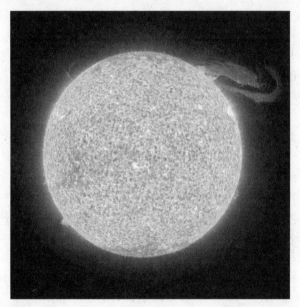

Figure 10.1—The Sun

Unimaginable Power

A star is a continuous explosion of awesome power. Before the invention of the telescope, known stars were relatively few. Obviously, there were many stories about how the stars came into being, but before we began to understand how immense the universe really was, a few thousand stars didn't seem much of a mental issue to grapple with.

But then we began to see the universe in a very different way. Within the space of a century or so, humanity was able to understand a little bit of the biblical concept that the stars of the universe were really virtually uncountable. And each of them was enormous and powerful.

> I will multiply your descendants as the stars of the heaven and as the sand which is on the seashore (Genesis 22:17).

> He counts the number of the stars; He calls them all by name (Psalm 147:4).

> Can you bind the cluster of the Pleiades, or loose the belt of Orion? Can you bring out Mazzaroth in its season? Or can you guide the Great Bear with its cubs? Do you know the ordinances of the heavens? (Job 38:31-33).

The power needed to create a universe with a billion galaxies, each with a billion stars, is beyond imagination. One of the most fundamental laws of our universe is that matter (mass-energy) cannot be created or destroyed. If anything is a law of science, that one surely is. The questions must be asked: How were these stars formed, and where did they all come from? If the mass-energy that we can see, test, feel, and measure cannot create itself, then where did this unmeasurable and absolutely infinite storehouse of power come from?

The commonsense answer is that a Creator did it. But that means supernatural power. That means that the Creator is outside and transcendent to everything that we mere humans can see or conceive of. The only way we are ever going to know anything about such a Creator is if He is willing to reveal Himself to us.

Spiral Galaxies

Galaxies exist in many shapes and sizes, and one of the more common galaxy configurations is a spiral. That is, the galaxy is composed of a central mass of stars with a series of arms spiraling away from the center. Secular scientists suggest that these arms take a long time to form and that a spiraling galaxy is about 10 billion years old. These galaxies appear throughout the universe. Most of them have been identified, named, and located spatially. Our own Milky Way is a spiral galaxy.

Here's the problem: Astronomers have made careful measurements of the motion within such galaxies, and it is well-known that the inner stars are rotating faster than the outer ones. Thus, the arms would soon wind up in the middle with the rest of the stars, making the galaxy a large lump of closely packed stars—not a spiral. The measured speed of the outer stars would spin the arms into the center in about 100 million years. That's one-tenth of the supposed age of many spiral galaxies.

Figure 10.2—Spiral Galaxy

Blue Stars

At the time of the apostle Paul, astronomers knew that "one star differs from another star in glory" (1 Corinthians 15:41). Recently, with the advancement of devices like the Hubble Space Telescope, astronomers have discovered many very bright and high-energy stars that have been named *blue stars*.

The exceedingly high rate at which these stars consume energy would dictate they cannot be more than a few million years old. That, of course, is way too young for the supposed 13.8 billion years of the universe's existence. So these beautiful stars are called stragglers because they are supposed to have formed much later in time than stars of other colors. Of course, no astronomer has ever seen any star form, whether blue, red, yellow, or white.

The supposed youth of these blue stars is not a problem for a creationist. In fact, if God created the vast host of stars only a few thousand years ago, then we would not only expect a wonderful variety of different stars but would delight at the special brilliance of these young and vibrant lights.

Exquisite Order

Organized systems or structures do not happen spontaneously. We never observe organization occurring by accident. No amount of undirected power or energy is enough to bring order out of chaos. Instead, an intelligent cause is required to direct the order. Try shooting a wristwatch with a bullet—the watch's order does not increase! The organization in a watch is what the watch-maker intelligently puts into it at the beginning. Likewise, if we drop a glass bottle of spoiled milk onto bricks, it quite naturally shatters into a more disorderly arrangement of chaotic glass fragments mixed with spilled spoiled milk. It could never reform itself into a more exquisitely sculpted glass container containing fresh milk.

The addition of enormous amounts of energy over huge amounts of time is not enough, either. A tired human eats to gain nutritional energy, but eating hot coals is not an adequate energy source because it fails to match and cooperate with the orderly design of the human digestive system. Experiences such as broken watches and spilled milk remind us that complexity does not happen by itself. In fact, our entire universe demonstrates that same truth. The earth's rotation, the moon's phase cycle, the Earth-sun distance, the placement of planets in the solar system, and the changing seasons are just a few of the ordered processes observable in nature.

Exquisite Functions

Hydrogen is considered the most plentiful element in the universe. Light from stars begins with hydrogen. The sun is a large ball—more than 100 times larger than the earth—of very hot hydrogen. Its energy comes from explosions of hydrogen. These are nuclear explosions, which are much more powerful than chemical explosions.

Gravity draws all the sun's hydrogen together, creating intense pressure. In the core of the sun, huge forces cause nuclear fusion reactions. Hydrogen atoms fuse together into helium and release enormous amounts of energy. The explosions do not cause the sun to suddenly blow up and then go cold. Instead, the laws of physics describe processes that hold our sun together. Gravity pulls the atoms back as each explosion pushes them away. This balance keeps the billions of stars in billions of galaxies burning—without exploding or burning out very often.

This is an amazing set of circumstances. Most explosions are not helpful and are not designed to produce a recurring sequence of events that seemingly function very well. Obviously, the various functions within the sun and other stars are more complex than the rather simple explanation provided above. However, compared to the functions within a living cell, the stars are quite simple. As far as our planet is concerned, the sun is the most important star, but can you imagine what the night sky would look like without the rest of them? Many of our earliest memories are of staring up into the dark sky with wonder. Stars serve as a reminder that the universe is magnificently beautiful. The vast and unmeasurable universe in which they are placed would insist that their Creator be even more grand and "past finding out" (Romans 11:33).

Measurable Clocks

Although the majority story is that the universe is billions of years old, there are a number of "clocks" in the universe that imply the universe is only several thousand years old. In addition to the blue star and spiral galaxy clocks mentioned earlier, comets provide a natural clock within our solar system. Every time a comet orbits the sun, it loses a portion of its substance. As the comet circles around the sun, the heat melts some of its material, and that material sloughs off as the tail, a long trail of melted ice and debris coming off the ball of the comet itself.

Figure 10.3—Halley's Comet

Obviously, after a certain number of orbits, the comet will melt away. Astronomers have studied many of them, and they are pretty regular. Probably the most famous is Halley's Comet, which has an orbit around our solar system that cycles every 75–76 years. Its orbit was first calculated by Edmund Halley in 1705. The last time it returned to the inner solar system was 1986. Each time it has come within Earth's view, it has appeared smaller. Some suggest that the next time it is scheduled to appear, in mid-2061, it may be really hard to see with the naked eye.

This is a serious problem for folks who insist the universe is really old. Comets cannot be very old because they cannot survive many orbits around the sun. To get around this dilemma, secular astronomers assume there is a vast cloud of comets near the edge of the solar system that releases new comets every so often. This imaginary source is called the *Oort cloud*, named after the astronomer who proposed it. The problem with this is that there is no observational evidence such a cloud exists.

Each year, our knowledge of astronomy increases with new evidence concerning the origin of our solar system, our galaxy, and our universe. While it is possible to make assumptions beyond what can be observed and verified, the assumptions should fit within the anthropic principle. (In other words, the observation must fit the nature of the intelligent observer.) Many of the secular assumptions are "way out there" and do not conform to rational thought.

Meanwhile, the heavens continue to bear witness to recent creation.

A Stable Universe

Empirical science depends on the dependability of processes. If the functions of our universe flipped and flopped all over the place—as is implied by the random theories of evolutionary origins—science as we know it would be impossible. In order for scientists to figure out how things work, it is necessary for them to assume that the same thing will behave the same way the next time it is analyzed. Once a certain process has been analyzed many times with the same effect happening each time, the process becomes known as a law of science.

Yes, some science is speculative in an attempt to think outside the box. That kind of science is really not empirical science but an intuitive experiment to see if something else works. These intuitive efforts are sometimes necessary even in ordinary life to understand how to overcome difficulties. However, once the basic laws of science have been proven over and over again, then those laws become the foundational building blocks of any and all theories and experiments within observational science. For instance, the First and Second Laws of Thermodynamics are overarching observations and are applicable to every functioning process known to empirical science. The law of cause and effect must be considered in every attempt to analyze or hypothesize operational functions. Even the so-called "pure" sciences must take into account the impact these laws have on rational thought.

The Laws of the Universe

Although there are many facts that have been uncovered about how various processes work, there are two all-encompassing laws of how energy works that have been demonstrated to be true in every imaginable way throughout the known universe. They are called the First and Second Laws of Thermodynamics.

We have touched on them in previous chapters as they apply to design, basic science, the days of the creation week, and the story the fossils tell us. However, these fundamental laws pervade the universe in such a way that they provide a constant absolute for *all* science and *all* rational evaluation of how things work. They are so pervasive that they have never been demonstrated to be violated in any way—and any attempt to suggest that "somewhere out there" there must be another set of laws is nothing short of foolishness.

The First Law of Thermodynamics

Thermodynamics is a compound word made from two Greek words that mean "heat" and "energy." Essentially, all energy is some kind of heat, even though there are scientists who theorize there is some cold, dark energy around somewhere. But for all practical purposes, everything that we can observe is heat-related energy of some kind—thus, the laws of *thermodynamics*.

Sometimes the First Law is called the law of the conservation of energy. Essentially, scientists have proven that energy can neither be created nor destroyed. It can, however, be changed from one form to another. Looked at from another perspective, it can be depended on that our universe contains the same amount (quantity) of energy that it had at the beginning, but that energy can be (and frequently is) changed from one kind of energy to another.

We classify energy in two main types: kinetic and potential. Kinetic energy is energy in motion, like wind and moving water. Potential energy is energy that is stored, ready to become kinetic energy. Kinetic energy is sometimes subdivided into classifications that are obvious, like mechanical energy or electrical energy. Perhaps it is worth stating that what we normally call matter is energy "doing" certain processes over time. The atoms and molecules of which things are made are really energy in motion through time.

All of these various classifications and expressions of energy are subject to the First Law. Energy in any form is not currently being created. Whenever an event happens, energy from several sources may be involved, but nothing new is being generated.

Humanity can do some wonderful things with energy. We can change the way energy behaves, we can use energy for a wide variety of new processes, but we cannot create new energy. It is not even possible to destroy energy. We can store it (potential energy), we can move it around (kinetic energy), but we can neither create more of it nor get rid of any of it.

The implications of this First Law are very important. The universe could not have created itself. Energy cannot make more energy. That presents the biggest problem of all. Where or what or who created the energy that surrounds us? Present measures of energy are incredibly enormous, indicating a power source so great that *infinite* is the best word we have to describe it. Natural processes did not exist before the universe came into existence. Something beyond nature must have created all the energy and matter observed today. The logical conclusion is that a *super*natural Creator with infinite power created the universe. There is no natural energy source capable of originating what we observe.

The Second Law of Thermodynamics

There is less available energy today than there was yesterday. The reason this proven observation is called a law is because *every* time any work is done, some of the energy used to do the work becomes unavailable or unrecoverable.

The fact that energy becomes unrecoverable is referred to as *entropy*, a compound term from Greek words that mean "in-turning." The work process caused energy to "turn inward" (figure of speech) so that the heat of the energy downgrades to the point where it cannot be recovered. In the biggest system (our universe), everything that happens conforms to this Second Law. Stars grow dimmer. Galaxies become less organized. Orbits decay. Our sun is burning out. Things die!

Sooner or later, the universe will lose its heat. Fortunately for us, the temperature of the universe is not zero. It is moving that way each moment, but it is not there yet. At some prior time, all the energy in the universe was available. Energy must have been created at some finite time in the past. Otherwise, it would have died long ago. The logical conclusion is that an infinite Creator made the universe a finite time ago.

But here's an important point: The decay process (the entropy) applies to everything, not just to heat. It applies to all organized functions (atoms, molecules, chemicals, flowers, trees, rats, rabbits, even people!). As a matter of fact, the entropy principle applies to information as well (computers, airplanes, fire trucks, DNA). Everything in the entire universe is subject to the First and Second Laws of Thermodynamics.

The First Law insists that the universe could not have created itself.

> In the beginning God created the heavens and the earth (Genesis 1:1).

> Thus the heavens and the earth, and all the host of them, were finished (Genesis 2:1).

> For by Him all things were created that are in heaven and that are on earth, visible and invisible, whether thrones or dominions or principalities or powers. All things were created through Him and for Him (Colossians 1:16).

The Second Law insists that the universe is not eternal.

> While the earth remains, seedtime and harvest, cold and heat, winter and summer, and day and night shall not cease (Genesis 8:22).

> We know that the whole creation groans and labors with birth pangs together until now (Romans 8:22).

> He is before all things, and in Him all things consist (Colossians 1:17).

> But the heavens and the earth which are now preserved by the same word, are reserved for fire until the day of judgment and perdition of ungodly men (2 Peter 3:7).

The beginning was brought into existence by an all-powerful, all-knowing, transcendent Creator who created time, space, and mass-energy. That fits the absolutely proven First Law of Thermodynamics. The Second Law, which is also absolutely proven, is borne out by the clear principle of decay and degradation of all mass-energy.

The fact that the decay processes are slow (things do not always die quickly) is borne out by the clear promise and effort of that same Creator who is holding all things together by "the same word" that created them in the first place (2 Peter 3:7).

Actually, it is a wonderful thing: Our universe is very stable. The processes of physics, astronomy, chemistry, biology, and geology are dependable. We can rely on things working the same way time after time. That makes science possible!

The Tri-Universe

We *know* the universe could not create itself and processes are always increasing in entropy (everything is dying). But even though we know that, we do not like the implications of a Creator. If, indeed, He really exists—an omnipotent, omniscient, omnipresent God of the entire universe—then everything (and everyone) is subject to His laws and His judgment.

The TRI-UNE God
Manifested by and Analogous to His Creation

Father = SPACE	Son = MATTER	Spirit = TIME
Invisible	Visible	Sensed and Felt
Omnipresent	Tangible	Understood
Source	Present Reality	Future
God Framed	God Manifested	God Experienced
Authority	Declaration	Appropriation

Deuteronomy 6:4

Figure 10.4—The Tri-Une God

That is hard for many people to digest. The Bible addresses this problem:

> The wrath of God is revealed from heaven against all ungodliness and unrighteousness of men, who suppress the truth in unrighteousness, because what may be known of God is manifest in them, for God has shown it to them. For since the creation of the world His invisible attributes are clearly seen, being understood by the things that are made, even His eternal power and Godhead, so that they are without excuse, because, although they knew God, they did not glorify Him as God, nor were thankful, but became futile in their thoughts, and their foolish hearts were darkened. Professing to be wise, they became fools, and changed the glory of the incorruptible God into an image made like corruptible man—and birds and four-footed animals and creeping things. Therefore God also gave them up to uncleanness, in the lusts of their hearts, to dishonor their bodies among themselves, who exchanged the truth of God for the lie, and worshiped and served the creature rather than the Creator, who is blessed forever. Amen (Romans 1:18-25).

Secular scientists conduct their research on the presupposition that nothing exists beyond the natural world. They do not believe that an ultimate Cause exists. Scientists at the Institute for Creation Research hold to the presupposition that the uncaused First Cause is the Creator, who exists outside of the physical creation He made.

Time is not eternal but created. To ask what happened in time before time was created is to create a meaningless false paradox. There was no "before" prior to the creation of the triune universe of time, space, and mass-energy. Yet even more amazing (and the universe is amazing) is the historical fact that this Creator-God, after purposefully creating the space-time-matter universe, chose to enter it in the God-human person of Jesus Christ for the sole purpose of providing the means by which humanity could have a very real and personal relationship with the very God who created the universe (John 3:16).

The Triune God

The opening verse of the Bible indicates that the Creator God is "plural" in that the plural noun *Elohim* is used. Later, on the sixth day, Elohim says that "they" (the plural Godhead) should create a being in "our" image and likeness (Genesis 1:26). Yet Moses, in his instructions to Israel about their worship of God, insisted that "the LORD our God, the LORD is one!" (Deuteronomy 6:4). Centuries later, the scholar Paul noted that the design of the creation itself was sufficient evidence to show the "invisible" things of God, even His power and divine nature (Romans 1:20).

The prophet Isaiah foretold that the coming Messiah would be a "stem of Jesse, and a Branch," and that the "Spirit of the LORD shall rest upon Him" (Isaiah 11:1-2). Later, Isaiah said the Messiah would say of Himself that "the Lord GOD and His Spirit have sent Me" (Isaiah 48:16). Finally, in Luke 4:18-21, Jesus Himself would quote a famous passage in Isaiah speaking of the Messiah and apply the passage to Himself: "Today this Scripture is fulfilled in your hearing."

> The Spirit of the Lord GOD is upon Me, because the LORD has anointed Me to preach good tidings to the poor; He has sent Me to heal the brokenhearted, to proclaim liberty to the captives, and the opening of the prison to those who are bound; to proclaim the acceptable year of the LORD, and the day of vengeance of our God; to comfort all who mourn, to console those who mourn in Zion, to give them beauty for ashes, the oil of joy for mourning, the garment of praise for the spirit of heaviness; that they may be called trees of righteousness, the planting of the LORD, that He may be glorified (Isaiah 61:1-3).

These and many other biblical sections underscore the Bible doctrine of the triune God—one God revealed to us in three Persons: the heavenly Father, the Son, and the Spirit. The Old Testament tends to emphasize the role of *Yahweh*, most often translated by the English term "Lord." The promise of the Messiah—the coming Redeemer, who would be the Son of God—is also frequently emphasized.

According to the Bible, the Creator is none other than the one who is named in the Bible as Jesus of Nazareth. He is the Jewish Messiah who was promised from the very beginning of the world as the Redeemer who would come to resolve the supernatural conflict between the God of the universe and the human race that had rejected His authority right at the very start of everything.

> In the beginning was the Word, and the Word was with God, and the Word was God. He was in the beginning with God. All things were made through Him, and without Him nothing was made that was made...And the Word became flesh and dwelt among us, and we beheld His glory, the glory as of the only begotten of the Father, full of grace and truth (John 1:1-3, 14).

God is the infinite, invisible, omnipresent Father, but He is also the Son who is visible, touchable, yet the perfectly holy Word who is always revealing and manifesting the Father. And He is also the Holy Spirit, always present to guide, convict, and comfort. He is the very real, eternal, invisible, omnipresent Father of all, yet visible and approachable by the Son and experienced and understood through the Holy Spirit. A majestic mystery but a wonderful reality! Three divine Persons, each equally and totally God.

As the Scripture declares, God does not change from one "person" into another over time, nor are there three independent but coequal persons, but rather a coequal, coterminus, coexistent Being. That is, they are indeed equal in power and status (none is "over" the other), they are always inseparable from one another, and they have existed with each other from and during all eternity. We are given insight into the relationship they share with each other by the titles that are most often used in the Bible when speaking about them individually.

Space-Time-Matter—Our Universe

We cannot adequately comprehend this reality with our finite minds, but we are compelled to acknowledge it, believe it, and rejoice. This reality of God's triune nature is somewhat analogous to the space of God's created universe. Space is comprised of three dimensions (length, width, height), each of which permeates all space. This structure helps illustrate the nature of the triune God. God is one God, not three gods, yet revealed as three Persons, each of which is eternally and completely God: "His invisible attributes are clearly seen, being understood by the things that are made, even His eternal power and Godhead" (Romans 1:20).

The "things" God made are nothing more or less than our universe. That created reality is the only valid illustration of the triunity that expresses the nature of our Creator. Other illustrations have been put forward by theologians and philosophers, but none of them are true trinities. Here are the most common examples.

NOT a Good Illustration for Trinity
 **Three states of matter**—liquid, solid, gas. The most common example used is the water molecule. Its normal state is liquid. Heat it enough and it will become a gas. Take heat away and it will become a solid. Three *different* conditions, but each condition exists only if the other two do not. In other words, water can change from one form into another but cannot be all three forms at the same time. It is a triad, not a trinity.
 **An egg.** This illustration is frequently used and often appears in various religious symbols because it is composed of three parts: the shell, the albumin, and the yolk. One thing, three parts. Yet, again, it is entirely possible to separate these parts, something often done for cooking. Crack and remove the shell, drain away the albumin to use for meringue, and use the yolk for an omelet. Again, it is a triad, not a trinity.
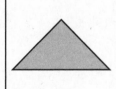 **A triangle.** This is quite often seen in religious symbols to represent the triune Godhead, but this symbol is easily shaped, destroyed, or disfigured—all at the whim of man. The triune Godhead *never* changes. "I am the LORD, I do not change" (Malachi 3:6). "Jesus Christ is the same yesterday, today, and forever" (Hebrews 13:8). "Every good gift and every perfect gift is from above, and comes down from the Father of lights, with whom there is no variation or shadow of turning" (James 1:17).

Figure 10.5—Incorrect Illustrations for Trinity

God's illustration of Himself is in the universe that He created! Space is both invisible and at the same time the matrix in which all of our reality exists. This space in which our universe exists is analogous to the heavenly Father. "No one has seen God at any time" (1 John 4:12). "For in Him we live and move and have our being" (Acts 17:28). God the Father is spirit, and "true worshipers will worship the Father in spirit and truth" (John 4:23). Christian doctrine has always insisted there is only one God (Deuteronomy 6:4), but that Creator God manifests Himself in three Persons: the Father, the Son, and the Holy Spirit.

Matter (mass-energy) is the visible and tangible revelation of the existence of space. We "see" space by means of the visible phenomena of energy arranged in molecular structures that are functioning, predictably, over time as matter that we can see, feel, and use. Just so, God the Son is the Word (John 1:14) who makes it possible for us to "see" God. The introduction of the title role for the Son of God is "the Word"—that which can be communicated. John introduces the Lord Jesus by this title when he declares:

> In the beginning was the Word, and the Word was with God, and the Word was God. He was in the beginning with God. All things were made through Him, and without Him nothing was made that was made (John 1:1-3).

This Word was and is the Creator, existing from all eternity past as God in every sense that the Bible speaks about God. But, for a very few Earth years (about 33), this Creator-God willingly emptied Himself of His position, power, and privileges so that He could become a human being just like the rest of us (Philippians 2:5-8). Thus:

> The Word became flesh and dwelt among us, and we beheld His glory, the glory as of the only begotten of the Father, full of grace and truth (John 1:14).

Just so, the Lord Jesus Christ, while He was on Earth, was completely human and "was in all points tempted like as we are, yet without sin" (Hebrews 4:15). In fact, He was so human that His disciples had a difficult time thinking of Him as the Word in flesh. On one occasion, Philip asked the Lord Jesus to "show us the Father, and it is sufficient for us" (John 14:8). I can almost hear the Lord Jesus sigh as He said to Philip: "Have I been with you so long, and yet you have not known Me, Philip? He who has seen Me has seen the Father; so how can you say, 'Show us the Father'? Do you not believe that I am in the Father, and the Father in Me?" (John 14:9-10).

Just as space is the only valid illustration of the heavenly Father, so matter (mass-energy) is the only valid illustration of God the Son. Just as matter reveals and helps us visualize space, so the Lord Jesus Christ, God the Son, reveals and helps us visualize God the Father. And just as matter (mass-energy) is "in" space, occupies space, and cannot be taken out of space, so God the Son is in the Father and the Father in God the Son. That is precisely why the Bible teaches that Jesus Christ is "all the fullness of the Godhead bodily" (Colossians 2:9).

Time is the means by which we experience our reality. Matter is really mass-energy operating in a very specific way through and during time. Were there no time, nothing would function—nothing would happen. Time is the "thing" that makes our reality real! Without time, there would be no beginning. Without time, there would be no present, past, or future.

Time is, beyond doubt, the most mysterious aspect of our universe. Lots of effort has been spent attempting to understand what time is or where it comes from. But about the best we can do is suggest that the source of time is the future, flowing through the present and into the past. Obviously, we live in the present, we have memories and see results of past occurrences, but the future is merely a hope or a dream or a vision of what might be. Movies about time machines notwithstanding, no one has ever gone back into the past or leaped forward into the future. Time, as far as our actual experience is concerned, exists in the present.

For example, I have an intellectual awareness of the concept of space. I speak of it in terms of height, width, and length. I know my body occupies space and that the various elements of my life (house, workplace, tools, friends, etc.) occupy their own position in space. Whenever I need or want to experience any of that, I must involve time and space. If I want to give my wife a hug or a friend a handshake, I must take my "mass-energy" (my body) across the space that separates us and experience the hug or the handshake. That simple event requires time. I must use time to cross the space between us. I must use time to move my body. I may see the other person in space, but until I use time to cross the space that separates us, I will never "experience" them.

Just so, the Holy Spirit is the "time" of the triune Godhead. It is He who brings about the experience of a relationship with God. The Holy Spirit is the One who brings conviction about the need for truth (John 16:8). It is the Holy Spirit who actually executes the creation of the new birth (1 Corinthians 6:11; 2 Corinthians 5:17; Ephesians 4:24). The Holy Spirit is the One who imparts the spiritual gifts of God to the believers (1 Corinthians 12:7). Indeed, the Holy Spirit is the One who guides into truth (John 16:13). And just like time, all we ever "see" or "sense" about the Holy Spirit is the *result* of what has been done.

> The wind blows where it wishes, and you hear the sound of it, but
> cannot tell where it comes from and where it goes. So is everyone
> who is born of the Spirit (John 3:8).

The physical universe is, in a very real sense, a trinity of trinities. Also, in a certain sense, human life is a trinity of body, soul, and spirit. In fact, triunity in various ways is often seen in the creation. Although no man could ever model the Godhead, God has "clearly" done this in His creation (Romans 1:20).

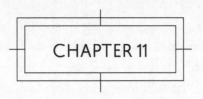

The Unique Earth

The last chapter looked at the wonder of the universe. Even a child can be filled with awe and joy at seeing the stars at night. Where did the power to put them there come from? Billions of galaxies fill the universe, consisting of billions of stars placed together in concentrated and organized groups. The amount of energy contained and displayed in the heavens is absolutely overwhelming. It's difficult to grasp the significance of what was done when the stars were put in place. The psalmist simply states: "By the word of the LORD the heavens were made, and all the host of them by the breath of His mouth" (Psalm 33:6).

Not only did God "breathe" out the heavens, He put them together in such a marvelous way that the entire universe speaks to us every day and night. There is a language in the majesty and order of the creation that continually tells us about the Creator Himself (Psalm 19:1-3; Romans 1:20). Most of what we see and hear is within our own solar system. That's what this chapter is about—the special home we call Earth and the specific ways God designed it for us.

Let's take a few minutes to tour our place in the universe.

Perfect Location

Abundant evidence of God's wisdom and provision can be found within our own galaxy. The spiraling arms and center of the Milky Way contain many stars set close together, giving it a characteristic brightness. Unlike many other galaxies, the Milky Way contains just the right balance of stars and planets needed to support life on Earth. Most stars are located in places with too much harmful energy for life. But our solar system is situated within the Milky Way in a position that is far enough from the central region to escape the immense radiation from the stars concentrated there.

Figure 11.1—Blue Marble Earth

Our solar system is located about two-thirds of the way out toward the edge of the Milky Way, where we are less likely to suffer collisions with other stars. Most of the stars in our galaxy are within the larger spiral arms or in the center. If our solar system were placed near the center of the Milky Way, we could not observe farther than a few light-years into the rest of the universe. The lower radiation in our vicinity gives us a clearer window to observe and study the rest of the universe and our own galaxy much better.

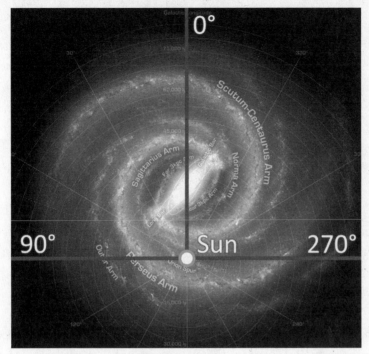

Figure 11.2—Solar System in the Milky Way

Unique in the Solar System

As far as science has discovered, planet Earth is unique in the entire universe. Certainly this is true in our own solar system. Nothing we have observed leads us to believe that there is any other planet like Earth. A brief survey of our neighboring planets reveals many contrasts. Mercury is the closest planet to the sun. It gets very hot on the sun-facing side and very cold on the other. It has a very slow spin. The side facing the sun is heated to 800 degrees Fahrenheit, while the side away from the sun is cooled to –298 degrees Fahrenheit.

The next planet, Venus, is similar to Earth in that it's about the same size and seems to be within a range from the sun that could allow it to be habitable. Many had hoped that Venus would turn out to be a lush, tropical world that might host exotic life. Yet once we finally got a spacecraft to fly by and drop probes onto the surface, we found it to be profoundly different than anticipated.

Venus is hotter than Mercury, though farther away from the sun. It has an atmosphere 90 times thicker than Earth's. Heat is trapped in clouds and heats the entire planet to 931 degrees Fahrenheit. It has a nasty atmosphere with supersonic winds. There's a mountain that's higher than Everest, volcanic flows that look like pancakes, and about a thousand craters. These craters, mountains, and volcanic features all appear to be the same age. That creates a real problem for planetary scientists who believe in long ages. Essentially, they have been forced to infer that the first 90 percent of the planet's evolutionary history is missing!

Mars is like Earth in many ways. A day on Mars is 24.7 hours. It is tilted 25 degrees, just two more degrees than Earth. At its warmest, it can get to be a comfortable 67 degrees Fahrenheit, but it gets very cold at night. It has two small moons. But Mars is smaller than Earth. Its gravity is only a third of Earth's. Unlike Earth, it has no atmosphere to speak of and no global magnetic field. What atmosphere it has is made of gases we cannot breathe.

Without much of an atmosphere, many meteoroids hit Mars. Everything that crashes onto Mars creates a shower of secondary particles that causes even more damage. Mars would be a dangerous place to take an evening walk. Also, since there is no liquid water on Mars, the dust devils generated by the space debris wander around the ultra-dry surface of Mars, blanketing the soil with toxic chemicals and charging the dust with static electricity. Delightful.

Jupiter is the largest planet in our solar system. It is 10 times smaller than the sun and 10 times larger than the earth. Jupiter spins faster than any other planet, with a day of 9 hours and 55.5 minutes. Its fast spin causes tremendous storms. The big red spot on Jupiter is actually a huge hurricane.

Saturn is the second-largest planet and has the largest set of rings. It is almost twice as far away from the sun as Jupiter. Saturn is a gas giant. As one descends into the atmosphere, the pressure, temperature, and gravity greatly increase. The core of the planet is boiling hot and radiates more heat out into space than it receives from the sun.

Uranus is tilted on its side with its axis pointed at the sun. If the earth's axis were pointed at the sun, one hemisphere would always be boiling hot and the other would be freezing cold. Uranus is four times as far from the sun as Jupiter and twice as far from the sun as Saturn.

Neptune is the farthest gas giant from the sun. It is almost four times larger than the earth. Its strong gravity traps harmful gases in its atmosphere. And then there's poor little Pluto, a dwarf planet. The *New Horizons* probe has given us absolutely stunning pictures of this intriguing little world—but it is absolutely void of anything living!

Every planet in our solar system proves Earth to be specially created for life. Yet even here most places are too hot, too cold, too far underground, or too far above ground to support much life. In the many thousands of miles of changing environments from the center of the earth to the edge of its atmosphere, there are only a few meters of habitable environment for most life forms, and therefore almost all creatures are forced to live there. Although in our solar system only the earth was made to be inhabited (Isaiah 45:18), even here only a thin slice is ideally suited for the majority of living things, including those we are most familiar with, such as mammals, birds, and reptiles.

This narrow section, though, is teeming with life. It is estimated that an acre of typical farm soil, six inches deep, has several tons of living bacteria, almost a ton of fungi, 200 pounds of one-cell protozoan animals, about 100 pounds of yeast, and the same amount of algae.

The Sun and Moon

Everyone can appreciate the sun's power. The sun lights our days so we can see nature all around us. The energy that is useful to life is a very small part of the kinds of energies that radiate from the sun. The visible portion of that energy enables human sight and is the best energy for the chemical reactions of life. It also powers plant growth, which is the foundation of almost all food chains on Earth. Even the energetic behavior of little bugs ultimately depends on the sun's power.

Of all the energy the sun gives off, only 0.45 billionth of its daily output strikes the earth. The sun provides the earth with energy estimated at over 239 trillion horsepower, about 35,000 horsepower for each resident.

Our sun belongs to a spectral class representing only five percent of all stars, a G2V yellow dwarf main sequence variable. That designation may be technical, but it emphasizes why our sun is so special. Many other stars in this class pulsate much more radically than the sun, giving off deadly flares. But the energy of the magnetic storms on our sun escapes between the granules instead of heating the photosphere. As a result, our sun's heat output, its solar constant, only varied by 6/100th of a percent during the entire observational period of 1974–2006.

Our sun is uncommonly stable.

The sun is a star among countless others, but in many respects it stands alone. It is the perfect lighthouse for the one planet we know harbors life. Rejoicing like "a strong man to run its race," it journeys across our sky each day, radiating its life-sustaining energy and declaring the glory of God (Psalm 19:1-6).

The earth's moon protects us from many of the rocks that cross our planet's path. The craters across the moon's surface demonstrate the number of times something has collided with the moon instead of with Earth. The moon's South Pole—Aitken basin—is the largest-known crater in our solar system, 8 miles deep and about 1500 miles across. The earth's moon is unusually large, serving as a stabilizing anchor for our planet. It prevents Earth from tilting too far from the gravitational attraction of the sun or Jupiter.

If the moon were much larger or nearer to the earth, the huge tides that would result would overflow onto the lowlands and erode the mountains. If the continents were leveled, it is estimated that water would cover the entire surface to the depth of more than a mile! If the earth was not tilted 23 degrees on its axis but rather was on a 90-degree angle in reference to the sun, we would not have four seasons.

Without seasons, life would soon not exist on Earth. The poles would lie in eternal twilight, and water vapor from the oceans would be carried north and south by the wind, freezing when it moved close enough to the poles. In time, huge continents of snow and ice would pile up in the polar regions, leaving most of the earth a dry desert. The oceans would eventually disappear, and rainfall would cease. The accumulated weight of ice at the poles would cause the equator to bulge, and, as a result, the earth's rotation would drastically change.

Just a "little" change (in the perspective of the universe) would render the earth unsuitable to support life.

We are protected by how our solar system was created. The sun and the moon were obviously designed to rule the daytime and the nighttime (Genesis 1:16), and their role in "telling" us about God is fairly easy to see if we are not blinded by an insistence on the unprovable position that "there is no God" (Psalm 14:1).

Unique Planet

Secularists like to consider Earth as just one among many millions of planets, occupying an obscure place in an insignificant galaxy in a sea of nothingness. The Bible teaches, however, that Earth is very special to the Creator, performing a crucial role in the universe today and playing an unending role in the cosmic saga.

Earth is the only planet circling our sun on which life as we know it could (and does) exist. Other known planets are either gas balls or are covered with lifeless soil or frozen chemicals. Unlike other planets, ours is covered with green vegetation, enormous blue-green oceans containing more than a million islands, hundreds of thousands of streams and rivers, huge land masses, mountains, ice caps, and deserts that provide a spectacular variety of color and texture. Some form of life is found in virtually every ecological niche on the earth's surface. Even in the extremely cold Antarctica, hardy microscopic organisms thrive in ponds, tiny wingless insects live in patches of moss and lichen, and plants grow and flower yearly. From the apex of the atmosphere to the bottom of the oceans, from the coldest part of the poles to the warmest part of the equator, life thrives here. To this day, no evidence of life has been found on any other planet.

The earth is immense in size, about 8000 miles in diameter, with a mass calculated at roughly 6.6×1021 tons. It is on average 93 million miles from the sun. If the earth traveled much faster in its 584-million-mile journey around the sun, its orbit would become larger and it would move farther away from the sun. If it moved too far from this narrow habitable zone, all life would cease to exist. If it traveled slightly slower in its orbit, the earth would move closer to the sun, and if it moved too close, all life would likewise perish. The earth's

365-day, 6-hour, 49-minute, and 9.54-second trip around the sun (the sidereal year) is consistent to more than a thousandth of a second!

The chances of a planet being just the right size, the proper distance away from the right star, etc., are extremely minute, even if many stars have planets circling them, as some speculate. The mathematical odds that all of these and other essential conditions happened by chance are astronomical—something like billions to one!

The Water Planet

Figure 11.3— Pacific Ocean. Over 70 percent of the earth's surface is water. It acts as a temperature regulator, absorbing heat during the day and releasing it at night.

Precision of design can be detected in even the most commonplace substances, like water. Our planet is close enough to the sun to provide the liquid water necessary for life. But if it were just a little farther away, that water would become ice. Or if a little closer, the "just so" liquid state would turn into steam. Our physical bodies are mostly water. Imagine what would happen if our planet's place in the solar system were switched with Mars or Mercury!

While water itself is a very small molecule (just a three-atom unit of hydrogen and oxygen), it is a primary ingredient of our planet. God's design of how water's specific molecules behave—and the impact water has on our entire planet—is an example of God's creative design and custodial presence on the smallest and largest of scales.

In contrast to virtually all other materials—the rare exceptions include rubber and antimony—water contracts when cooled only until it reaches roughly 39 degrees Fahrenheit. Then, amazingly, it suddenly begins to expand until it freezes. Because of this rather unusual anomaly, the ice that forms in seas, oceans, and lakes stays near the surface. That's where the sun can heat it during the day and the warm water below melts it in the summer. That helps keep the large water bodies in liquid form. If ice did not float on the surface of water, the floors of the oceans and lakes would be covered with glaciers of ice that would never melt. Surface ice also helps regulate the climate by reflecting energy.

As a liquid, water's temperature range is perfect for cycling water from the oceans to the land. Water requires a lot of energy to evaporate into a vapor, and it releases this energy when it condenses back into liquid. This hydrological cycle balances temperatures in the earth's climate, as well as inside living cells. If less energy were required for evaporation, then streams, rivers, and lakes would evaporate away quickly.

Liquid water is necessary for life processes on Earth and explains why the planet is so fertile. The earth is the only known planet with huge bodies of water. Seventy percent of its surface area consists of oceans, lakes, and seas surrounding large land masses. Some of the planets we have been able to study contain water in some form. None have liquid water, although a few may have contained liquid water in the past, as evidenced by erosional features. Even though there is internal heat in many of these planets and moons, the water they have is either in a mixture of gases or trapped in huge ice masses that are absolutely nonlife supporting.

Water is unique in that it can absorb enormous amounts of heat without a large alteration in its temperature. Its heat absorption level is about ten times as great as steel. During the day, the earth's bodies of water rapidly soak up the sun's warmth; thus, the earth stays fairly cool. At night, they release the vast amounts of heat they absorbed during the day, which, combined with atmospheric effects, keeps most of the surface from freezing solid at night. If it were not for the tremendous amounts of water on Earth, temperature variations would be far greater each day and night. The large oceans on Earth are necessary for life to exist here.

Another unusual design element called the *Coriolis effect* produces ocean currents. Essentially, our planet is spinning (rotating) all the time. That spin generates a force that pushes perpendicular to the direction of motion and to the axis of rotation. This force makes the motion of the ocean currents go toward the right north of the equator and toward the left in the south. That, along with the unique properties of water, ensures that most of the ocean stays in a liquid form, allowing the innumerable water creatures to live and thrive.

Some random happening, right?

Clouds function as Earth's curtains, helping to balance the temperature. They block the sun when the temperature becomes too hot and let the sunlight in when it becomes too cold. When the earth is hot, more water evaporates from the oceans and turns into clouds. These clouds reflect more energy and the earth cools. As the earth cools, clouds cool and condense into rain and snow. With fewer clouds, less energy is reflected. The energy reaches the earth and warms it. The earth has the most diverse collection of reflecting and absorbing surfaces in our solar system.

This is one more stunning demonstration that the "LORD by wisdom founded the earth; by understanding He established the heavens" (Proverbs 3:19). The unique features of water, all working together to form the properties of this most basic of life-supporting compounds, cannot justly be called coincidences or random accumulations. Water was created for our planet and for our life.

The Miracle of Air

Most of us never give a second thought to the air we breathe. It is just here, and we breathe in and out without anticipation of any problems—until we can't get enough of it for some reason. Swallow a bit of water down the wrong pipe, and air becomes really important.

Air is a mixture of gases, some of which are not very good for us on their own. But the mixture we normally breathe is close to perfect for life. If it were much different, life would cease to exist on Earth. For instance, if the oxygen in the atmosphere were 17 percent instead of 21 percent, or there were too little carbon dioxide, we would die. If the atmospheric pressure were much higher or lower, nothing would work like it currently does. Air is really a miracle of precision and design.

The air close to the earth's surface is heated by light energy from the sun. After the air is warmed, it becomes less dense (expands) and floats upward. That feature enables the air near the earth's surface to maintain a temperature range suitable for life to exist. On the other hand, if air reacted in the opposite way when heated, if it contracted rather than expanded and became denser, the temperature on Earth's surface would become unbearable and most life could not survive for very long. If that opposite condition really were the case, the temperature a few hundred feet above the surface would be extremely cold, and people and animals living in the mountains would die. The only habitable region would be a thin slice of air on the surface.

But even in that tiny slice of atmosphere, the plants and trees necessary to support life could not survive. They would be in the cold zone. Birds would have no resting place, food, water, or oxygen. If our air worked differently than it actually does, nothing would live—or, from the evolutionary perspective, nothing would have come to life in the first place. However, because God designed our air specifically for this planet, life can exist here.

But that's not all.

The movement of warm air rising upward from the surface creates air currents (wind) that carry away carbon dioxide from areas that produce more of it, such as cities and volcanoes, and move oxygen to the large urban population centers. Considering the way the atmosphere maintains a relatively uniform temperature, whether there is a cooling or a warming tendency, it seems like the atmosphere has a built-in thermostat to maintain thermal equilibrium. Amazing. One would think there was an engineering design that had anticipated the need for cleaning out pockets of "bad" air and bringing in "good" air.

Sometimes the intricacy of God's design escapes all but the scientists who study the specifics of our atmosphere. The Creator really did have in mind the balancing of atmospheric chemicals when He made microbes. Bacteria and fungi are required for such vital processes as the nitrogen and carbon cycles. Using cleverly crafted biological machinery, microbes can break triple and double bonds on certain chemicals so that these very specific chemicals can be converted into other absolutely necessary chemicals. This very precise process works dynamically with plants and animals to regulate methane, ethane, and carbon dioxide levels around the planet with ceaseless and seamless vigilance.

Some will no doubt ask why we should care about this rather invisible activity. Well, whoever cares about staying alive should pay very careful attention!

The main component of Earth's atmosphere is molecular nitrogen. Fortunately for all land life, when two nitrogen atoms bond together, they become a gas at Earth surface temperatures, which render them inert. Inert is good. Inert means that the atoms will not react with the tissues of our bodies. Oxygen reacts much more readily, which means that too much oxygen will severely damage our lung tissues—which is one of the reasons that doctors are really careful not to prescribe breathing pure oxygen too long. It seems that the oxygen in our atmosphere is kept at a very breathable (and unharmful) level just about all over the planet.

And then there is carbon dioxide, which is formed in the atmosphere as nitrogen bumps into radiation from the sun. That wonderful process provides just about the right amount for plants to use in their photosynthesis function to produce just enough oxygen along with the atmospheric oxygen for lung-breathing creatures to use. Then we pump out carbon dioxide when we exhale, which the plants use and recycle. Of course, if carbon dioxide levels dropped, plants would have a decreasing source of carbon with which to make our food. Too much carbon dioxide becomes toxic. Microbes found in Earth's soils and oceans maintain just the right gases in just the right proportions for life. Cool, huh?

God deserves the credit for this—not eons of random atoms bouncing around hoping for something to happen.

God even foresaw the problem of space debris that peppers our planet constantly. If our atmosphere were much thinner, many of the millions of meteors that now burn up would crash on the earth's surface. Those rocks from space would cause death, destruction, and fires. It seems like our planet was designed with a rather effective shield that eliminates just about anything that might injure us. How could this precise protection come about through random processes?

Those who insist on an explanation that excludes God in their thinking will always be perplexed at what they discover. In the meantime, step outside underneath the gentle sun, breathe the sweet air, and thank God for His "wonderful works to the children of men" (Psalm 107:8).

The Speech of the Day, the Knowledge of the Night

The day-to-day faithfulness of constant stability and dependable processes is a speech without words that testifies to God's care and provision. What may often be overlooked by the "day unto day" routine (Psalm 19:1-2) of our existence is that the very dependability of each day's processes is a wonderful testimony to the design, purposes, and faithfulness of the Creator. The whole core of evolutionary naturalism is randomness—an unknowable, undependable chaos and disorder. The universe, on the other hand, is very stable!

- The sun rises in the east and sets in the west— always.

- The earth turns on its axis and cycles through its day at the same speed every time—always.

- The dependable clockwork precision of the tides regulates much of our life—always.

- The seasons come and go, planting and harvesting follow each other dependably, life is conceived and born with regularity—always.

Figure 11.4—The Universe Is Stable

After the awful judgment of the great Flood of Noah's day, God gave a solemn promise to Noah, and through him to all living creatures. With that promise, God placed in effect the same creative power that brought the universe into existence (Colossians 1:17), but He now focuses His grace and mercy on keeping the universe stable until He finalizes His plans for eternity (2 Peter 3:7).

> The LORD said in His heart, "I will never again curse the ground
> for man's sake, although the imagination of man's heart is evil
> from his youth; nor will I again destroy every living thing as I
> have done. While the earth remains, seedtime and harvest, cold
> and heat, winter and summer, and day and night shall not cease"
> (Genesis 8:21-22).

This wordless language is easily read by all humanity and openly declares that God is awesomely omnipotent and omniscient, and at the same time lovingly compassionate and faithful. All living creatures depend on it.

God's Protection

Life is fragile, yet the protection of life can be seen in the careful design of our physical environment. Our bodies need many forms of protection from exotic dangers such as rocks falling from space to mundane considerations such as temperature control.

If our earth had a thinner atmosphere, our planet would be hit with lethal amounts of incoming rocks and harmful radiation. Mercury, Pluto, and the moon have almost no air at all. Their surfaces are scarred with craters from the impacts of giant boulders, little pebbles, and small grains of sand. The surfaces of these planets are very hot when facing the sun, and very cold when facing away. If earth had a thicker atmosphere, our planet would be boiling hot. The weight of the atmosphere on Venus and the "gas giant" planets (Jupiter, Saturn, Uranus, and Neptune) is very heavy.

Earth has just the right mixture of nitrogen and oxygen in its atmosphere. Venus and the gas giants have the wrong kinds of gases for humans (or any other life forms) to survive there. Venus's atmosphere is mostly carbon dioxide. The gas giants are mostly hydrogen and helium. The other planets have little or no "air" at all. Truly, the very air we breathe is an invisible yet universal witness to God's protective providence.

Even though we can see through it, our atmosphere acts as a filter. It allows in the sun's radiation that is useful to life and at the same time mostly blocks the radiation that is harmful to life. Only a fraction of the radio waves and some of the visible light and infrared radiations are blocked, but almost all of the harmful ultraviolet rays, x-rays, and gamma rays never reach us.

We have been given an atmosphere that protects us. It provides just the right amount of air and warmth. It allows the sunlight to reach the plants that feed us. Our transparent atmosphere not only protects us, it allows us to the see the stars and wonders of the heavens. The question is: Are these marvelous devices merely accidents, or are they evidence of incredible design by a Creator?

The list is endless. God has provided overwhelming evidence of His care in the design of our universe, our earth, all living things—but especially humans. Everywhere and everything bears the fingerprints of an omniscient Designer who loves and cares for His creation.

God's Provision

Our sun has been placed at the perfect location within our galaxy, and our planet has been placed at the perfect location within our solar system. Our planet was created to protect the life that God placed here. Even the atmosphere and oceans of our planet have been carefully designed to provide the right amount of energy and fresh water.

The provision of every good thing in nature needful or useful for humans or other creatures comes from our Creator. God provides everything we require. Consider this: Why does the earth provide edible food in the first place? If the planting and harvesting of crops were not so commonplace, we would (or should) regard the growing cycles of corn, beans, fruit trees, potatoes, or any other plant as amazing miracles.

The sun's energy warms our planet. Hot air blows from areas heated by the sun to cooler areas. The sun's energy brings rain. Water evaporates from the ocean and falls to the land as it cools. The sun powers the winds that move the water vapor to the land. The sun's energy renews the air. With that energy, plants convert carbon dioxide into oxygen. The sun's energy grows food. Plants capture sunlight and store it in sugar, starch, and fat.

Figure 11.5—Wheat

Bread in one form or another is often the most basic form of food in many human societies, past or present, so much so that it is often called "the staff of life." Old, dried cakes of bread have even been found in a number of ancient archaeological sites. That ordinary food, so common throughout the world, has been made from many different kinds of grain. The wheat or barley or other grain is first ground into flour, then mixed with water, then baked into cakes or loaves. Other ingredients are often added to produce different varieties, but each type of bread almost inevitably becomes the most essential foodstuff of that society.

There was one special time when God's chosen people had to live in a hostile desert environment for 40 years and could neither plant grain nor produce bread. In answer to their prayers, however, God "satisfied them with the bread of heaven" (Psalm 105:40). That refers to the wonderful manna that miraculously appeared on the ground each day in the wilderness. It was actually called "the bread of heaven" and "angels' food" (Psalm 78:24-25).

Whether a unique provision like manna or an ordinary provision through the growth of the grain that we take for granted, God provides it all, "for He makes His sun rise on the evil and on the good, and sends rain on the just and on the unjust" (Matthew 5:45).

Because God's wisdom is displayed in the universe, and also in our human ability to comprehend that universe, we owe our great Creator-God an ongoing debt of creaturely thanksgiving. The cause of our universe coming into being and of its continuing to operate as it does is a dynamic display of the Creator's wisdom, some of which we can discover and understand. The unfathomable amount of applied knowledge (wisdom) that was used to invent the universe and to preprogram its interactive workings is a source of wonder beyond the imagination.

If we choose to believe we are the product of chance and random processes (evolution), where man is perhaps merely the highest order of animal, then we will possess a materialistic and relativistic philosophy. On the other hand, if we choose to believe that our brain was created by a Master Intelligence, then we will have a theological worldview, one that should prompt us to use our minds to understand His purpose for His creation, as well as the workings of the marvelous universe He has provided for us.

This was, after all, the conclusion of no less than Johann Kepler, a creationist and arguably one of the greatest scientists, who described the practice of science as "thinking God's thoughts after Him."

We live in a time when knowledge of the heavens is expanding rapidly. This knowledge should lead us to praise God for His amazing provision and protection. The cause of the laws of nature is not found in nature, but beyond nature. If left to chance, it is unlikely that any place in the universe could support life. God created our planet for life to thrive. As we learn how special our planet is within the entire universe, we learn of our Creator's faithfulness to us.

CHAPTER 12

The Big Picture

O f all the Bible's teachings, perhaps none is more controversial than the account contained in the early chapters of Genesis. Most major religions of the world acknowledge some sort of god or Great Spirit who was responsible for the beginning of things. The majority of them recognize that "good" is better than "bad"—and even acknowledge some form of evil, usually perceived as a force existing in a dualistic war with good. Most political systems are organized around codes of laws that are remarkably similar to the Bible's Ten Commandments.

During the past three centuries, however, academia has become more and more atheistic, insisting that science has eliminated the need for any kind of supernatural answer to creation. The concept of a personal god has been relegated to myth or psychological need, and the universities of the major countries of the world have become secular rather than religious—even though Europe and the United States still speak of "God blessing" our respective lands.

For all practical purposes, the idea that an omnipotent, omniscient, transcendent Creator brought everything into existence by His own power and under His own authority and for His own purposes is derided and dismissed as utter nonsense. Mankind is nothing more than a highly evolved derivative of some apelike creature, having developed over millions of years somewhere in the southern portion of the continent of Africa. That there has been a recent planetwide flood, designed by a holy Creator to rid the planet of a human population gone corrupt and violent, is laughed into the smallest corners of supposedly uneducated evangelical churches.

The Bible takes note of this very condition.

> Scoffers will come in the last days, walking according to their own lusts, and saying, "Where is the promise of His coming? For since the fathers fell asleep, all things continue as they were from the beginning of creation." For this they willfully forget: that by the word of God the heavens were of old, and the earth standing out of water and in the water, by which the world that then existed perished, being flooded with water. But the heavens and the earth which are now preserved by the same word, are reserved for fire until the day of judgment and perdition of ungodly men (2 Peter 3:3-7).

Please note several key points the Bible makes about these scoffers and the things they deny:

- Their basic philosophy is based on a denial of any kind of miraculous event.
- Their "proof" is that everything is always the same as it has always been.
- They "willfully forget" several demonstrable issues.
- The initial universe was created "by the word of God."
- The initial world was different, "standing out of water and in the water."
- The initial world was destroyed by "being flooded with water."
- The present world is "preserved by the same word."
- The present world will be judged and purged by fire of "ungodly men."

The past chapters have provided a general review of the enormous amount of evidence verifying the creation of our universe by an omnipotent, omniscient Designer. The evidence for design is overwhelming. The staggering data supporting the creation of life, purpose, and order are everywhere. The basic laws of science itself, proven hundreds of times in every conceivable way, have demonstrated that the universe could not create itself and it is not irrationally old. Indeed, there is evidence that any and all thinking people would recognize—unless they are willing to deliberately forget that evidence.

These facts have long been known to secular proponents of evolutionary naturalism. Any number of quotes from evolutionary scientists could be provided to prove that point, but there really is no need since the Lord Jesus Christ Himself insisted there was sufficient evidence in Scripture to demonstrate the truth of its pages. After openly healing and demonstrating His power to create, not merely amaze with tricks or "magic," Jesus said: "If they do not hear Moses and the prophets, neither will they be persuaded though one rise from the dead" (Luke 16:31).

We are faced with a choice between philosophies, a preference toward one presuppositional belief system over another. One is in diametrical opposition to the revealed text of Scripture. Any method that uses the cruel, inefficient, wasteful, death-filled processes of the random, purposeless mechanisms of naturalistic evolution contrasts radically with the God described in the pages of the Bible. In spite of this, some attempt to harmonize the two worldviews. Amazingly, it is Christian scholars who are the most prone to try blending the two systems of thought, though none of their efforts are satisfactory.

We must either resolve the conflict or reject one of the two opposing views.

Authentic Text

The Bible's text proclaims that it was overseen ("inspired") by God in a way that used selected humans to write its original words (2 Timothy 3:16-17; 2 Peter 1:21). That supernatural process resulted in the recording of the precise information God intended for us to know about Himself and about ourselves (Deuteronomy 29:29; 2 Peter 1:3). God also providentially ensured that this "Book of books" was satisfactorily transmitted and reproduced (Psalm 138:2; Matthew 24:35).

Many powerful men over the centuries have tried to discredit or destroy the Bible. All have failed. There is more evidence for the authenticity and accuracy of the Scriptures than for any other ancient book. No one who has studied these issues doubts the genuineness of the Bible. Many, however, reject its message.

New Testament Manuscripts

There are more hand-copied manuscripts of the Bible in existence than for any other literature of antiquity. The New Testament was written in the first century AD. There are some 20,000 manuscripts in existence. The earliest textual evidence we have was copied 100 years after the original.

- Caesar's *Gallic Wars* was written in the first century BC. There are only 10 manuscripts in existence. The earliest textual evidence we have was copied 1000 years after the original.

- Aristotle's *Poetics* was written in the fourth century BC. There are only five manuscripts in existence. The earliest textual evidence we have was copied 1400 years after the original.

There are many writings of the church fathers that quote various sections of Scripture; we could reconstruct the entire New Testament from their writings alone. There were millions of man-hours spent in cross-checking the manuscripts. There remains only one percent of all New Testament words about which questions still exist, and none of these questionable passages contradicts any Bible teaching.

Old Testament Manuscripts

The Old Testament has been more accurately transmitted to us than any other ancient writing of comparable age. The ancient scribes were very meticulous. There were only 1200 variant readings in AD 500, when the Masoretes produced an official text. There are other versions that confirm the accuracy of the Masoretic Text.

Samaritan Pentateuch: 400 BC
Septuagint (Greek): 280 BC
Dead Sea Scrolls: AD 0
Latin Vulgate: AD 400

Figure 12.1—Old Testament Manuscripts

The quotations from pre-Christian writing confirm the text. The New Testament accepts the Old Testament as authentic, affirming the traditional authors, quoting from at least 320 different passages, and confirming the supernatural events cited in the Old Testament.

Document	Written	Earliest Existing Manuscript	Current Number of Manuscripts
Gallic Wars (Caesar)	First century BC	1000 years later	10
Poetics (Aristotle)	Fourth century BC	1400 years later	5
New Testament	First century BC	100 years later	20,000

Figure 12.2—Document Comparison

Biblical Data Is Testable

Historical evidence routinely includes ancient literature, business records, and government documents analyzed in conjunction with linguistics, geography, and archaeological analysis of physical objects (pottery, coins, remains of buildings, etc.) using forensic science techniques. After many millions of man-hours of research and evidence analysis, archaeology has repeatedly confirmed the reliability of the Bible, and even of Genesis. For example, Abraham's birthplace, Ur, has been excavated, and careful scholars have located the site of the long-wrecked Tower of Babel. The Bible has been proven geographically and reproven historically accurate, in the most exacting detail, by external evidences.

Historical Accuracy

The biblical record is full of testable historical and archaeological data, unlike the sacred texts of other religions. Wherever such historical information is cited, the data has proven to be precise and trustworthy. It has been subjected to the minutest scientific textual analysis possible to humanity and has been proven to be authentic in every way.

The Bible has been a significant source book for secular archaeology, helping to identify such ancient figures as Sargon (Isaiah 20:1), Sennacherib (Isaiah 37:37), Horam of Gezer (Joshua 10:33), Hazar (Joshua 15:27), and the nation of the Hittites (Genesis 15:20). The biblical record, unlike other "scriptures," is historically set, opening itself up for testing and verification. Nineteenth-century critics used to deny the historicity of the Hittites, the Horites, the Edomites, and various other peoples, nations, and cities mentioned in the Bible. Those critics have long been silenced by the archaeologist's spade. Few critics dare now to question the geographical and ethnological reliability of the Bible.

The names of more than 40 different kings of various countries mentioned in the Bible have all been found in contemporary documents and inscriptions outside of the Old Testament, and can be interpreted as being consistent with the times and places associated with them in the Bible. Nothing exists in ancient literature that has been even remotely as well-confirmed in accuracy as has the Bible.

Scientific Accuracy

Although much controversy surrounds the early chapters of Genesis, empirical (observable, testable, repeatable) science verifies the Bible's information. Either the Bible is wholly reliable on every subject with which it deals, or it is not the Word of God. Although the Bible is obviously not a science textbook, it does contain all the basic principles upon which true science is built. The Bible abounds with references to nature and natural processes and thus frequently touches on the various sciences.

One often hears of mistakes or errors in the Bible. Seldom, when confronted, is an example provided by the skeptic. When such "errors" are cited, they fall into three kinds of alleged mistakes: (1) mathematical rounding, (2) relative motion, or (3) miracles. Obviously, mathematical rounding is both scientific and in constant use today, as is the use of relative motion for all sorts of navigation and distance calculations. And to deny the miraculous is to assume that one is omniscient.

Just as the Bible has become a source book for history and archaeology, so it is also a source for the foundational principles of science. Those who ignore the information of Scripture will be "always learning, and never able to come to the knowledge of the truth" (2 Timothy 3:7). Much of the content of this book deals with the scientific accuracy of the information recorded in the pages of the Bible.

In the Creator's design, plants were made for food, and animals are living evidence of the Creator's wonder and diversity. There is no hint, of course, in the Genesis account that God equated the replicating systems of Earth with the living creatures later created on Days Five and Six of the creation week. Much has been written to justify this position, but neither the Scriptures nor science supports it. There is a vast difference between the most complex plant and the simplest living organism. If one uses the biblical distinction of life (blood, Leviticus 17:11) as the wall between plant and animal, the differences are even greater.

The gulf between dirt and plants is huge! No naturalistic scheme can adequately account for such wonder. But according to God's words, they do not have life. Plants do replicate within their kind, but so do certain crystals and some chemicals. They replicate within kind, but they are nowhere said to possess *chay* (life) or *nephesh* (soul), the Hebrew words for living things. Job 14:8-10 is cited as evidence that plants die like people die, but that passage most certainly does not use the words for life. The supposed comparison is really a contrast between plant and man.

The food created by God as a good product and part of the process to maintain life cannot be equated with the awful sentence of death pronounced by the Creator on His creation. Animals and man have life. Plants and planets do not.

Worldwide Destruction by Water

The language of Genesis 6–9 demands that the great Flood of Noah be understood as a planet-covering, geologically destructive, yearlong water cataclysm. That global flooding left enormous evidence of the event.

There is a great divide between two major systems of belief on the biblical Flood in the days of Noah. There are those who say it is either a purely mythological event or else a local or regional flood. Then there are those who accept the biblical record of the Flood as a literal record of a tremendous cataclysm involving not only a worldwide deluge but also great tectonic upheavals and volcanic outpourings that completely changed the crust of the earth and its topography.

The Old Testament record of the Flood, which both Christ and Peter accepted as real history, clearly teaches a global flood. For example, the record emphasizes that "all the high hills under the whole heaven...and the mountains were covered" (Genesis 7:19-20) with the waters of the Flood. We are also told that "all flesh died that moved on the earth...all that was on the dry land" (Genesis 7:21-22). Noah and his sons had to build a huge Ark to preserve animal life for the postdiluvian world, an Ark that can easily be shown to have had more than ample capacity to carry at least two of every known kind of land animal. (Marine animals were not involved, of course.) Such an Ark was absurdly unnecessary for anything but a global flood.

God promised that "never again shall there be a flood to destroy the earth" (Genesis 9:11). He has kept His word for more than 4000 years, if the Flood indeed was global. Those Christians who say it was a local flood, however, are in effect accusing God of lying, for there are many devastating local floods every year.

Accurate Predictions

The Bible contains many, many prophetic predictions, most of which are quite detailed. Either they come true, or they do not. If one prediction is accurate, it might be called coincidence. When dozens (even hundreds) come true, the odds become astronomical.

The purpose of prophecy in the Bible is given in Isaiah 46:9-10:

I am God, and there is none like Me, declaring the end from the
beginning, and from ancient times things that are not yet done.

Supernatural predictions are evidence provided to us for verification. Not a
single prophecy from the Bible has been proven false. And there are many more
prophecies yet to be fulfilled in the future. For example, an amazing prophecy is found in Revelation 11:9. In AD 90, the prediction was made that many
nations would view the same event within a few days' time. Today, billions of
people from around the world can simultaneously view the same event through
mass communication. When the prediction was made, communication and
transportation across the Roman Empire took months.

All prophecies from the Bible that have reached their point of fulfillment
have been verified to be true, and hundreds have been fulfilled—like Micah
5:2, which foretold the birthplace of Christ hundreds of years before the Lord
was born.

Also, in 332 BC, Alexander the Great conquered the island fortress of Tyre
by building a causeway from the old mainland city. This fulfilled the prophecy in Ezekiel 26:4-5, written hundreds of years before. At the time of Ezekiel,
Tyre was the capital of Phoenicia, and the island fortress had not yet been built.
Ezekiel predicted:

> They shall destroy the walls of Tyre and break down her towers; I
> will also scrape her dust from her, and make her like the top of a
> rock. It shall be a place for spreading nets in the midst of the sea.

Two hundred years later, Alexander scraped away everything, leaving bare
rock.

And of course we have seen the fulfillment of hundreds of prophecies related
to the birth, life, death, and resurrection of Jesus Christ.

Human Stewardship

The first command given to humanity was to rule, subdue, and "have
dominion" over the earth. That delegated authority contains the fundamental
warrant for all honorable human endeavors as stewards of Earth. This dominion mandate, found in Genesis 1:26-28 and later repeated and amplified to

Noah in Genesis 9:1-7, is still in force. It is not a despotic dominion, as some have insinuated, but a responsible stewardship.

Areas of Human Stewardship	
Science	Education
Technology	Humanities
Commerce	

Figure 12.3—Areas of Human Stewardship

In order to subdue the earth, we must first understand its processes. Research is the foundational occupation for fulfilling the divine mandate. Then this knowledge must be applied in technology (engineering, medicine, agriculture, etc.). It must be implemented for use by all (business, commerce) and transmitted to future generations (education). The creation should also be described and praised in the humanities and fine arts.

The mandate reaffirmed to Noah after the Flood included the additional institution of human government, a change made necessary by the entrance of sin and death into the world. Thus, all the occupations we now call the social sciences (law, civics, counseling, etc.) have been added to God's authorized vocations.

Science

The command to subdue does not imply that the earth was an enemy, but rather, that it was a complex and wonderful world to be ordered and controlled for man's benefit and God's glory. Man was to keep the earth (Genesis 2:15), not exploit and waste its resources. To subdue it first requires understanding it. The disciplines of science uncover how things work. In order for mankind to subdue the earth and have dominion over it, humanity would eventually have to explore every region of it.

Performing the function of subduing and exercising dominion over the physical and biological creation necessarily implies the development of physical and biological sciences (physics, chemistry, hydrology, etc., as well as biology, physiology, ecology, etc.). Thus, the work involved suggests the study and understanding of the created world—or, as Johann Kepler reportedly put it, "thinking God's thoughts after Him."

Since sin entered the world, profound changes have taken place in all of God's created domains. The ground itself was cursed (Genesis 3:17), as were the living creatures (Genesis 3:14). The principle of decay and disintegration began to operate in physical systems. Mutations, disease, and death began to debilitate biological systems. No longer is science merely required to understand the function and organization of Earth; it must now attempt to uncover the original designs of those processes and to learn how to repair the increasing damage being done.

Factual and quantitative data in all areas of study are accessible to all men with the capacity to pursue them. The interpretive and philosophical applications of such data, however, depend primarily on the worldview that is embraced.

Technology

The command to rule requires effective use in the service of mankind. The disciplines of technology involve the development and application of all science. This requires the development of physical and biological technologies (engineering, agriculture, medicine, etc.). These activities under the stewardship of the dominion mandate imply the complementary enterprises known by the modern terms of science and technology, research and development, theory and practice. The application and utilization of the physical and biological processes and systems, as learned from scientific study, should be used for the benefit of mankind and the glory of the Creator.

The social sciences (psychology, sociology, etc.) and their respective technologies in organized human societies (economics, government, politics, etc.) have become significant. These fields come within the bounds of the dominion mandate and can be wonderful disciplines. But, as with scientific research, factual and quantitative data in all areas of study are most accurate and useful in technological development. The interpretive and philosophical applications, however, can be either tainted or enhanced by the "heart" attitude toward the Creator.

Commerce

Adam and Eve were placed in the Garden and told to "tend and keep" it (Genesis 2:15). They were not told how to do so, only that it was their responsibility before the Creator to maintain and develop what had been provided for them. As the population of Earth grew, it would be necessary to develop skills to make tools and talents available to others. That procedure, in modern terms, is commerce.

Science is charged with the responsibility of researching the forces and processes of the earth to determine how things function. Technology tackles the task of developing useful tools and techniques for the application of the information gained in research. Commerce (business) is the complementary discipline necessary to distribute the resulting commodities, thus falling under the "fill the earth" portion of the mandate.

There are a number of commerce-related instructions throughout the Scriptures. We are told not to be "lagging in diligence" but be "fervent in spirit, serving the Lord" (Romans 12:11). Someone who "excels in his work" will "stand before kings; he will not stand before unknown men" (Proverbs 22:29). In one sense, business (commerce) is the familial responsibility of every person, and we are told to "lead a quiet life, to mind your own business, and to work with your own hands" (1 Thessalonians 4:11).

Given the somewhat sordid reputation of certain businesses, it would be well if all commerce would heed the Golden Rule: "Just as you want men to do to you, you also do to them likewise" (Luke 6:31). There is no doubt those words were intended to be implemented by humanity when the mandate to fill the earth was first given.

Education

The knowledge of science, the skills of technology, and the techniques of commerce must be transmitted to others. It is important that true knowledge and wisdom, once known, not be either lost or corrupted. Each generation, therefore, has the responsibility to transmit its knowledge of truth, undiluted and undistorted, to the succeeding generation. This is the ministry of teaching.

In God's economy, the primary responsibility for educating the young is in the home (Deuteronomy 6:6-7; Ephesians 6:4; 2 Timothy 3:15). The church also bears a complementary and extended responsibility to identify and equip God-called teachers as needed for all aspects of its educational ministries (1 Timothy 3:15). It is significant that there is no reference in the Scriptures to school as a separate institution established by God.

That fact does not necessarily mean that parents and pastors have to do all the actual work of teaching. It is certainly appropriate for them to employ qualified tutors and trainers, but the control of the educational process should remain primarily with the home and secondarily with the church. When it is not, it becomes a tool of social power (government) to indoctrinate rather than educate.

The gift of teaching is identified in all three Bible lists of the gifts of the Spirit (Romans 12:4-8; 1 Corinthians 12:1-31; Ephesians 4:7-16). This gift focuses on the teaching of the Scriptures, of course. However, we must not forget that the Bible provides the framework for all teaching. All physical, biological, and spiritual reality is created and maintained by God in Christ and revealed by the Spirit. All teaching, no matter how profound, attractive, or eloquent, should be tested by its fidelity to the Word of God.

Thus, the wonderful threefold goal of teaching must be as follows:

- to transmit the truth in fullness and purity
- to train the student with love and wisdom
- to glorify Christ, in whom perfect love and absolute truth will be united forever

Humanities

The recording of man's achievements through literature, drama, art, etc., should all focus on God's glory. The humanities and fine arts are the spiritual and emotional extensions of the knowledge and technological condition of society. While the disciplines of science and technology are fairly grounded in factual and quantitative data, the farther one gets from that which is "true" to that which is "applied," the more likely the sin nature will distort or contaminate the discipline.

That contamination affects the humanities and fine arts in even greater measure. These professions cannot even use the empirical data developed by secular persons, as can be done with the social sciences, because there are practically no empirical data involved in the humanities and fine arts. In this realm, pretty much everything is based on either human reasoning or emotions, with the exception of the actual mechanical techniques of writing, composing, painting, or performing. But reasoning and emotions come from the mind and heart, which, in the secular person, are without the benefit of the godly mind (1 Corinthians 2:14).

As the world has advanced, the growing secularization of society has increased. This is relatively easy to observe in the great art museums of our large cities. As one moves from the older galleries to the more modern ones, the movement of art from realism to abstract and from godly to profane is easy to see. One does not have to be an art critic to observe the trends.

Perhaps it would be helpful for the Christian person to remember: "Whether you eat or drink, or whatever you do, do all to the glory of God" (1 Corinthians 10:31).

Government and Politics

In God's renewal of the dominion mandate to Noah after the Flood, man was authorized to develop the institution of human government. The authorization for capital punishment given in Genesis 9:6-7 entails the ultimate oversight of human relations through government, politics, sociology—indeed, all legitimate human endeavors. With the authority to impose capital punishment as the penalty for murder, the authority to invest that "sword" in mankind was permitted (Romans 13:1-4).

This ultimate in governmental authority, of course, implies also that human government was now responsible to regulate other human interrelationships as well, since uncontrolled, self-centered activities could otherwise quickly lead to violence, murder, and even anarchy. Laws define how governments and people should interact.

Almost all societal or moral laws are derived from or reflect the biblical Ten Commandments, both directly and in applications of the implications extrapolated from those commandments. This is especially true of the last six of the commandments, which deal directly with man's relationship to his fellow man.

Politics describes how governments and people actually interact, especially over money and power. Governmental institutions, which include our legal systems, are a mix of law and politics. This is partially because of their use of persuasive pressure (and enforceability) of law to influence the actual behavior of others. American government was mostly founded on Bible-friendly political principles by creationist patriots (most of whom were Bible-revering Protestants, as the US Supreme Court once admitted). Many judges now view law itself as inherently secular and "evolving."

To the extent that government officials no longer respect God as the ultimate Authority, they functionally substitute their own power for His, using the evolutionary logic that "might makes right" instead of the Bible-friendly rule-of-law logic that "right justifies might."

The Bible's Message

There are more than 3000 different religions in the world, most of which claim to teach the way to eternal happiness. It has often been said that each of them provides a different path to the same end, and that men are free to choose the path that best suits their own disposition and culture. The Word of God is insistent that this is not so!

The Bible declares that the God of the Bible is the only true God (Isaiah 44:6; 45:5-6) and that Jesus Christ is the only way to God (John 14:6). All other religions, while stressing their "paths," would allow for some other contingency. The Bible states that it is the only true revelation, that its words are not to be changed (Proverbs 30:5-6; Revelation 22:18-19), and that its words are the basis of all judgment (John 12:47-50).

Recent Creation

The Bible has a unique account of origins and early Earth history (Genesis 1–11). All other accounts are either evolutionary or pantheistic, with eternity of matter as the beginning. The biblical account of origins is unique in both quality and quantity of information. Other religions are based on the subjective teachings of their founders. Biblical teachings are based on objective and demonstrable facts.

The first 11 chapters of Genesis speak of the creation of the universe, the fall of man into sin, the worldwide Flood of Noah, and the language-altering event at Babel. There is much evidence that these events actually took place. Although some would suggest that the biblical account of creation is either allegorical or analogous to the evolutionary story, the text itself does not permit such an application.

The language of Genesis 1 and 2 is technically precise and linguistically clear. Any reader would understand that the author of those pages intended to convey a normal six-day creation involving God's supernatural intervention both to create (something from nothing) and to make and shape (something basic into something more complex). Three days (Days One, Five, and Six) involve creation. Three days (Days Two, Three, and Four) involve the organization, integration, and structuring of the material created on Day One.

Creation Week	
Creation Days	Organization Days
Day 1: Heavens, earth, light, darkness	Day 2: Earth's water and atmosphere
Day 5: Sea and marine creatures	Day 3: Land and plants
Day 6: Land creatures and man	Day 4: Sun, moon, stars

Figure 12.4—Creation Week

Life was created on Day Five, a life in which all animals and man share. A special image of God was created on Day Six that only humans have. The movement from "simple to complex" may appear to follow evolution's theory, but the specific order (water >land >plants >stellar and planetary bodies >birds and fish >land animals >man) most emphatically does not.

The Hebrew word for day (yom) is used some 3000 times in the Hebrew Bible and is almost always used to mean an ordinary 24-hour night-day cycle. On the few occasions where it is used to mean an indeterminate period of time, it is always clear from the context that it means something other than a 24-hour day (day of trouble, day of the Lord, day of battle, etc.). Whenever it is used with an ordinal number (first, second, etc.), it always means a specific day, an ordinary 24-hour day.

The language of Genesis 1 appears to have been crafted so that no reader would mistake the word use for anything other than an ordinary 24-hour day. The light portion is named "day," and the dark portion is named "night." Then, the "evening and the morning" is Day One, Day Two, etc. The linguistic formula is repeated for each of the six days, a strange emphasis if the words were to be taken as allegorical or analogous to something other than a day-night cycle.

When God wrote the Ten Commandments with His own finger (certainly the most emphatic action ever taken by God on behalf of His revealed Word), God specifically designated a seventh day to be a Sabbath day (rest day) in memory and in honor of the "work six days, rest one day" activity of God Himself during the creation week (Exodus 20:11). In that context, spoken and written by God Himself, the creation week can mean only a regular week of seven days, one of which is set aside for rest and is to be observed as a holy memorial.

Sin Caused Death

The biblical record is very precise: Adam's sin introduced death into the world (Romans 5:12). A major platform of those who hold to long evolutionary ages is that death is a normal part of the original creation. Their position is that the fossil remains are a record of eons of natural development rather than the awful debris of a worldwide, yearlong sentence of destruction executed by an angry Creator. Naturalistic interpretations must have death as a good mechanism that produces the "most fit." The Bible makes it clear, however, that death is an enemy (1 Corinthians 15:26) and a curse pronounced on all creation (Genesis 3:14-19). That awful judgment was because of Adam's rebellion (Genesis 3:17; 1 Timothy 2:14) and was not a part of God's original creation.

Death by the design of God is foreign to the revealed nature of God. Why would anyone want to suggest that God "authored" death in His creation— other than to somehow fold into that creation account an agreement to the eons of death that is required by an evolutionary hypothesis? The Bible states that creation was designed to "clearly" show us His invisible nature and Godhead (Romans 1:20).

The "groaning and laboring" (see Romans 8:22) of the universe began with the curse that the Creator pronounced on the earth because of Adam's sin. In fact, the entire tone and message of Scripture turns at Genesis 3. The curse was on the ground that would fail to yield its normal good. Thorns and thistles are indicators of that failure so that even the environment would require the "sweat of your face" to conduct life (Genesis 3:17-19). The death that God inserted into His flawlessly functioning universe started a process that the apostle Paul extends to the whole universe. Death and its all-encompassing impact is said to be the "last enemy" that will be destroyed before Christ assumes eternal rule over the universe (1 Corinthians 15:26).

If pain, suffering, and death had been present for long eons before the rebellion of Adam, then a whole sweep of biblical teaching is thrown into the black hole of allegory. Death becomes the good function that weeds out the "unfit." Hundreds of Bible passages relating to the necessity of Christ's death on the cross are twisted. In the Bible, physical death is specifically identified as absolutely necessary to accomplish the atonement of sins. These two views of the role of death cannot be merged into some sort of hybrid theology. Death is either God's judgment and punishment for sin, or it is nothing more than a normal function of biology.

Supernatural Salvation

There is no question that the Bible teaches it was necessary for Jesus Christ to die physically in order to accomplish the payment for our sins (Hebrews 2:14-18). If death is normal or good, even if it is merely relegated to a spiritual effect, then the physical death of Jesus Christ becomes unnecessary and meaningless.

Perhaps the most resisted message of the Bible is that it is impossible to be forgiven of our sins except by the supernatural gift of holiness obtained through the substitutionary death of Jesus Christ.

No one can come to Me unless the Father who sent Me draws him; and I will raise him up at the last day (John 6:44).

Jesus said to him, "I am the way, the truth, and the life. No one comes to the Father except through Me" (John 14:6).

God, who is rich in mercy, because of His great love with which He loved us, even when we were dead in trespasses, made us alive together with Christ (by grace you have been saved) (Ephesians 2:4-5).

Pursue peace with all people, and holiness, without which no one will see the Lord (Hebrews 12:14).

Christ...suffered once for sins, the just for the unjust, that He might bring us to God, being put to death in the flesh but made alive by the Spirit (1 Peter 3:18).

Actually, it's pretty simple. Adam and Eve refused to believe that God was telling them the truth and died because of their rebellion. God still loved them and all the people who would come into the world through them, so He provided the *only* solution possible: He gave Himself to solve the problem. He came into the world as the Lord Jesus, took our own form and nature, lived our life, was subject to every kind of temptation and problem humans could ever face, did not blow it like Adam did, willingly accepted unjust condemnation and death—for our sakes—and then, to prove that He was really God in the flesh, came back again from death (after paying our "wages"—Romans 6:23) as the resurrected Lord.

Now He sits in heaven as the Advocate (defending lawyer) on our behalf, acting as the eternal High Priest interceding for us, all the time preparing a place for us to live with Him forever. One day He—that same Jesus who died for us and rose again from the grave—will come to earth again as King of kings and Lord of lords to end the rule of the enemy and make a "new heavens and a new earth in which righteousness dwells" (2 Peter 3:13)!

Conclusion

There are five principles you can understand and apply to your own life from a right understanding of origins.

First, you are not an accident. You are a wonderfully designed and magnificent human being, endowed with the responsibility and intelligence to care for this planet.

Second, you are not an impersonal collection of molecules with mere chemical reactions for brains. You have blood in your veins. You move, you emote, you think, you love and hate and do math and make music and make mistakes. You are alive.

Third, you are not an animal. There is so much difference between human beings and animals. The differences are profound—and scientific studies are proving that more and more each day. Don't ever think of yourself as an animal. You bear the image of the Creator God.

Fourth, you are unique. There is nobody else in the entire universe like you. God has placed you here for a specific purpose, and no one else in the world can do what you do. Find out what that is. Learn what only you can do. Get rid of all that evolutionary baggage. You are God's creation.

Finally, because you are not an accident that resulted from the unguided actions of random processes—because you are a human being created in God's own image, unique in all the universe—God loves you. He loves you with an eternal love that will never go away. No matter what you have done or think you are, God has made it possible for you to become His child.

Jesus had two important things to say about this. One is an invitation. The other is a promise.

> Come to Me, all you who labor and are heavy laden, and I will give you rest. Take My yoke upon you and learn from Me, for I am gentle and lowly in heart, and you will find rest for your souls. For My yoke is easy and My burden is light (Matthew 11:28-30).

> This is the will of Him who sent Me, that everyone who sees the Son and believes in Him may have everlasting life; and I will raise him up at the last day (John 6:40).

INDEX

IMAGE CREDITS

Figure 1.1—Bigstock (edited)

Figure 1.2—NASA/JHUAPL/SWRI

Figure 1.3—Bigstock (edited)

Figure 1.4—Bigstock

Figure 1.5—Bigstock

Figure 2.1—Fossil Tree and Lawn—Credit ICR

Figure 2.3—Bigstock (compiled and edited)

Figure 3.1—Lucy, Wikipedia (https://commons.wikimedia.org/wiki/File:Lucy_blackbg.jpg)

Figure 3.2—Ida, Wikipedia (credit: Jens L. Franzen, Philip D. Gingerich, Jörg Habersetzer1, Jørn H. Hurum, Wighart von Koenigswald, B. Holly Smith)

Figure 3.3—Homo naledi (credit: Lee Roger Berger reseserch team)

Figure 3.5—Bigstock

Figure 3.6—Bigstock

Figure 4.1—public domain

Figure 4.2—Bigstock

Figure 4.3—ICR

Figure 4.4—Bigstock (compiled)

Figure 4.5—ICR

Figure 4.6—Photos from Fotolia.com were edited and arranged into this graphic

Figure 4.7—ICR

Figure 5.5—ICR

Figure 6.3—Credit: John Morris

Figure 6.5—Credit: Henry M. Morris III

Figure 7.1—iStock

Figure 7.2—Dino outlines from Bigstock / chart credit: ICR

Figure 7.3—Bigstock

Figure 7.4—public domain

Figure 7.5—Bigstock

Figure 7.6—public domain

Figure 7.7—Bigstock (mosasaur illustration)

Figure 7.7—ICR (skull photo)

Figure 7.8—Bigstock

Figure 7.9—Bigstock (both Spinosaurus and Kronosaurus)

Figure 8.1—public domain

Figure 8.2—iStock

Figure 8.5—Jake Hebert

Figure 8.6—ICR

Figure 9.4—iStock

Figure 9.5—Ra—Bigstock

Figure 9.6—Bigstock

Figure 10.1—NASA

Figure 10.2—NASA

Figure 10.3—NASA

Figure 10.5—Bigstock images placed in chart

Figure 11.1—NASA

Figure 11.2—NASA

Figure 11.3—NASA NOAA GOES Project

Figure 11.5—Bigstock

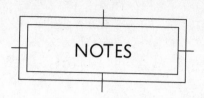

NOTES

Chapter 1—Creation or Chaos

1. Richard Dawkins, *The Blind Watchmaker* (London: W.W. Norton, 1986).

2. Anders Garm and Dan-Eric Nilsson, "Visual navigation in starfish: first evidence for the use of vision and eyes in starfish," *Proceedings of the Royal Society B* 281, no. 1777 (2014), 20133011.

3. Darwin's letter quoted in Jerry Bergman, *The Dark Side of Darwin* (Green River, AR: Master Books, 2011), 118.

Portions of this chapter were adapted from the following sources:

Brian Thomas, "Amazing Animal Eyes," *Acts & Facts* 42, no. 9 (2013): 16.

Frank Sherwin, "Blue-t-ful Beetles, Birds, 'n Butterflies," *Acts & Facts* 35, no. 6 (2006).

Frank Sherwin, "Spiral Wonder of the Spider Web," *Acts & Facts* 35, no. 5 (2006).

Henry M. Morris III, *Exploring the Evidence for Creation* (Dallas, TX: Institute for Creation Research, 2009).

Chapter 2—Origin of Life

1. Dani Cooper, "When did life begin?" *ABC Science*, September 17, 2009, www.abc .net.au/science/articles/2009/09/17/2689221.htm.

2. Henry M. Morris, "The Urge to Submerge," *Acts & Facts* 24 (1995).

3. Henry M. Morris, "Like the Most High," *Days of Praise,* November 6, 1992.

4. Jeffrey Tomkins, "The Mystery of Life's Beginning," in *Creation Basics & Beyond* (Dallas, TX: Institute for Creation Research, 2013), 185.

Portions of this chapter were adapted from the following sources:

Henry M. Morris III, *Your Origins Matter* (Dallas, TX: Institute for Creation Research, 2013).

Henry M. Morris III, *Six Days of Creation* (Dallas, TX: Institute for Creation Research, 2013).

Chapter 3—Human Life

1. Ben Stein, *Expelled: No Intelligence Allowed,* directed by Nathan Frankowski (Premise Media Corporation, L.P., 2008), DVD.

2. Richard Dawkins, *The Selfish Gene* (Oxford: Oxford University Press, 1976), 21-22.

3. "*Australopithecus* a Long-Armed, Short-Legged Knuckle-Walker," *Science News* 100, no. 22 (1971), 357.

4. James Randerson, "Fossil Ida: Extraordinary find is 'missing link' in human evolution," *The Guardian,* May 19, 2009, www.theguardian.com/science/2009/may/19/ida-fossil-missing-link.

5. "Fossil Skeleton Known as Ida Is No Ancestor of Humans," Associated Press, October 22, 2009.

6. "'Missing link' primate isn't a link after all," Associated Press, October 21, 2009.

7. "Lovejoy Helps Unveil Oldest Hominid Skeleton That Revises Thinking on Human Evolution," *e-Inside,* October 5, 2009, einside.kent.edu/?type=art&id=92233.

8. Bruce Bower, "Ardi's kind had a skull fit for a hominid," *Science News* 183 (2013), 13.

9. *Imagineering* is the term used to speak of the work done by Walt Disney Imagineering Research & Development, Inc., which is the design and development arm of The Walt Disney Company. Its headquarters is located in Glendale, California, and there are field offices in other locations, including the Disney World Resort in Florida.

10. Jeffrey P. Tomkins, "Epigenetic Study Produces 'Backwards' Human-Ape Tree," *Creation Science Update,* August 16, 2013, http://www.icr.org/article/7680/; Jeffrey P. Tomkins, "Human and Chimp DNA—Nearly Identical?" *Acts & Facts* 43, no. 2 (2014): 20.

11. Jeffrey Tomkins, "Epigenetics Proves Humans and Chimps Are Different," *Acts & Facts* 42, no. 1 (2013): 11-12.

12. Ibid.

13. Peter Singer, "All Animals Are Equal," in *Animal Rights and Human Obligations*, 2nd ed., Tom Regan and Peter Singer, eds. (Englewood Cliffs, NJ: Prentice Hall, 1989), 148-62.

14. "Are Animal and Human Life Equal?," *ABC News*, August 31, 2001, abcnews .go.com/ThisWeek/story?id=132601&page=1.

15. "About Us," Nonhuman Rights Project fact sheet, www.nonhumanrightsproject .org/about-us-2/.

16. C.S. Lewis, *Prince Caspian* (New York: HarperCollins, 1994), 233.

17. Randy J. Guliuzza, "Made in His Image: Human Gestation," *Acts & Facts* 38, no. 2 (2009): 10.

Chapter 4—The Fossils

1. George Wald, "The Origin of Life," *Scientific American* 191, no. 2 (1954): 48.

2. "Statement on Evolution," Society for the Study of Evolution, cms.gogrid.evolu tionsociety.org/content/education/statement-on-evolution.html.

3. "The Teaching of Evolution," NSTA Position Statement, National Science Teachers Association, www.nsta.org/about/positions/evolution.aspx.

4. "NABT Position Statement on Teaching Evolution," National Association of Biology Teachers, www.nabt.org/websites/institution/?p=92.

5. "The Paleontological Society Position Statement: Evolution," Paleontological Society, paleosoc.org/about/policy/the-paleontological-society-position-statement -evolution.

6. Ibid.

7. Carl Dunbar, *Historical Geology*, 2d ed. (New York: John Wiley & Sons, Inc., 1960), 47.

8. Richard C. Lewontin, "Billions and Billions of Demons," *The New York Review of Books* 44, no. 1 (1997): 31. Emphasis in original.

9. Ibid.

10. David B. Kitts, "Paleontology and Evolutionary Theory," *Evolution* 28 (1974): 467.

11. Charles Darwin, *On the Origin of Species* (London: John Murray, 1859), 189.

12. Daniel I. Axelrod, "Early Cambrian Marine Fauna," *Science* 128, no. 3314 (1958): 7.

13. Alfred S. Romer, *Vertebrate Paleontology*, 3rd ed. (Chicago: University of Chicago Press, 1966), 15.

14. Larry Vardiman, Andrew A. Snelling, and Eugene F. Chaffin, eds., *Radioisotopes and the Age of the Earth: Results of a Young-Earth Creationist Research Initiative* (El Cajon, CA: Institute for Creation Research and Chino Valley, AZ: Creation Research Society, 2005).

15. Robert T. Bakker, *The Dinosaur Heresies* (New York: Zebra Books, Kensington Publishing Corp., 1986), 296-97.

16. George Gaylord Simpson, *Tempo and Mode in Evolution* (New York: Columbia University Press, 1944).

17. Steven M. Stanley, *The New Evolutionary Timetable: Fossils, Genes, and the Origin of Species* (New York: Basic Books, 1981), 71.

18. David Raup, "Conflicts between Darwin and Paleontology," *Field Museum of Natural History Bulletin* 50, no. 1 (1979): 25.

19. Douglas J. Futuyma, *Science on Trial* (New York: Pantheon Books, 1983), 197.

Chapter 5—Noah's Flood

1. For more information about Flood legends, see John Morris, *The Global Flood* (Dallas, TX: Institute for Creation Research, 2012), 67-75.

Portions of this chapter were adapted from the following source:

Henry M. Morris III, *The Book of Beginnings, Vol. 1: Creation, Fall, and the First Age* (Dallas, TX: Institute for Creation Research, 2012).

Chapter 6—The Age of Earth

1. George Wald, "The Origin of Life," *Scientific American* 191, no. 2 (1954): 48.

2. Carl Sagan, *Cosmos* (New York: Random House, 1980), 30.

3. Data in this table came from Henry Morris, "The Young Earth," *Acts & Facts* 3, no. 8 (1974).

4. Larry Vardiman, Andrew A. Snelling, and Eugene F. Chaffin, eds., *Radioisotopes and the Age of the Earth: Results of a Young-Earth Creationist Research Initiative* (El Cajon, CA: Institute for Creation Research and Chino Valley, AZ: Creation Research Society, 2005), 414.

5. John R. Baumgardner, "^{14}C Evidence for a Recent Global Flood and a Young Earth," in *Radioisotopes and the Age of the Earth: Results of a Young-Earth Creationist Research Initiative,* eds. Larry Vardiman, Andrew A. Snelling, and Eugene F. Chaffin (El Cajon, CA: Institute for Creation Research and Chino Valley, AZ: Creation Research Society, 2005), 587-630.

6. Brian Thomas and Vance Nelson, "Radiocarbon in Dinosaur and Other Fossils," *Creation Research Society Quarterly* 51, no. 4 (2015): 299-311.

Chapter 7—Dinosaurs

1. Hillary Mayell, "'Mummified' Dinosaur Discovered in Montana," *National Geographic News*, October 11, 2002, news.nationalgeographic.com/news/2002/10/1010_021010_dinomummy.html.

2. Tim Clarey, "Tracking Down Leviathan," *Acts & Facts* 44, no. 7 (2015): 14.

Chapter 8—The Ice Age

1. Jake Hebert, *The Ice Age and the Flood: Does Science Really Show Millions of Years?* (Dallas, TX: Institute for Creation Research, 2014).

2. Ibid.

Chapter 9—Ancient Civilizations

1. See Genesis 2:4; 5:1; 6:9; 10:1; 11:10, 27; 25:12, 19; 36:1, 9; 37:2.

2. Iraq's Ancient Past: Rediscovering Ur's Royal Cemetery. University of Pennsylvania Museum of Archaeology and Anthropology, www.penn.museum/sites/iraq/?page_id=50.

Portions of this chapter were adapted from the following source:

Henry M. Morris III, *The Book of Beginnings, Vol. 2: Noah, the Flood, and the New World* (Dallas, TX: Institute for Creation Research, 2013).

Chapter 10—Origin of the Universe

Portions of this chapter were adapted from the following source:

Henry M. Morris III, *Exploring the Evidence for Creation* (Dallas, TX: Institute for Creation Research, 2009).

Chapter 11—The Unique Earth

Portions of this chapter were adapted from the following source:

Henry M. Morris III, *Exploring the Evidence for Creation* (Dallas, TX: Institute for Creation Research, 2009).

Chapter 12—The Big Picture

Portions of this chapter were adapted from the following sources:

Henry M. Morris III, *The Book of Beginnings, Vol. 1: Creation, Fall, and the First Age* (Dallas, TX: Institute for Creation Research, 2012).

Henry M. Morris III, *Exploring the Evidence for Creation* (Dallas, TX: Institute for Creation Research, 2009).

Henry M. Morris III, *Your Origins Matter* (Dallas, TX: Institute for Creation Research, 2013).

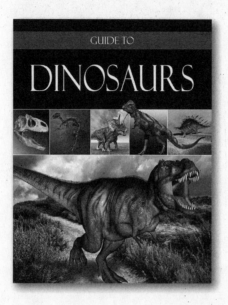

How do fish breathe and birds fly? Why do some animals migrate and others hibernate? And what happened to the dinosaurs and other extinct animals?

The animal kingdom is a massive and amazing part of God's wonderful creation, with creatures that fly, swim, slither, gallop, swing through trees, and much more. Discover the fascinating details of what makes each animal unique and how they are engineered to live in their own habitat.

GUIDE TO

CREATION

Planet Earth is one amazing place. It has everything from high mountains to deep canyons, frigid ice caps to searing deserts. And it's inhabited by living creatures of all shapes, sizes, and colors. Then there's outer space, with spectacular arrays of planets, stars, and galaxies that are countless millions and billions of miles away.

Where did all these come from? Some point to the Bible's famous words, "In the beginning, God created..." Others say it all "just happened" by chance through random, unguided processes.

What does the evidence say? And more importantly, does that evidence agree with both the Bible and science?

To learn more about Harvest House books and
to read sample chapters, visit our website:

www.harvesthousepublishers.com

HARVEST HOUSE PUBLISHERS
EUGENE, OREGON

Angels spoke to men. 3 or more - Gabriel
Came Down & spoke to Mary